JJ

JJ

JOHN JAMESON

FOUNDER OF THE MOST FAMOUS
IRISH WHISKEY IN THE WORLD

Brian Jameson

First hardcover & paperback editions September 2023

Cover design & typesetting by riverdesignbooks.com

Cover images: John Jameson and Margaret Jameson by Henry Raeburn
Map by Helen Cann
Illustrations by Ciaran Murphy
John Jameson's Seal by Quentin Peacock
Permission has been secured for all other images used

Hardcover: ISBN 978-1-7394419-1-3
Paperback: ISBN 978-1-7394419-0-6
Audiobook: ISBN 978-1-7394419-3-7
Ebook: ISBN 978-1-7394419-2-0

Published by Mad Alice

www.brian-jameson.com

Dedication

This book is dedicated to Donna-Maria, the love of my life, who advised and encouraged me but, on occasion, was driven to the limits by my preoccupation and was tempted to dig up my ancestor and bash him over the head with a big spade.

Table of Contents

❧ John Jameson's Seal in 1792 ❧

JJ's Family Baggage

GRANDPARENTS

Grandfather:
James Jamisone
b. Alloa 1685

Married *1709*

Grandmother:
Joan Clark
b. Alloa 1685

PARENTS

Father:
William Jameson
b. Alloa 1718

Married *1737*

Mother:
Helen Horn
b. Kinross

SISTER

Margaret Jameson
b. Alloa 1739

UNCLE & AUNTS

Uncle:
Thomas Jameson
b. Alloa 1711

Aunt:
Margaret Jameson
b. Alloa 1714

Aunt:
Joan Jameson
b. Alloa 1716

COUSINS

William Jameson, the son of Thomas Jameson & Elizabeth Stewart
b. Alloa 1732
A preacher in the Secession Church

Married: Mary Wilson, daughter of William Wilson, a founder of the Secession Church.

William & Mary Jameson's Children:
Elizabeth
John Jameson, a preacher of the Gospel at Methven Perth
William Wilson Jameson, a distiller in Alloa who then moved to Ireland.

Peggie's Family Baggage

HAIG GRANDPARENTS
James Haig Merchant *1691 - 1748*
Mary Mackenzie *1691 - 1743*

STEIN GRANDPARENTS
John Stein Distiller at Kennetpans *1697 - 1773*
Margaret Caldom *1699 - 1747*

FATHER
John Haig
Tobacconist *1720 - 1773*

MOTHER
Margaret Stein *1729 - 1794*

HAIG UNCLES AND AUNTS

George	Janet	Mary	Robert	Cecily
1719-1752	*1722-1804*	*1723-?*	*1725-1773*	*1727-1808*
	Married George Peirson Tobacconist			

STEIN UNCLES AND AUNTS

Robert	Ann	Magdalen	James	Andrew	Alison	John	Janet
1733-1816	*1734-1798*	*1727-1808*	*1740-1804*	*1741-1828*	*1743-1799*	*1745-1835*	*1747-1835*
Distiller Kincaple			Distiller Kilbagie & Russia	Distiller Hattonburn		Distiller Kennetpans & Ireland	
			Son John Stein Distiller Canonmills & MP			Son John Stein Distiller Ireland	
						Daughter: Isabella Stein Married John Jameson II	

BROTHERS AND SISTERS

James	Mary	John	George	Ann	Robert	Janet	Caldom	Andrew	William
1755-1833	*1756-1803*	*1758-1819*	*1760-1774*	*1761-1802*	*1764-1845*	*1766-1828*	*1767-?*	*1769-1824*	*1771-1847*
Distiller Canonmills Lochrin & Sunbury	Married Andrew Mackenzie Haig Agent in London	Distiller Lochrin & Bonnington		Married John White, Cotton Mill Owner In Penicuik	Distiller Dodderbank	Married John Philp a Stein business partner	Married James Millar	Distiller Tulliallan	Distiller Kincaple & Guardbridge
Married Helen Higgins		Married Christian Jameson			Married Caroline Wolseley				Married Janet Stein (1st Cousin)
									Son John Haig Distiller & founder of John Haig & Co. Cameron Bridge
									Grandson 1st Earl Haig

The Jameson Family in Alloa

'JJ' & 'Peggie'
Married 12th September 1768

JJ & PEGGIE'S SIXTEEN CHILDREN

Margaret b. 1769
Married William Robertson of Eyemouth
Three Children
d. 1805

Robert b. 1771
Lawyer
Land Agent
Sheriff Clerk
d. 1847

John b. 1773
Lawyer
Distiller Tulliallan & Bow St.
Married Isabella Stein (1st Cousin)
Ten Children
d. 1851

Helen b. 1775
Lived in Alloa
d. 1847

William b. 1777
Lawyer
Distiller Marrowbone Lane
d. 1822

Mary b. 1779
d. 1781

James b. 1781
Lawyer
Banker
Distiller Marrowbone Lane
Married Elizabeth Woolsey
Six Children
d. 1747

Andrew b. 1783
Distiller Fairfield
Married Catherine Jameson & Margaret Millar
Eight Children
Grandson Guglielmo Marconi
d. 1757

George b. 1784
d. 1786

Anne b. 1786
Married Francis Stupart
Three Children
d. 1861

Janet b. 1787
Married John Woolsey
Nine Children
d. 1861

Francis b. 1789
d. 1790

Elizabeth b. 1791
d. 1791

Henry b. 1792
d. 1801

Mary b. 1794
d. 1800

Alison b. 1797
d. 1802

John Jameson's Timeline and Ancestral Line to the Author

1740 Birth of John Jameson.

1745 Bonnie Prince Charlie's Jacobite Rebellion.

1758 John Jameson becomes a writer in Alloa.

1760 George III becomes King of Great Britain and Ireland.

1767 John Jameson becomes Sheriff Clerk of Clackmannanshire.

1768 John Jameson marries Margaret Haig.

1775 American War of Independence.

1788 Collapse of Haig and Stein distilleries.

1789 John Jameson purchases Lochrin distillery in Edinburgh.

1798 United Irishmen Rebellion.

1800 William Jameson distils at Marrowbone Lane, Dublin.

1801 Kingdoms of Great Britain and Ireland merge.

1805 Bow Street distillery purchased by the Jameson family.

1815 The Battle of Waterloo.

1823 Death of John Jameson.

1837 Victoria becomes Queen of Great Britain and Ireland.

1845-49 The Great Famine of Ireland

1878 *Truths About Whisky* published.

1899 John Jameson & Son v. William Jameson & Co.

1901 Marconi receives the first transatlantic radio signal.

1914-18 WWI.

1916 Easter Rising.

1920-1933 Prohibition in the United States

1924 *The History of a Great House* published by Bow St.

1939-45 WWII.

1966 John Jameson merges into Irish Distillers.

1971–75 Distilling moves to Midleton County Cork.

1988 Pernod Ricard takes over Irish Distillers & John Jameson.

1995-2007 Celtic Tiger period of high economic growth in Ireland.

John Jameson's success continues.

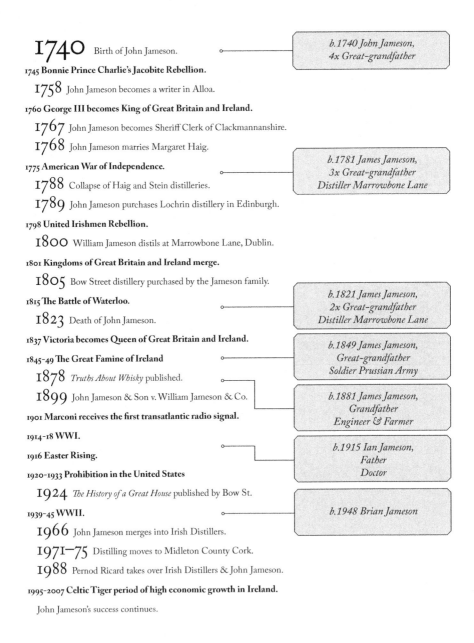

b.1740 John Jameson,
4x Great-grandfather

b.1781 James Jameson,
3x Great-grandfather
Distiller Marrowbone Lane

b.1821 James Jameson,
2x Great-grandfather
Distiller Marrowbone Lane

b.1849 James Jameson,
Great-grandfather
Soldier Prussian Army

b.1881 James Jameson,
Grandfather
Engineer & Farmer

b.1915 Ian Jameson,
Father
Doctor

b.1948 Brian Jameson

Preface

T HE WRITING OF THIS BOOK arose from not believing everything
I was told.

John Jameson was a revered ancestor of mine. My family's account
of his life seemed to follow without question the version promoted by
his whiskey brand. But brands are there to suit their marketing needs,
and my curiosity took hold to seek out his real story.

The research consumed me and could have continued uninterrupted
into the twilight. Fortunately, the pandemic came along, and I had to
abandon the cosy archives of stacked animal hides and knuckle down
to write out my discoveries.

There was plenty of help bringing to life the dry legal documentation that maps out the John Jameson story. The eighteenth century,
an awakening age of agricultural, industrial, and political revolutions,
provided the backdrop; his contemporaries of writers and commenta-
tors gave anecdotes and travel tips; the Jacobite and United Irishmen
rebellions left their mark as they erupted within John Jameson's earshot.

I am not a whiskey sommelier and have made only the simplest of
references to its creation. Although there is much here for the whiskey
buff to ponder, it is a tale also for those who do not drink for whatever
reason.

Whiskey or whisky?
Within this book, when referring to Irish whiskey, an e has been
included in the spelling, and when referring to Scottish whisky, the e
has been omitted.

Chapter 1

An Introduction Face to Face

Back through the socks of time; Rainbows, donkeys, and Duffy's Circus; The National Gallery of Ireland; Truths about whiskey.

PARENTS AND GRANDPARENTS ARE TIME travellers who can take us back to before we were born. My mother's father, whom we all called Pop, had his own time-travelling armchair in our house. There he would sit, puffing his pipe as he took us, his grandchildren, into darkest East Africa on military exploits, off winning his Military Cross, playing polo with maharajas in India, and losing an eye as he was shot at as a dispatch rider. His glass eye replacement would occasionally pop out when he became emotional. Our favourite story was Pop's shipwreck on the Irish Sea and his swimming to an upturned lifeboat where he pushed off a dead sailor to save himself.

The story told, we would leave Pop to snooze and dream of those days so long ago, until his smouldering pipe would set fire to the time-travelling armchair, and we would rush in to save him and hoist him back to the present.

1

As a children's TV director, I once quaintly demonstrated time through the pairs of socks that one might have been gifted every Christmas. One hundred pairs of these gifted socks could easily be visualised, pegged to a washing line. At a glance, you could see for one hundred years.

A stroll down the washing line today, I can meet my young, fresh, and flourishing grandparents away from their faded photos.

Two washing lines, and I can see two hundred years of socks stretching back in time. A walk along these two hundred years of Christmas gifts, and I can call on my four times great-grandfather JJ. Back then, old JJ could fill me in on a few fundamental facts before he popped it.

"Grandpa, what school did you go to?" I would ask.

Back along the socks of time to my 1950s childhood, I arrive at Salisbury in Wiltshire, England. Pleasant, but not embraced by my Irish mother, Patsy Shaw. But still, for me, it was my home and where I always return to in my dreams.

Our house, shaded by a copper beech tree, was looked down upon by a glorious cathedral that chimed its ancient clock for us at every quarter hour.

The city contained nice wicker basket carrying people, hunting and shooting people, and doggy people. The Barkers a few doors down from our number fifteen were doggy people. Mr Barker was so doggy that I believe he eventually morphed into a pedigree Cocker Spaniel, following Mrs Barker and pooping wherever he pleased.

I attended a preparatory school run for the benefit of masochists and paedophiles. The tall, asylum-styled school building at the top of a hill was built of red brick to match the uniform. My attendance as Jameson minor was not voluntary in my brick-red, frequently doffed cap.

Amongst the staff, there were exceptions. A few ex-militaries were quite decent and applied themselves to our education with gusto. Major Gay gave us an eyewitness account of how he had won the Battle of El Alamein in his tank. Colonel Puff told us his tale of shooting a German pilot with a rifle from his biplane.

At the school, the Christian religion featured fiercely, and I, as Jameson mi, was convinced for a time that I was Jesus. Another boy, Richard Dawkins, became the nation's leading atheist.

'You become what you are told,' said the poet Lawrence Hoo.

My parents told me I was Irish. They weren't lying, because they were both Irish-born. I believed them. I liked being Irish in England; I felt different from those around me.

My first trips to the family land were spent cooped up and sealed into a Morris Oxford. There, with my brother, sister, mother, and father, we journeyed to Liverpool to embark on the Belfast ferry. My doctor dad puffed on his pipe whilst we choked towards the port and death from dense clouds of Erinmore tobacco.

As my dad drove and puffed, he would sing us 'Paddy McGinty's Goat'. This was long before the Val Doonican rocking chair version, and it had an Anglo-Irish patriotic feel, with Paddy's goat sinking a German U-boat and joining the Irish Guards in France.

Our Liverpool arrival burst through the Mersey Tunnel to the sights of trams, steam trains, overhead railways, cranes, masts, and funnels. The dockside cobbles clattered with nose-bagged horses giving off a thick opiate smell of straw and dung.

Exotica.

Here I thought I saw the future when, in fact, I was smelling the past.

The long, sleek *Ulster Prince* was more of a ship than a ferry. We climbed up the wooden gangway from the shore and passed through an opening cut into the steel wall. One step, and I was in heaven.

Our car was rolled onto netting packed around with straw sacks and swung up by a steam crane, high, over, and down to the deep hold.

Inside, where stewards wafted, Irish linen was tucked crisp into bunks and ironed onto tables.

Opposite our vessel was the green *Munster* set for Dublin.

My brother and I would watch, mesmerised, as the two ships' bilges were pumped out, and jobbies from the Republic and Ulster would meet, swirl, and waltz together around Liverpool's Prince's Dock.

Later, as we slept, we were lifted gently down through the locks to the River Mersey, where we sailed over the Irish Sea to the land of my mum and dad.

Ireland – rainbows, donkeys, and Duffy's Circus.

Relatives were visited from the north to the south, from the east to the west; loughs were fished, and sand was exported in shoes.

Granny and Grandpa lived with our clergyman uncle, Charlie. He had various large rambling rectories with tangled, mysterious gardens. One awoke to the sweet smell of a damp pantry and a breakfast of eggs, soda bread, potato cakes, and Irish bacon. Grandpa was moustachioed, with plus fours. A Glasgow-trained engineer, he could craft anything from wood and would make his grandchildren penny whistles.

There was always music. Granny sang operatic arias. Grandpa, sucking on an unlit cigarette, entertained us with his rollicking version of 'Slattery's Mounted Foot'.

Brocko, an old, floppy, honey-coloured Labrador, padded around after Grandpa Freddy as he trimmed the paraffin lamps.

The first glimpse I had of my four-times great-grandfather JJ was at my cousin's home near Dundalk. Milestown house was plantation large and long. Inside was a delight of a billiard room, a squash court, bedrooms with basins, a drawing room of sinking sofas, Irish coffees, and views over a jetty and bat-flown river.

The approach to the house was by an avenue of lime trees. This, I fancy, was a nod to my great-grandfather JJ. His own home was on a walk of lime trees.

Whether JJ had ever visited my cousin's house is uncertain, but his presence was there. Not just through the linden avenue, but from his gravelly gaze as one entered the hall.

JJ looked down through the oaked gloom with a growl.

In crumpled shorts and socks askew, I smiled up.

The old man grunted. Next to him, Great-grandmother Peggie calmed.

'Ye auld fool! Don't scare the poor wee laddie,' she said.

I must have looked worried, but I worried no more. Old JJ was quite safe to grunt and groan away within his ancient gold and green mouldy picture frame.

I gave the old man not another thought as I skedaddled off to explore the social swirl of wild mushrooms, gymkhanas, and dances in food-stained, mothballed dinner suits.

For a few short days, I was connected to the past and my father's childhood. As the bats flitted, tales were regaled, facts manipulated for laughter, and myths created.

On every trip to Ireland, I was seduced more. The Angelus bell on the radio, the show bands, the strumming of rebel songs, and the breathing of that air drugged with Atlantic salt and peat fumes.

Uncles, aunts, and cousins, and cousins and cousins. Everyone was related to someone or other. People were also related to things: biscuits, the radio, tyres, and cigarettes.

We were related to the whiskey.

And there he was, John Jameson. In bars, on bottles, emblazoned on doors and mirrors, etched into brass, and painted on tin signs. Not a town or village was without his presence—the name of a brand and the daddy of a clan.

And here he is today, sitting up high at the National Gallery of Ireland. He looks down at me. It is the same portraiture as that in my cousin's house but more pristine.

JJ looks younger than I remember, but, then, I am older. He is less growly, too, and his eyes are amused. Indeed, from deep within, I think I can detect a chesty chuckle.

A large canvas depicting the 'Death of Milo' trapped in a tree trunk separates John Jameson from his wife, Margaret Haig.

Peggie looks wistfully across at him. She is resigned to the naked squirminess of Milo between them.

"The naked auld fool," she mutters.

How close they are to me. With an ear to the canvas, I could hear their story. But there is no need. The National Gallery has kindly provided a sixty-three word synopsis of JJ's life. It reads like my prep-school school report:

> *Jameson came from Clackmannanshire, Scotland, like his wife Margaret, whom he married in 1768. After many years practising law, he came to Dublin, in 1780, where he founded his distillery at Bow Street, Smithfield. This became John Jameson and Son in 1810. He is depicted as vigorous, even in old age, following his return to Scotland, which would explain the choice of artist.'*

This short synopsis has misconstrued JJ's life like a prep-school school report. But the gallery is not to blame.

A book was produced in 1878 called *Truths About Whisky*. It was produced by four Dublin distilleries, including John Jameson & Son and William Jameson & Co. It is a deliciously informative book that extolls the virtue of pot-still Dublin whiskey and how to spot counterfeits.

However, when it comes to the 'Truths' about the origins of the two Jameson whiskey companies at the time, the book is less than truthful. It suspiciously, in one case, even takes the Fifth Amendment and claims ignorance.

Just fifty-five years after the death of John Jameson, John Jameson & Son says of itself:

> *'Its origin cannot now be traced.' – 'There is no one living who knows, and there is no discoverable documentary evidence to show what was the date of the foundation, neither can we even say at what date prior to 1802 the distillery passed into the hands of the ancestor of the present proprietors.'*

The denials are preceded with the whimsical, of which there is a fluff of truth:

'There is a tradition that it was founded by three gentlemen, one of whom was a baronet and another a retired general, but that they were unsuccessful in their enterprise and lost their capital.'

For William Jameson & Co., the book says of the distillery:

'Messrs. Wm. Jameson and Co. has been in the possession of the family of the present proprietors since the year 1779.'

No truth whatsoever.

So, what ghastliness were the proprietors of the two distilleries and, indeed, members of my family trying to hide and sweep under the carpet?

A crazed serial killer in the attic? Descent from a family of werewolves? Or maybe, was the whiskey an offshoot from a hand gel?

I suspect that the reason was no more than a marketing wheeze.

The longer a company has been established, the more dependable it sounds. In the case of whiskey, it is the ageing that brings it to its excellence. An old whiskey company with a long lineage adds an extra ambience.

1780 was a popular date for many companies to become established. Pawnbrokers, breweries, fire insurance, wine merchants, opticians, grocers, sliversmiths, wool growers, and chemists all scrambled to become established in 1780. Some maybe had.

John Jameson & Son, of course, could not claim to have been established on any such date as their book of 'Truth' had already stated:

'There is no discoverable documentary evidence to show what was the date of the foundation.'

Eight years later, it appeared that documentation had finally been discovered, probably at the bottom of an old family wardrobe. John

Jameson Whiskey then began to be advertised as having been 'Established' during that prolific year of 1780.

Wee fibs grow into whoppers until the perpetrator believes it themselves. 1780 stuck, and today it is labelled and engraved onto bottles of Jameson Whiskey. 'Established 1780' is a curious nineteenth-century marketing fabrication with which I have no quibble. It adorns the bottles of an extremely good whiskey. It has been there for one hundred and thirty years. It has claimed squatters' rights.

My quibble is with how other misrepresentations have attached themselves to that date and presumed all kinds of wrong suppositions. This misinformation has been repeated and embellished to infiltrate tourist guides, whiskey buff books, websites, dissertations, university bibliographies, and whiskey tours.

We have been put off the scent, but the intrigue remains. How did a small-town Scottish lawyer become linked to a billion-pound irish whiskey?

John Jameson's chosen motto as a lawyer was 'Truth Wins'. To my dear old four-times great-grandfather JJ, whom I share with hundreds of others, it is only fair that your tale is now told as truthfully as possible.

Walking back through time, along the pairs of gifted socks and stockings, there will be conjecture, but it will be pegged up with all the facts I have discovered.

'Veritas Vincit.'

John Jameson by Henry Raeburn
(National Gallery of Ireland)

From deep within, I think I can detect a chesty chuckle.

The Prospect of the House & of the Town of Alloa. Engraving by John Slezer
(Reproduced with the permission of the National Library of Scotland)

Alloa – *'The way to the sea.'*

Chapter 2

Buried and Born in Alloa

1740–45

Alloa – 'The way to the sea'; Royal myths and ancestry; Kirkyard neighbours; the birth of John Jameson; Early years; A trip to the harbour.

ALLOA IS A SEAPORT TOWN on the north bank of the River Forth in Scotland.

The Forth is a river that rises and tumbles down from Ben Lomond and the Trossachs. Bubbling through moorlands, forests, and lochs, the waterway rushes into alliances with various other rivers and then begins to slow to take in the lush scenery of the Lowlands. Meandering beneath Stirling Castle, the Forth loops onwards and eastward in a most extraordinarily haphazard way. Eventually, after an overindulgent twenty miles to a crow's six, the Forth pulls itself together at Alloa.

At Alloa, the river widens into a firth, and the Firth of Forth flows on into an arm of the German Ocean. Alloa – derivative from the Gaelic, meaning, 'The way to the sea.'

Two miles inland from Alloa are the Ochil Hills, a range of small, tufty mountains whose toes wriggle into the fertile green valley of the Forth. These hills border the north of 'the wee county' of Clackmannanshire and provide a backdrop to its parishes and villages.

Beneath the Forth valley can be mined the black gold of coal.

Along the coastal shallows can be panned the white gold of salt.

Beneath the waters can be caught the rich silver of fish.

Here, John Jameson's ancestors were attracted, came, and settled.

But from whence did they come?

It is curious that a family who couldn't quite recall when their distilleries were founded in the recent past could, nevertheless, trace their ancestry back to royalty and King James the First of Scotland.

As a child, I was told the swashbuckling royal tale that James the First of Scotland had a bastard son who married a pirate's daughter. I then imagined that after a rum-swigging wedding, this son of James and the pirate's daughter sailed away to raise a family of younger pirates from whom I was descended.

Cool!

A more developed version of this story tells the tale that James the First had two bastard sons. These bastard brothers were commanded by their fornicating father to chase off pirates and Norwegian immigrants. They obliged, and for their services, they were granted a coat of arms, a version of which has attached itself to bottles of Jameson Whiskey.

It is hard to discover the foundations for these stories, but James Stewart was captured by pirates as a child and handed over to Henry IV of England. This tale may have triggered the pirate stories in the Jameson myths.

I also suspect that John Jameson would have disowned any association with a fornicating ancestor, due to his strict religious upbringing.

JJ had his own, far less grandiose, tale as recorded in the 'Memoir of Dr Jamieson'.

In his comfortable old age, JJ had sat down for a chinwag with the Reverend Dr John Jamieson. Dr Jamieson was the learned author of the *An Etymological Dictionary of the Scottish Language* to which JJ had subscribed. Dr Jamieson was also a relative of JJ's but had inserted an 'i' into his name during a fit of adolescence.

Together the two like-minded men discussed their shared ancestry.

The first of their tribe, so they believed, had settled in Orkney and Caithness. This was during the twelfth century when there was a migrant influx from Norway and Denmark.

But as JJ puffed away at his clay pipe, he took delight in telling a subsequent tale.

"Now Reverend, did ye hear tell the history of oor founding faithers, the brothers?"

"Romulus and Remus?" smiled Dr Jamieson.

"Ach no Sir, there were three of these brothers."

JJ continued to enjoy telling this scholarly gentleman something he didn't know.

"They were sailors from the north. And as sailors, they possessed all the restless curiosity o' that race. But when they arrived in these most agreeable waters o' the Forth, the three brothers decided to bade and went no further. Ane brother settled north o' the river n' twa to the south."

"And when was it do you suppose, Mr Jameson, that they came here?" enquired Dr Jamieson.

"Alas, I can give you no firm date, Doctor, but since then, from these three brothers, oor families have multiplied considerably, both to the north and the south of this great water."

JJ's tale of the journeying brothers would resonate within his lifetime.

As for the coat of arms on a bottle of Jameson Whiskey, through the centuries, the tribes of Jamieson, Jameson, Jamison, and Jimison have collected a wide assortment of coats of arms, crests, and seals. In common, they have depicted all kinds of ships, from roman galleons with oars to sleek sloops with sails. There is none that I know of to date that displays a funnel.

When John Jameson wrote his many letters, he sealed them with wax stamped with his trademark bearing his crest and monogram. At the centre was a proud, three-masted eighteenth-century merchant ship. Above the ship was the Latin motto, 'Sine Metu' ('Without Fear'). Below the ship, prominently monogrammed, were the initials JJ.

Seafaring was in JJ's blood; the sea had led the family 'Without Fear' to Alloa; the sea had given many their livelihoods; the sea was a part of JJ's life, too.

Today, John Jameson's residence in Alloa remains within the whiff of the sea, half a mile inland at the kirkyard of the old parish church of St Mungo's. The church has been dismantled, leaving behind a tower topped off with a bell-shaped roof. Here is the memory of the bell that once tolled to summon JJ to worship, weddings, and funerals.

JJ's kirkyard neighbours have fertilised an advancing tangle of growth that threatens to smother their memorials forever. Where descendants care or history decrees, the triffids are kept at bay.

The Erskines of Mar, the dominant local family, have escaped the rampant vegetation. They have built themselves a well-maintained mausoleum to the east of the bell tower.

Next door to this deceased toff's dormitory is a tall, simple, but impressively Palladian tomb. A wrought iron fence gives the property its dimensions, and two Ionic columns frame the roll call for those piled up beneath. At the head of this household, with his age at death neatly chiselled but with an extra year cheekily added on, lies John Jameson.

John Jameson's proximity in death to his neighbours, the Erskines, suggests an association in life.

The Erskines of Alloa House and its tower had a claim to the ancient Earldom of Mar. They were a foremost Jacobite family who owned Alloa.

Significant was John Erskine, commonly numbered as the 6th Earl, who was a visionary genius of a man.

An architect, an urban planner, a musician, a politician, and a soldier, he was one of those toffs who was irritatingly good at everything.

Born in 1675, this Erskine laid down many of the legacies that led Alloa into the Industrial Revolution. Principally, before steam power was established, he constructed the Gartmorn Dam. This provided hydropower for coal mining, woollen mills, and other industries. By his design, this same force of water swept down and flushed the silt from the harbour.

Alloa became a gateway to the oceans.

The Earl was well-liked by his servants and tenants. Having a slight aristocratic spinal deformity gave him a distinct walk. He was thus affectionately nicknamed, Bobbing John.

A Protestant, he adopted the Episcopalian variety rather than the Presbyterian. This pleased his highland tenants as being halfway to Catholic.

The halfway house he espoused politically, too. He had a pragmatism that frequently changed his allegiances between Whig, Tory, Jacobean, and Hanoverian.

And why not?

But his detractors were quick to seize upon his infirmity's 'Bobbing' nickname.

Bobbing John was one of the authors of the Act of Union between Scotland and England in 1707. However, the Earl changed his tune after discovering that the Union was not delivering what it promised – namely, free trade for Scotland.

In 1715, Bobbing John became an earnest supporter of Scottish independence under the flag of the Old Pretender James Stuart. From his Braemar estates, he raised the highland clans for the 1715 Jacobite rising.

Unfortunately, near Alloa, the Earl's considerable gifts gave out. At the Battle of Sheriffmuir, he could not bring about a decisive victory.

The Earl fled to France whilst at home his titles and lands, including those in Alloa, were confiscated for his treason.

But that was not the end of the Erskines of Mar. They were toffs.

Bobbing John's brother, James Erskine Lord Grange, came to the rescue. Judge, binge drinker, wife kidnapper, and libertine, Grange bought back the confiscated lands for his nephew and niece.

His niece, Lady Frances, he married off to his son and Frances's first cousin James.

By the time John Jameson was born, twenty-four years after the battle of Sheriffmuir, Bobbing John's children, Thomas Erskine and Lady Frances, were back in residence at Alloa Tower. Through their patronage, the land, town, harbour, and even the jail were at their behest.

JJ was born into a feudal world.

JJ's father, William Jameson, was a feuar, a tenant who rented land that could medievally be paid for in grain.

William rented a field from the Erskines on the outskirts of Alloa at Gubber, where he raised sheep. William would supplement his income by subletting leased tenements, lending money, and buying and selling various goods. He was a small-time merchant and entrepreneur.

William Jameson's relatives were sailors, shoemakers, tanners, farmers, and preachers of the gospel.

JJ's beginnings were solid but not well-to-do.

'October 5, 1740. William Jameson & Helen Horn in Alloa had a lawful son baptised before the congregation called John.'

John Jameson was only a few days old as he squealed in shock from the cold kirk water brusquely sprinkled on his head. In eighteenth-century Scotland, registering a birth before God was the most pressing and important part of postnatal care. It followed birth swiftly.

Survival was slender. JJ had just one sibling, an elder sister called Margaret. Margaret, it seems, did not live beyond her childhood.

For Helen and William Jameson, their new bundle of worry was to be their one and only son. JJ would not be allowed to forget his debt to God for his existence.

1740 Scotland was not a wealthy land. A highwayman would be better off robbing himself. Frugality was the norm, a way of life, and religiously desired.

The Jamesons' cottage at Woodgate was small, thatched, with a low ceiling, wooden floored and uncarpeted. The furniture was rough-hewn and sparse. Beds were in recesses or boxed in the wall. The old tenements of today's Scotland still mirror those snug Scottish ways of sleeping.

Wee JJ was born into an uncrowded, cosy world.

From the first mewling, advice was near at hand from neighbours and extended family. Close also was mother and father's rough, worsted comfort and body odour.

Slowly, JJ became aware of the rural universe that surrounded him: the thick, dark woods of fir trees creeping towards the house; scary horned cows, staring sheep, barking dogs, flustered chickens; the click of the spinning wheel, the rattle through the walls of rats and mice.

Everywhere there was mud and the scent of human excrement.

The weather dominated; the seasons obeyed. Winter cut cold, and the plaids were wrapped tight. Spring, like Brigadoon, pranced forward, swirling with the giddy inhalation of herbs and flowers, their varieties now long extinct. Summers of long days, hay, and the lazy ripening in the fields. But when days grew pleasantly warm, the haar wickedly huffed out its air-conditioned chill from the Forth. Through the hanging mists, or from the belligerent rain, or sudden snow came a snigger: 'Sae ye think it is bad now, do ye? Well, it can only get wurst.'

Diet was sustaining but hardly adventurous. Broth, beef, cabbage, and mutton were the staples. Potatoes and turnips were a rarity.

In summer and autumn, meat was eaten fresh. At Martinmas, cows and sheep were slaughtered and salted by the fleshers. During the winter months till May, the thrifty would methodically eat their way through their beast from nose to tail. Visits to certain aunts and uncles would be timed as to what part of their cow they were eating that day.

Sweets and puddings were unheard of.

In the absence of culinary delights, there were alternative high points for wee JJ. One was exploring the myriad paths and lanes where a story could be found around every corner. A stone where Kenneth King of Scots raised his standard, a stone where a wizard was burnt, a stone where Robert the Bruce carelessly left a glove, and another stone he sat upon.

There were towers and castles, too, as witnesses to Scotland's past. Mary Queen of Scots had spent her childhood just down the road at Alloa Tower.

History, legend, and myth were crouched down, ready to leap out into the present and fill the mind of a small Scottish boy.

But the highest high point for JJ was a trip with Papa to the port, away from the stifle of woods to the free breeze of the sea. They would go down the track to Alloa, jumping the deep ruts made by the coal wagons. Through the crooked streets of the town, they navigated to Sailors Walk. A broad avenue of Bobbing John's lime trees led straight down to the shore.

The harbour was a place that promised imaginings of the lands beyond horizons. Robinson Crusoe's diarist, Daniel Defoe, reported, *'At Alloa, a merchant may trade to all parts of the world.'*

Offshore were ships of impossible size, rocking and waiting at anchor. At the pier, others were crammed, with their cluttered masts, crowding the sky. Overhead, sailors whistled and clambered the rigging. The air was steeped in tar, from the vessels, from the sails, from the ropes, from the sailors' hair.

Sights, sounds, and smells surrounded the small boy to feed his imagination and ambitions forever.

Barrels were rolled and swung, delivering anything from nails to salted beans to French brandy. The barrel, the two-thousand-year-old shipping container, that one day would reveal another priceless feature and play its part in the small boy's story.

Uncontained were the clouds of emphysema-giving dust as the local coal was shovelled onto barques. Off it would sail down to Leith to stoke the fires of Edinburgh.

The traffic clattered as spindly-legged packhorses arrived from Glasgow. Their loads of Virginia tobacco would be weighed, distributed, and shipped down to England or Europe and beyond.

The four-year-old JJ stood with his hands on his hips, his stocky head turning in widening wonder. Off the shore, he saw the thrill of a ship setting sail. Sail upon sail opened out and filled with the wind, whilst below this giant wooden chest of drawers was powered gradually forward. What wee boy would not want to one day captain such a vessel?

"Papa," said JJ.

"Aye, Johnny?" said his father.

"Ane day," said JJ with certainty, "ah shall be a sailor tae."

"Aye, mibbie," his father replied with an elusive shrug.

The time would come for one last glimpse of the excitement, and then Papa would take JJ's hand for home.

"Papa," said JJ.

"Aye, Johnny?" said his father.

"This is ma best day ever." And for JJ, it always was.

Away from the salt sea, they would go through the smell of coal fires, flesh cooking and sweet dung. Once more, the wee boy was surrounded by trees where that night, he would dream of oceans.

John Jameson's Tomb by Ciaran Murphy.

John Jameson's residence in Alloa today

John Erskine Earl of Mar by Ciaran Murphy

Bobbing John, JJ's Jacobite churchyard neighbour.

Chapter 3

The War

1745–46

1745 – James Erskine, MP for Stirling, advises James Francis Stuart and his son Charles that the time is ripe to seize the throne; Charles Edward Stewart lands in Scotland; John Jameson witnesses a circus coming to town; Charlie enters Edinburgh; Battle of Prestonpans; Thuggery and the workings of War; Alloa becomes a bridging point; Charlie retreats; Cannon fire at Alloa; 1746 – Battle Alley; Culloden; John Jameson becomes a Jacobite by default.

'YOU BECOME WHAT YOU ARE TOLD,' said the poet Lawrence Hoo. JJ was told he was Scottish and that God would be merciful if he were honest and good. Then, as he approached his fifth birthday, the world changed. War erupted. Fear and uncertainty arrived. God didn't seem quite so merciful.

When JJ was born in 1740, the Kingdoms were involved in the War of the Austrian Succession, which was to continue until 1748. It was a massive war of toffs that spread throughout Europe and to America, but it kept well away from Alloa.

In 1745, another war of toffs and succession began to brew. Prince Charles Edward Stuart was planning to take advantage of the disruption in Europe and seize the British throne for his father, James.

From near Alloa, an ally arose. Bobbing John's brother, the libertine James Erskine of Grange, now MP for Stirling, was feeling miffed. Grange had courted both Prime Minister Walpole and the Hanoverian Prince of Wales to regain the Alloa Mar Earldom for the family. But to no avail.

James Erskine's closet Jacobite loyalties kicked in. Changing tack, he wrote to James Stuart to encourage his son Bonnie Prince Charlie that the time was ripe to strike with troops away on the Continent and opinion divided at home.

Charlie agreed with James Erskine's counsel but ignored the advice that up to ten battalions of French soldiers would be needed.

In July, Charlie set sail with just two ships.

From Nantes, Charles was aboard the small but armed brig *Dutillet* to link up at Belle-Île with the larger frigate *Elisabeth* with its sixty cannon and seven hundred men. Together as they swung by the *Lizard*, the Royal Navy's HMS *Lion* spotted the two and fired.

Charlie's *Dutillet* skippered out of range.

A bloody pounding then began between the *Lion* and *Elisabeth*. Both large ships were severely damaged with many killed and wounded. The *Elisabeth* had no alternative but to limp back to Brest with all the expedition's arms and men.

Charles was impatient; he didn't want to lose face. To James Erskine's and others' dismay, Charlie on the *Dutillet* sailed off up the Irish Sea to battle on alone for the throne.

On 23 of July 1745, upon the dazzling white sands of the island of Eriskay, Charles Stewart the Bonnie Prince first set foot in Scotland.

Off Eriskay, nearly two hundred years later, in 1941, the SS *Politician* was to neatly flounder with a cargo of twenty-eight thousand cases of whisky. Both events were the beginnings of the stuff of legends.

From this flat island, Charles and seven companions made their way over the Hebrides Sea to the mainland and loch Nan Uamh. Here the turquoise waters lap their way inshore. Through rocks of silvers and browns, the Loch leads inwards to the luscious greens of mythical hills and the mountains beyond. When the midgies lie low, this is a landscape that pulls you in from the ocean to capture and entangle you as you glimpse a paradise. Scotland bewitches. Small wonder, then, that when the locals had advised Charlie with his crazy ideas to:

'Gang hame!'

Charles replied, 'But I am home.'

Having landed, the privateer *Dutillet* set sail again, leaving Charlie and his seven companions alone on this remote Scottish shore with ambition and little else.

But what Charlie lacked in arms, army, and wealth, he made up for with a rightful Scottish cause. Excepting for a forty-year ban on Catholics for succession, Charlie's father James's claims to the thrones had legitimacy.

The Catholic Exclusion Law had replaced a Scottish Stuart King with a German Hanoverian King. That coupled with the forty-year-old union of England and Scotland, there was much that stuck in the gut of the Highlander, Lowlander, Catholic, and not-so-Catholic.

Charlie immediately set about fly leafing, and from then on, the speed of Charlie's success was astonishing. From the initial stone-walling on arrival, Charles eventually won over the heart of clan chief Donald Cameron of Lochiel, and then others followed. In less than a month after his landing, he had gathered an army.

On 19 of August 1745, at Glenfinnan, where, one hundred and fifty years later, Concrete Bob McAlpine would build his famed railway viaduct, standards were raised. Fifteen hundred toughie highlanders roared their support for this bonnie laddie, all sweetness of looks and freshly landed from France. It was brandy galore to all.

Back in Alloa, the vibrations of war were already felt.

On 20 of August, General Sir John Cope, the commander in chief of Scotland, arrived with his government forces in nearby Stirling. Wee JJ could watch an army on the move. The flashy red coats, the marching, the drumming, and the endless procession of supply wagons; it was a circus coming to town.

For Papa and Mama, there was unease. Alloa was strategically placed with a convenient ferry crossing. Any conflict could impact their family's safety.

Having strengthened the garrison at Stirling Castle, Johnnie Cope marched north to meet the foe.

Meanwhile, Charlie's Jacobean cause was gathering momentum as more highland chiefs and lords joined him. With the chiefs came their servants and tenants. Two guineas advance and nine pence a day was the pay. Sanctions or threats were added to press a tenant when needed. The Scottish rebellion to arms was well on its way.

Johnnie Cope sped northwards, travelling along the military roads built to suppress such uprisings.

Charlie sped southwards by also taking advantage of these conveniently paved ways.

South of the Corrieyairack Pass, General Cope baulked at the opportunity for a confrontation and swerved off to Inverness.

Charlie now had a free run down to Edinburgh.

On 4 September, Charles paused at Perth. Here he appointed Lord George Murray and the Duke of Perth his lieutenant generals. Murray's flop over to Charlie's side was a coup. A veteran of Bobbing John's campaigns, he was highly skilled, although the Bonnie Prince often underappreciated him.

Up north, Johnnie Cope suddenly realised that he was going the wrong way. At Aberdeen, he ordered ships to take his army back south again.

At Alloa on 14 September, wee JJ heard distant cannon fire. Charlie had arrived in Stirling with another circus. Whilst the Lord Provost was entertaining Charles in the town, the troops up at the castle were none too pleased with the lack of an invite, and they were firing off shots.

The world was turning upside down and in quick time.

Three days later and Charlie's men were outside Edinburgh demanding surrender. When a city gate was opened to let a coach through, in rushed the Jacobites, who overpowered the guard. The government troops had already fled the streets, so Edinburgh was Charlie's. At the Palace of Holyroodhouse, the Prince set up shop.

Johnnie Cope, in the meantime, had landed with his army in Dunbar, having left his tents behind in Aberdeen.

With the first proper battle of the '45 rebellion looming, General Cope's forces were a template for the Keystone Cops. The story goes that Cope's troops were told to leave their swords at Stirling Castle to avoid drawing attention to themselves. Untrained, the commanders forgot the powder for the artillery and, on discovering that the shot for the muskets was the wrong size, ordered it to be chewed down to make it fit the musket barrels. Then there was confusion as to how to fire the cannons. The gunners would sometimes place the ball before the powder or set off the powder without the ball.

On 20 September 1745, the opposing armies caught sight of one another just east of Edinburgh near Prestonpans on the Forth. Three thousand government troops were assembling on the open coastal plain when the Jacobites arrived on a ridge above them. The Bonnie Prince was all for charging down to attack. Luckily, General George Murray managed to dissuade him by pointing out that between the two armies, there was a marsh.

That night, Charlie and his generals planned an early wake-up call. At three in the morning, the highlanders awoke, emptied their bowels, crept along a narrow track through the marsh, and swung round behind

Cope's forces. As the sun rose from the east, so did the Jacobite army
– surprise!

"Hey! Johnnie Cope, are ye waukin' yet?"

With stabbings, screaming, spurting blood, and heads lopped off,
the Battle of Prestonpans was over within half an hour.

Johnnie Cope fled to Berwick to be the first to deliver the news of
his defeat.

The garrisons at Edinburgh and Stirling castles remained in government hands, but now they were isolated and not at home to callers.

In just two months from when he first landed, Charles Edward
Stuart had raised an army and conquered Scotland. Remarkable.
What next?

Charlie returned to his Palace of Holyroodhouse and planned the
conquest of England.

A portrait by Alan Ramsay was part of the publicity pack for the
requisitioning of the English throne. Soft and powdered with no hint
of battle or tartan, the twenty-five-year-old looks out as fresh and rosy
as a baby's bottom and dreams of England.

But as Charlie planned and preened before the oil paints, his cohorts
went about their rougher business. Thuggery goes with the workings
of war, and thuggery was employed to keep the show on the road and
down to England.

Transport was critical for battle, and horses were needed for the
hundreds of wagons and the cavalry. Farmers were targeted, and their
horses and fodder were seized without a receipt and often on pain of
death. In Alloa, there was immediate concern that fields could not be
ploughed nor crops sown for the spring.

But as Charlie lorded the land, government ships continued to rule
the waves. Admiral Byng dominated the Forth, and he administered
his own indiscriminate thuggery.

Unable to get a good shot at Leith, Basher Byng sent a fifty-gun ship
to blitz the small fishing village of Newhaven. Innocent lives were lost,
homes destroyed, and livelihoods shattered, and for no good purpose.

For many, this action showed that the government in London had turned against the whole Kingdom of Scotland. For the local Newhaven Fishwives, the bombardment probably contributed to their collective Tourette's.

Byng's squadron on the Forth was a good reason for the Jacobite artillery supplies to be landed well away to the north at Montrose and Stonehaven. These arms were then transported overland and south to Edinburgh. For speed, the goods still needed to be ferried over the Forth.

Alloa was the chosen crossing point. Alloa was now in the front line and within the sights of Basher Byng.

To secure the crossing, the men of Alloa were pressed into service as navvies. Together with the Highlanders, they raised extensive defensive earthworks on either side of the passage. The veteran Jacobite, Lord George Murray, came to supervise the operation. Murray ordered up and topped off the newly raised batteries with fourteen Swedish canons.

Basher Byng was kept at bay as his ship of war, *The Happy Jennet*, skulked just out of cannon range. Pappa William kept wee JJ well out of range, too. Trips down to the harbour ceased.

But then, towards the end of October, the momentum towards Charlie's march to annex England increased. As supplies were funnelled through Alloa, the largest circus of all arrived in town. It would have only been fair that wee JJ could witness history in the making.

JJ would watch in awe as three hundred wagons loaded with armaments and supplies swayed through the streets. Commandeered horses and cattle accompanied in their droves.

Escorting the procession were four hundred warriors from Cluny MacPherson's Highlanders. This fearsome division of Charlie's conquering army, with their broadswords, targes, belted plaid, and their defiant tartan swing, captivated and enthralled. Any child would have been smitten. JJ watched unwaveringly, his cheekbones high and his eyes buttoned deep in thought. Would he become the captain of a ship or a highland warrior?

Through the hours, the mesmerising miles-long convoy churned forwards to be ferried over the Forth. The stench of steaming dung rose and hung in the air as the last stragglers brought up the rear.

Maybe a small five-year-old boy with unruly, thick dark hair, cow-licked at the crown, returned for one last look.

All seemed safe when, out from nowhere, came the sudden panic and hysteria of thrashing hooves and coats blazing red. Captain Aber-cromby from Stirling Castle had snatched his opportunity.

A father whisked up his child to safety as the burn of steel flashed within a breath. A sword sliced deep across the shirted breast of a high-lander. In a streak, skin flapped forward to expose the flesh, frozen in shock before the blood and life streamed out. For a moment, a child had glimpsed the horrors of war. The spectacle was now no longer so thrilling.

The raid evaporated as rapidly as it had appeared.

The press reported that Captain Abercromby returned to Stirling with prisoners, baggage, letters, horses, and some cows. Hurrah!

As military supplies arrived in Edinburgh, Charlie was impatient to get going. He convinced himself that once in England, further support would materialise. With an unhelpful royal belief in divine guidance, he chose this time to ignore the earthly advice from his generals.

On 30 October, the Bonnie Prince left Edinburgh for England.

The Highland Guard at Alloa withdrew, taking their cannon. The opportunity was now open for the Stirling garrison to gallop off to Alloa once again. Great sport was had as they sank the boats that had transported the armaments over the Forth.

Such galloping, sabotage, and fringe fighting was making Alloa a jittery neighbourhood.

For Papa William Jameson, paralysis of trade was creeping in also, as supplies and markets were severed with local weavers and spin-ners immobilised. Off Greenock, Virginian ships were dangerously marooned, bringing Alloa's lucrative tobacco industry to a halt. Revenue officers either submitted or fled as taxes were syphoned into Charlie's coffers.

Papa William could have been enlisted by either side at any time, whatever his sentiments. His livestock was there for the taking from whatever army was passing by at the time. For JJ and his family, there was fear. The future felt unsafe. Papa William longed for the old status quo.

Nearing Christmas, Charlie's escapade into England had stalled. The support that the Prince had insisted would come never materialised.

There was no sign of French assistance from the Continent, but there were plenty of signs of government troops returning. At Derby, Charlie learnt that there were no fewer than three armies on his case.

With Hogmanay approaching, the numbers in Charlie's army were depleting. On the insistence of Lord George Murray, the Bonnie Prince had no alternative but to retreat to Scotland.

Charlie marched back up the West Coast towards Glasgow. Not many friends were made on the way.

Accommodation for large armies is a problem. B&B for a Jacobite meant refusing to pay the bill and leaving with the owner's bed linen and their shirts, too.

The Bonnie Prince was a charmer, but any slight snub to him could result in callous behaviour from his henchmen.

On one such night, Charlie had decided to entertain himself and his chums at Lord Douglas's Castle in Lanark. Douglas had a slightly different political perspective from the Prince and preferred not to socialise.

Having drunk Douglas's wine cellar dry, Charlie left after breakfast the following day.

As a bread-and-butter letter, Charlie's henchman remained to humiliate the lord and abuse his tenants. They then took away any items to their liking, including horses, his Lordship's breeches, and his butlers' stockings.

On 3 January 1746, the Bonnie Prince left Glasgow with, among other things, a requisitioned printing press. Maybe a memoir was on the way or an alternative publication to the government-favouring press.

South of Stirling, Charlie set up his headquarters at Bannockburn.

Alloa was within Battle Alley. Bannockburn, Stirling Bridge, Falkirk, and Bobbing John's Sheriffmuir were just a few battles fought within trotting distance. Now a new local battle was on the horizon.

From Edinburgh, General Hawley and a large army of newly arrived government troops set forth.

Once again, Alloa became a critical ferrying point for the Jacobites and their supplies from the north. Local Alloa carpenters and wrights were pressed into constructing new flat-bottomed boats to transport cannons and other artillery.

On 8 January, Alloa was in the direct line of fire and attack. Government troops and sloops arrived to challenge the Highlanders at their ferrying point. A rebel brig, loaded with two large cannons, was setting sail for Stirling. Government troops intervened and in the crossfire, a life and a leg were lost. In the confusion, the government boat grounded, and the brig escaped with its cannon to set about the siege of Stirling Castle.

Wee JJ heard many an explosion.

Downstream at Airth, government cannon fire destroyed houses and killed eighteen. Upstream, Stirling Castle was under siege with cannon fire from both sides. For everyone in the Alloa neighbourhood, it was best to keep your head down and not to walk around town wearing your team's colours.

On 17 January 1746, eight miles south at Falkirk, Charlie and his troops clashed viciously with General Hawley's army. The weather was foul, and as the rain soaked, so did blood. Horses were cruelly butchered as Highlanders attacked the cavalry with their dirks. They grabbed and stabbed, and Hawley's men fled from the frenzy. The Bonnie Prince, it seemed, had won the Battle of Falkirk Muir.

Unfortunately, Charlie failed to capitalise on the action and went back to bashing cannon balls up against a rock wall at Stirling.

Meanwhile, another blueblood from the rival house of Hanover was arriving on the scene. Charlie's cousin, Prince William, the Duke of Cumberland, was advancing with five thousand German soldiers to relieve the Stirling garrison. Happy families.

Cumberland was a sausage of a man with a fashionable habit of dressing up in the drawing-room curtains that belied his butchering instincts.

With his army rapidly leaking men, the Bonnie Prince wisely decided to avoid a clash. The Jacobites headed north to winter for a while and to replenish the troops.

Alloa breathed a sigh of relief as the never-ending military activity of armies coming and going – of cannons firing and limbs flying – subsided.

Soon wee JJ could sleep more soundly, go down to the shore again, and not be greeted by the menace of heavy artillery.

As the April buds burst, history took hold with a blood fest at Inverness. At the Battle of Culloden, Charles Edward Stuart was defeated by Butcher Cumberland. It was a celebration of blasting, slashing, stabbing, slicing, and garrotting.

Cumberland then set about living up to his butchering name in a merciless spree of hangings, burnings, imprisonments, and deportations for anyone with a twitch of a Jacobite. Of course, these victims were mainly your common folk, because your toffs could afford to take a ticket abroad and wait for a pardon.

The toffs up at Alloa Tower had concealed any excitement for the Bonnie Prince and quietly resumed their rural affairs. As soon as he saw how hopeless the rebellion was, Uncle James Erskine of Grange flopped back to supporting the Hanoverians.

As for the Bonnie Prince, he would be touring the highlands in the first incarnation of Charlie's Aunt. As he cross-dressed from place to place, he left a legacy of extensive trails for 'Visit Scotland'. Eventually, Charlie weaved his way home to the Continent and a decent brandy.

Bonnie Prince Charlie. Painting by Alan Ramsay
(IanDagnall Computing /Alamy Stock Photo)

The Bonnie Prince – Fresh and rosy as a
baby's bottom.

John Jameson would remember the rebellion of 1745 for the rest
of his life. The herding of hooves, the smells, the sounds, the slicing
of steel, the marching, the drumming, the distant explosions, and the
uncertainty would haunt him. Maybe it was simply the circumstances,
but John Jameson, his children, and his grandchildren all swerved joining the military.

Long before the Bonnie Prince decorated shortbread tins, Charlie
became a legend and a symbol of Scottishness.

JJ was told he was Scottish; JJ would become a sentimental Jacobite
by default.

Chapter 4

An Education

_____

1746–53

John Jameson goes to school; The curriculum; John Francis Erskine and Sheriffmuir; Navigation or bookkeeping; Religion; The Alloa riot; Mr Moir's School; John Jameson secures an apprenticeship with Mr Rollo.

"**G**RANDPA, WHAT SCHOOL DID YOU GO TO?"
No reply.

Fundamental facts are missing from John Jameson's life up until the age of sixteen. However, a picture emerges from where he began, to what he became, and from what was available in Alloa.

From the age of six, JJ started his schooling in earnest. There were none of the niceties of a gradual familiarisation with education through kindergarten or nursery school. Nor did he have those gentle early learning years of creating hedgehogs from egg boxes. Preschool instruction at home concentrated on the practical, such as how to strangle a chicken.

On JJ's first day at school, lunch was wrapped in a cloth, and he was sent off at five thirty in the morning to return home at six that night. For wee Johnny J, the day was full of daunting confusion. He was pushed and jostled into an exuberance of new faces, names, customs, and outsized by all.

Crowding into the school room, boys slammed down onto benches in a mix of ages, abilities, and social classes. They nudged, kicked, and laughed together, whilst the small first-timer felt like a foreigner amid those who knew it all.

The clatter and the chatter vanished abruptly as the dominie's swift presence alighted at his tall, intimidating desk. All in black with a frock coat draped in academic gown, the parish schoolmaster bent, crow-like, to scrutinise his new arrivals.

Wee Johnny J trembled under the shadow of the dark spectre from whom he had arrived to discover the wonders of the world.

The dominie gave a quick rundown of what he expected of the poor little mites and the punishments he could inflict at his discretion. The punishments sounded a little more extravagant than those offered in my day of getting the whacks or having a board rubber bounced off your skull. A whipping or a flogging were the terms in regular use.

The first day at school then shot off to a rollicking good start with prayers and prayers and prayers, and the shorter catechism learnt by rote and belted out by heart.

Throughout the day, the schoolmaster multitasked between a wide variety of subjects. His older scholars would sit with the younger ones, becoming occasional classroom assistants.

Good hearing was vital, so JJ tried to avoid having his ears boxed. If ever his mind wandered to dream of captaining his ship to save Mr Crusoe, he would be lifted by the hair, dangled, and dropped to the floor.

It was tough nurture, but wee Johnny J was determined and soon got into the swing of learning.

Although the discipline was harsh, the boundaries were known so that a flogging would have been rare for the canny wee JJ.

The days were long, with ample time for JJ to acquire the rudimentary skills of reading, writing, and arithmetic. Religious studies underpinned all subjects.

Then came an awareness, followed by the learning of Latin, Greek, French, geography, history, and the classics. Latinity was what all scholars would be judged by on leaving, and Latinity was JJ's strength. JJ was also a meticulous calligrapher.

To verify JJ's academic achievements through his youth, there is no need to look for evidence in school assessments. His skills acquired through his education can be seen over the decades in his handwritten documents in Latin.

But it wasn't all work. JJ would grow up with his school chums, many of whom he would know throughout his adult life. One such was John Francis Erskine of Mar.

John Francis Erskine was about a year younger than JJ and was the grandson of Bobbing John. John Francis lived at Alloa House, the mansion with its illustrious and ancient tower. John Francis was from a very different background from that of JJ.

But rural life was a great leveller. There was a diverse mix within the parish schools, from the sons of noblemen to labourers and all those in between.

As boys, John Francis's and JJ's paths would have crisscrossed.

Unlike JJ, John Francis possessed a horse of his own. He had a natural affinity for the beast. Later, his university friend James Boswell was to nickname him 'The Horse'.

One might imagine that the seven- to eight-year-old Johnny Erskine and JJ took off together for a spin on the steed.

A quick hoist up for JJ, and off they would gallop. No fancy saddle, just gripping legs around the horse's flanks, grabbing onto Johnny Erskine up front and pounding forward.

They would fly, along the Great Perth Road, from river and town to the desolate moor of Kinbuck and Sheriffmuir.

At Sheriffmuir, the sounds of battle still echoed forty years on. Wee Johnny Erskine would jump from the horse and run to his secret stash of rotting armoury. Broken swords, their basket hilts intact, rusty dirks ready to stab, and the prize of his boulder-hidden collection, an abandoned Lochaber axe. Pole wizened, blade dangerously slipping, the boys took turns to wield it.

With battle shrieks, they dragged red coats from their horses and chopped them to pieces.

"Death to Captain Abercromby!" screamed John Francis Erskine.

"Death to Captain Abercromby!" screamed JJ.

In their eighteenth-century Japs and Jerries, the boys lost themselves.

For Stuarts, for Scotland, for Jacobites all, and the ghost of Bobbing John.

Muddied and battle weary, JJ returned to his home and the reality of mutton stew and the Bible.

At the ages of ten or eleven, the toffs left the parish schools for the English establishments of Rugby, Westminster, and Eton. Spruced up, they lost their vernacular, and their Jacobite battles vaporised into myth.

JJ remained in Alloa to take advantage of all the parish school could offer.

Alloa was 'The way to the sea', and so was the Alloa Parish school. 'Navigation, a Complete Course' was offered at the school for one pound and one shilling. For JJ, this was an opportunity to lay the foundations for a career on the oceans. As a ten-year-old, there was the chance to follow a family tradition and captain the ship of his dreams one day.

But JJ's success in his studies pointed to a land-based occupation. Fingers trapped, mangled, and broken in a pulley block could forever ruin the chances of a desk job with a quill.

Papa William was not about to chuck away his considerable investment in his only son. JJ's mum, Helen Horne, would also want her boy's future safe on shore.

As an alternative to the navigation course, the school offered bookkeeping. JJ's ambitions and dreams of captaining his ship were beginning to disappear. The dutiful son sighed and knuckled down to master the maths and logistics of the ledger with ease. Bookkeeping would be another foundation stone for John Jameson's life ahead.

The Christian religion featured prominently in JJ's growing up. For the Jamesons in Alloa, there were various versions to choose from. But some varieties came with hefty penalties.

To be Episcopalian was synonymous with being a Jacobite, and your church was likely to have been burnt down by the butcher Cumberland. Additionally, to prevent any religious cross-infection, worship had to be conducted in pandemic bubbles of no more than four persons.

To be a Catholic would incur losing your civil rights.

Presbyterianism was the government-recommended version of Christianity and came relatively penalty-free. That was provided you could endure the strictures of austere worship in often overcrowded premises.

The Jamesons followed the government guidelines and attended the local kirk of St Mungo.

Papa William's nephew, another William Jameson, was a preacher of the gospel who had chosen a slightly different path. He had joined an offshoot of the Presbyterian Church of Scotland, the Church of Secession. The Seceders had a gripe with the establishment. They were against the rights of the landowners to appoint the minister of their choice to the Kirk. They were, in effect, anti-aristocratic and demonstrated this by refusing to doff their hats to the gentry. With their opinions came the seeds for rebellion and revolution.

In 1750, JJ's tenth year, the monotony of the Sabbath day was broken when a new minister was appointed at St Mungo's.

The local landowners had chosen the Reverend James Syme as the new incumbent. Mr Syme was a particular favourite of George Abercromby, a toff from next door Tullibody and a relative of the infamous galloping Captain Abercromby from Stirling Castle. Mr Syme had recently tutored George's son Ralph, and the family championed him.

Members of the Alloa congregation took up the Seceders' call that they should all have been consulted on the new minister's appointment. Other grass root grievances also fed into their anti-establishment anger. On the land, farms were increasing in size, and tenants were being moved on. In the coal fields, colliers were trapped, by law, into their scantily paid jobs. At the Alloa Kirk, there was severe overcrowding. Those with the money bought their seats, and the poor could not enter the door to worship. It was all things bright and beautiful and the poor man at the church door, without a voice, opinion, or pew to kneel and pray in.

Sunday, 16 September 1750, when Mr Syme was to be admitted as a minister, the mob arose. According to the *Aberdeen Journal*, they consisted '*mostly of coaliers and the lowest sort of people*'.

As the riot erupted, the ringleaders carried off the keys of St Mungo and locked themselves in the bell tower. Here they rang the church bell continuously all day.

Outside, much to the glee of a young JJ, the mob prevented entry into the church so that the Rev. Warden from Gargunnock could neither deliver his edict nor his barn-storming sermon.

The Abercromby family were furious, and there was a skirmish. George and his father, Alexander, were assaulted and injured. One of the rioters then damaged a chaise. Luckily, there were no tyres yet invented to be slashed.

The church bell continued to be rung, and a flag was raised from the steeple for the victory that Mr Syme's settlement as the minister had been prevented.

It was one–nil to the Seceders.

That was, of course, short-lived. Three militia companies were sent off to Alloa to ensure Mr Syme could take up his post.

The riot ringleaders, consisting of two shoemakers, two weavers, a baker, a coal hewyer, and the wife of a maltman, were arrested. They were marched off to Edinburgh, incarcerated in the Tolbooth, tried, and sentenced.

Most of the ringleaders were transported to His Majesty's plantations in America. Anyone discovered returning within seven years would be whipped down Edinburgh High Street and transported back. As for the leaders of the Seceders, they continued to preach the gospel.

By age ten, JJ had witnessed a full-blown rebellion with war and a revolutionary riot.

When JJ was eleven, another Abercromby favourite had returned to Alloa. Mr James Moir was a schoolmaster who had once again tutored the young Ralph.

Unusually, George Abercromby, a leading unionist, had entrusted his son's education to Mr Moir, a renowned Jacobite. But Mr Moir was an exceedingly good schoolmaster, so George ignored his 'peculiar' beliefs.

Each year James Moir took on twelve scholars, and for their twelve-hour day, it was advertised that:

> 'Besides the Latin, Greek and French Languages, and a particular attention to the knowledge of our own, he (Mr Moir) teaches the Use of the Globes, Geography ancient and modern, Writing, Arithmetic, and the elements of Geometry, and, if desired, Navigation and Book-Keeping. He likewise spends an Hour every day, on the Mythology and antiquities of the Oriental, Greek and Roman Nations; History and Chronology ancient and modern, and with the more advanced Scholars, Books proper for informing and improving their tastes in the Belles Lettres, will be read. Each scholar pays Five pounds sterling per Quarter and a Silver Spoon at Entry.'

In 1752, five pounds was the price for a single twelve-day coach journey to London. Five pounds and a silver spoon would have been a considerable sacrifice for the Jamesons but worth it. A year or so with Mr Moir would smooth off the rough edges of JJ's education and give him a broader view of the world.

By the age of twelve, it was time for JJ to leave schooling behind, commit to his future, and earn his way. JJ's academic strengths pointed him to the possibility of a career in law.

The diarist James Boswell, who was the same age as JJ, had also looked to a career in law. But Boswell was a toff with money and connections. He was able to study at Edinburgh, Glasgow, and Utrecht universities with frequent gap years abroad. He eventually became an advocate.

With little money and few connections, JJ's ambitions needed to be more modest. His goal was to be a writer and admitted as a procurator in the county courts. In essence, JJ set out to become a country solicitor.

The first step was for JJ to obtain an apprenticeship in a local law office. University lectures could come later, as and when required.

The competition was keen. The gentry often used local law offices as finishing schools for their sons to pick up a few legal tips before running their estates. A law office would only take on a young apprentice if they could be of use from the start. JJ had to impress.

In the small town of Alloa, it wasn't easy to doctor your CV. Your character was carried before you. Recommendations from teachers, the kirk, and neighbours all gave weight.

The young thirteen-year-old John Jameson had a reputation as a hard-working, honest, and polite young man. He could also demonstrate to any prospective employer his fluency in Latin and impeccable handwriting.

JJ's ability to listen and to write what he had heard accurately, neatly, and instantly gave him the credentials of an excellent shorthand typist or a top-of-the-range word processor.

Robert Rollo was a long-established writer in Alloa. When the young laddie walked into his office, he recognised that JJ had the skills that could be put to work immediately.

At the age of thirteen, JJ became Robert Rollo's 'servitor'.

They were humble beginnings that were to become the opportunity of a lifetime.

As JJ ventured forth for his first morning at work, he felt like a king for the day.

Unlike his Seceder cousin, JJ doffed his cap to the gentry and everyone else besides.

Chapter 5

Apprenticeship

1753–61

Learning the business of a writer; Befriended by Katharine Bruce; James Stein joins John Jameson as a fellow apprentice; Studying in Edinburgh; James Stein's scallywag ways; John Jameson becomes a writer at the age of eighteen.

Arriving for work at Robert Rollo's house and his office was a step up into another world for John Jameson.

As well as a procurator and a notary public, Robert Rollo was also the Sheriff Clerk of Clackmannanshire. The Rollo house was the administrative centre for the county and its court, where all the legal and fiscal records were kept.

In addition to his county business, Rollo's activities varied, including conveyancing, marriage contracts, deeds, bills of exchange, neighbourly disputes, bankruptcies, and the sale of ships and estates.

The Rollos were an old Clackmannanshire family, and Robert Rollo had been the Sheriff Clerk of Clackmannan for a good forty years.

The house was large, stone-built, two-storied, with steep slated roofs and many chimneys. It was set within the old town and just north of Alloa Tower on the high road to Clackmannan.

For the young JJ, it was a little too far from the sea to his liking, but the large garden of Ash and Sycamore trees would occasionally catch the breeze to sail him away on his daydreams.

Back down to earth and onto dry land, JJ's work was all-consuming.

As he copied contracts, wills, bonds, tacks, and leases, JJ began to learn and enjoy the lawyer's way with words and the power that a piece of parchment could wield. How the written article netted the deal and nailed it to certainty. The dry, pedantic lawyer's style, JJ relished, too. He had no trouble grasping the logic of it all.

'To each his own.' – This was Robert Rollo's chosen motto as a notary, and he and the young JJ hit it off instantly.

Rollo's free-styled philosophy tumbled through into his work. His office was a masterclass in disorganisation, with papers scattered and documents frequently getting lost. Much had to do with Mr Rollo's deteriorating eyesight. The young JJ, with eyesight keen, could often rescue the county from bankruptcy by discovering a lost bill under a slice of mouldering cherry tart.

With just Mr and Mrs Rollo and their twenty-three-year-old daughter Janet, the young JJ was a diversion for the household. Captivated by and relishing the comparative luxury of his surroundings to those of his upbringing, JJ caused much amusement. He couldn't help but feel the smoothness of the furniture and be transfixed by the paintings. The unusual extravagance and pride of a new carpet on the floor caused JJ to beg the question.

"Surely, such a floor covering is merely a convenience for rats to nest beneath?"

Such observations would cause the Rollos to erupt into laughter. JJ's dry comments and observations were unintended at first to amuse, but by creating laughter, they were the seeds for his quiet wit.

It wasn't long before JJ became one of the family.

A mile or so down the road from Rollo's house was Clackmannan, the head town of the county. It was little more than a village, with one broad high street of ill-kept and dilapidated houses.

At one end of this high street was a clock tower attached to a tolbooth with a gaol beneath and the county court above. The building was no less run down than the rest of the town, but within it, the sheriff courts were held throughout the year. Here Robert Rollo presided as Clerk of the Court together with the Sheriff-Depute or his substitute as the judge.

The apprenticed JJ attended these court sessions and slowly began to absorb the business and formalities of the county court. From theft to debt, JJ learnt how the laws of the land were applied.

Two other essential proceedings were held inside the draughty Sheriff's courtroom: the parliamentary elections and the Fiars Court.

The Fiars Court was a yearly event where fifteen county gentlemen braved the February freeze to fix the price of the various grains and crops from the preceding year. Those chosen by the Sheriff to act as jurors in the proceedings included tenant farmers, merchants, factors, millers, maltsters, and distillers.

Frequent attendees at these Fiars Courts were members of the Stein family. The Steins were farmers who rented land from the local toffs and lairds. John Stein was a feuar like JJ's father, but his farm down by the Forth at Kennetpans was large. Here, John Stein indulged in an offshoot and a favourite pastime for farmers, distilling. Mr Stein's distillery was substantial, and he took a specialist's pride in his alchemy, which he passed on to his sons.

It was probably at the Fiars Court at Clackmannan that the young apprentice clerk John Jameson first became acquainted with the Steins and the distilling business. This introduction would have given JJ a unique perspective on the importance that the price and quality of grain played in distilling whisky.

Here, as the assembled entrepreneurial jurors deliberated and Mr Stein passed around a warming wee tiple, the young JJ may well have choked on his first nip of whisky, too.

In addition to the knowledge he learnt in the courtroom, there was another realm revealed to the young apprentice in Clackmannan.

At the other end of the High Street to the Tolbooth and crumbling along with the rest of the town was Clackmannan Tower. Here was the seat of the chieftains of Clackmannan.

Henry Bruce was the last of the line of these chiefs, and he had fought in the 1745 rebellion for Bonnie Prince Charlie. He had escaped the harsh penalties of defeat by being concealed for many years within the vaults of the tower. But his survival was probably due more to his wife's forceful character than to his concealment.

Katharine Bruce was a famed Jacobite and proud Scot. Katharine and Henry were good friends of the Rollos, and therefore an introduction for the young adolescent JJ was in order.

When JJ visited the tower for the first time, he was in awe. On entering the lofty stone hall, JJ looked up to see a large portrait of the ginger-whiskered King Robert the Bruce. Hammered up on the wall also was the 'Tree of the Family of Bruce' displaying Katharine and Henry's direct descent from the King.

JJ bowed low to Katharine.

"M'Lady, I am deeply honoured to have the pleasure of your acquaintance," he stuttered.

"Noo, thir's a braw laddie," smiled Katharine. "A'though he has a strange way o' talking?"

JJ was relieved. To progress in society, language had to be twisted into the English vernacular; Katharine would have none of that. Katharine spoke in the broad Scots of her age.

"Come 'n' sit next to me, laddie," winked Katharine.

The Rollos had warned JJ that the outspoken Jacobite could also be a little forward in other matters, too. When the young spindly Henry Dundas begged to kiss the hand of the revered sixty-year-old, it was said that she had scoffed.

'What's wrang wi' mah mooth, man?'

Calls on Katharine Bruce were always entertaining. In her possession were other family artefacts. There was the Robert the Bruce battle helmet and the two-handed sword that he had wielded at Bannockburn. Onto those whom Katharine favoured, she would shakily and dangerously lower this monster weapon to dub them knight. Later, she would famously honour the Scottish bard Robert Burns in such a way.

The young JJ enjoyed Katharine's company much. Katharine would joke and nudge the serious, thoughtful young man until she got a smile. He listened to her forthright opinions and admired her tolerance, of which *Tait's Edinburgh magazine* would later say:

> *'Differences in politics and religious faith provoked no resentment nor produced an alienation of affection.'*

Together with Rollo's motto, 'To each his own', JJ carried these sentiments for the rest of his life.

Whether Katharine ever dubbed JJ with the great sword is not recorded. However, a more beneficial honour than to be dubbed a knight was that JJ became Katharine's family lawyer.

As JJ continued his apprenticeship, he was joined in Mr Rollo's office by a fellow apprentice, James Stein. Jim was the second son of old John Stein, the distiller at Kennetpans. Jim had no intention of becoming a procurator or an advocate, but his father sensibly thought that a knowledge of the law might serve him well in his businesses of the future. It was so to be.

Jim was a scallywag but a clever one.

Scallywag Jim was the same age as JJ, and their signatures appear together on the many deeds and agreements from the Sheriff Clerk's office as '*Servitors to the said Robert Rollo*'. But Jim and JJ were total opposites. Jim was gregarious and a risk-taker, whereas JJ was thoughtful and canny. Whilst JJ would be happy to sit for hours and listen to tales from Katharine Bruce, Jim would prefer to be cutting about chasing the local lassies. JJ was content enough to wander around in his brown woollens, whereas Jim would spend his father's money on the latest fashion.

But opposites attract, and as history was to prove, the two young men got on well together and appreciated their differences. On the other hand, it is hard to imagine that Mr Rollo enjoyed Scallywag Jim's forthright confidence and maybe found him a little too dangerous at times.

As JJ progressed through his teens during the 1750s, so did the country. With improved agriculture in fields and kitchen gardens, along came a wider variety of crops. The greater use of imported sugars, spices, and fruits meant that the culinary wilderness of JJ's childhood began to be replaced by an enjoyment of food and a budding discernment.

The new elevated company JJ kept, with the likes of the Rollos and the Bruces, would have influenced his tastes, too. For the first time, John Jameson would have sampled that favoured tipple of the gentry, a brandy. Here he would have discovered a spirit to savour rather than to choke on.

As a young clerk, John Jameson proved conscientious, diligent, and meticulous. To praise is not a particular Scottish practice, but JJ knew his talents were acknowledged, and his confidence grew. With Scallywag Jim as a second clerk in Rollo's office, JJ could now be released more frequently to concentrate on his studies.

JJ's love of ships was incorporated into his further education by hitching a lift on one of the many vessels sailing down from Alloa to Leith. A walk or a stagecoach ride would then take JJ up into Edinburgh for a short stay to attend the latest course of lectures at the university.

Edinburgh University was very accommodating in the range of public lectures you could join, from Law to Medicine to Hebrew. If you were thrifty, you could even have your cornea operated on for nothing whilst at the same time attending a discourse on the eye.

The Faculty of Law was moderately young at the university but vibrant. The first stop for JJ was the ever-popular lectures on Scots law given by John Erskine of Carnock.

More advanced and non-compulsory were Robert Dick's teachings on civil or Roman law. These lectures, at the time, were delivered in Latin, with which JJ had no problem.

During JJ's studies, Edinburgh was still cramped within its city walls and awaiting improvements. The university buildings were dilapidated, and it would be a good thirty years before Robert Adam's new build.

Since the Union at the beginning of the century, the city had slumped. With no local parliament, it ceased attracting the fashionable and smelt. The stink was unbelievably disgusting. It was no wonder that the powdered Bonnie Prince moved on so fast in 1745.

Sewers had been an unheard-of feature in many towns since Roman times. However, with its stacked-up sandstone skyscrapers, Edinburgh had a novel answer to the quick flush. It was called chucking your full potty 'oot the windi'.

'Gardyloo!' was the famed and frequent cry you might hear before receiving a splattering of high-velocity shit from nine stories up.

But the esteemed capital had one other delight to turn a stomach inside out. The North Loch was a water feature bordering the city that was to never appear in an edition of the fisherman's magazine *Trout and Salmon*. Intended as a defence, the Nor Loch now manufactured, beneath its surface, weapons of mass destruction. Into its depths were dumped every bloated, rotting carcass or missing person. In wet weather, dead cats, dogs, and fleshers offal rained down from the city above to enhance and spice up the loch's treacherous odour beneath. For this future World Heritage site, 'Auld Reekie' was not an affectionate term. Thankfully, the North Loch was soon to be drained, and the city would be free to break out and develop anew.

For now, JJ enjoyed the smelly old city with its steep, narrow closes and wynds. It had a good social mix, where lawyers and lords shared their lofty tenements with every other trade, from cartwrights to candle makers to chimney sweeps.

Once you were inside a cosy vintner or an inn, the unbearable city stench would waft away on tobacco smoke and conversation. Old and young would puff on their clay pipes as they discussed the latest war abroad or the new rationales in science and philosophy.

Occasionally, JJ would take a brandy. This distilled, matured spirit from the grapes of France, weathered by its travel across the salty German Ocean, was savoured on a smoky palate of best Virginian.

Apart from good brandy, there were other pleasures to tempt. The mid-1700s was a sex-riddled age. *The History of Tom Jones* had been published ten years before, and the pursuit of the fairer sex would have forever been on a young man's mind.

JJ's contemporary, the diarist James Boswell, records frequently indulging in the flirtations of the age, and whenever he considered safe the full libido. Unfortunately, Boswell's candid account of his romp with a Covent Garden actress Louisa Lewis left him with stage fright and a good dose of the pox. These were the dangers that JJ would not have been so inclined to dabble with. Unlike Boswell, JJ was a small-town boy, and his advancement relied heavily on his reputation. To the Edinburgh ladies of pleasure, JJ doffed his hat and nothing else.

On his return to Alloa, JJ left the dissertations of Hume, Smith, and the Scottish Enlightenment culture and took up his conversations with Scallywag Jim. James Stein was wildly ambitious, and as the two young men walked the quay at Alloa, talk would turn to trade and the prospects of future fortunes. JJ's love of the sea and ships flowed easily into these discussions.

In Alloa, there were many local shipowners, including Scallywag Jim's family. That was no big deal, as a boat was a part of the everyday transportation of goods. They were the white vans, the HGVs, the monster trucks of sea haulage.

Vessels from Alloa and Leith made frequent tobacco runs to the Continent and back. Therefore, it wouldn't be too fanciful to believe that JJ and Scallywag Jim might have taken a trip together to Amsterdam during the summer recess. The coffee shops served coffee in those days, and the taverns sold excellent Dutch beer. As a souvenir, Scallywag Jim would have brought home a flagon of the very individual and refined Dutch gin to his distiller father at Kennetpans.

By the time he was eighteen, John Jameson's name had begun appearing as a writer in Alloa in the Clackmannan Sheriff Court Book. JJ had started to ply his trade in law, but his studies continued.

As JJ made his way between university and the Clackmannan Sheriff court, he came to the notice of another Bruce. Robert Bruce of Kennet was a neighbour and relative to Katharine but with differing political views. Bruce was an advocate in Edinburgh and lectured at the university as a Professor of Public Law and the Law of Nature and Nations.

In JJ, Bruce noticed diligence and reliability, and began championing his future.

JJ gained invaluable experience from Bruce and his and other lawyers' offices.

Scallywag Jim, whilst continuing to carry out his apprenticeship with Mr Rollo, came to someone else's notice; the Reverend James Frame at the kirk in Alloa.

The kirks had their separate courts from those of the Sheriff. They had the state-backed remit to police the local morals. Every Sunday, the minister and his gentlemen elders took a trembling top-shelf look at the latest scandalous case of fornication.

In December 1760, unmarried Alice was called before the Alloa Kirk Court to confess that she was five months pregnant. The father-to-be, she said, was '*Mr James Stein apprentice to Mr Rollo*'. She explained, to the eager group of voyeuristic men, that '*the child was begat on the tenth day of July last in the wood of Alloa*'.

Scallywag Jim was summonsed to appear a fortnight later.

Disarmingly, Jim acknowledged the guilt of fornication with the said young Alice, but the guilt in the wood of Alloa, he added, was upon the eighth day of October. He told the court he had never had anything to do with Alice before or since that date. The heartless scallywag had, at a stroke, distanced himself by three months from the responsibility of fatherhood and given Alice a reputation she didn't deserve. Young, charming, and ambitious, James Stein revealed his ruthless streak to succeed.

JJ was ambitious, too, but evidence suggests that he cautiously kept his breeches tightly buttoned in the process.

In March of 1761, JJ's promoter Robert Bruce of Kennet became the next Sheriff of Clackmannan. JJ's network of influential contacts was growing.

Katharine Bruce by Ciaran Murphy

'What's wrang wi' mah mooth, man?'

Parliament Close, Edinburgh, 18th century
(history docu photo /Alamy Stock Photo)

Edinburgh, with its stacked-up sandstone skyscrapers.

Chapter 6

Good Prospects

1762–68

*John Jameson qualifies as a notary public; Robert Rollo dies;
John Jameson becomes the Sheriff Clerk of Clackmannanshire;
John Francis Erskine returns to Alloa; John Jameson becomes
Bailie of the Town; Tea is taken with Margaret Haig; John
Jameson marries Margaret (Peggie) Haig.*

WITHIN THE LEGAL PROFESSION, THERE were strong family cliques. JJ had no direct family links to the law and no impressive family tree to nail up onto the wall like Henry and Katharine Bruce. Marrying the judge's daughter might have been a good career move, but so far, he had come all this way on his own merits.

At the age of twenty-two, JJ decided to advance his career further. Having submitted various testimonials on his professional proficiency, he presented himself before two lords of session in Edinburgh. In a rigorous trial of skills, Lord Nisbet and Lord Coalston put JJ through his paces. Unfazed by them or the Latin tongue, the twenty-two-year-old impressed Nisbet and Coalston. On 11 January 1763, JJ qualified as a notary public.

John Jameson N.P. now had the authority to draw up all those differing legal documents that cause others to go squint-eyed or stuff away in the hopes that they will disappear; conveyances, bills of exchange, deeds, marriage contracts, everything and anything that no one else can be bothered to understand but must have. JJ's chosen motto when qualifying as a notary public was: 'Veritas Vincit', or 'Truth Wins'.

Robert Bruce of Kennet continued to promote JJ, but in the summer of 1764, he moved on from his post as Sheriff of Clackmannanshire to be elevated as Lord Kennet to Senator of the College of Justice. That summer, JJ moved back to Clackmannanshire Sheriff Clerk's office to give Robert Rollo a hand.

Robert Rollo was growing very old. The laughter had disappeared within the rambling Rollo house on the Clackmannan high road. Mrs Rollo had passed away, and the years were taking their physical toll. Robert Rollo was now almost completely blind.

The Sheriff Clerk's office had gone beyond chaotic. It was difficult to understand quite how the county's business had been able to stumble along for so long. JJ set about putting affairs back into order. Papers were unstuck, parchments sorted, bundles of rolls separated, and all placed into presses.

Added to that, over the past sixteen years, poor old Rollo had failed to report and record court proceedings correctly. To the relief of all, JJ reinstated the correct system and restored confidence.

After two years of hard graft, JJ was rewarded. Robert Rollo gave way to the stubbornness of age and appointed his one-time apprentice, John Jameson, as his Depute for Sheriff Clerk.

Sheriff Clerks continued at their post until their death. Unlike the Sheriff, it was a heritable job. Mr Rollo had just one child, his daughter, Janet. There was no immediate male successor. However, Bruce of Kennet and Mr Rollo believed that JJ was the most suitable candidate.

JJ confided confidently to George Sandy, the Under Keeper to the Signet, that '*he had the Clerkship in his Eye*'. But it was not a foregone conclusion. Bruce and JJ were sidestepped.

A fellow judge with a mouthful of a name, the Honourable James Erskine of Alva Lord Barjarg, was eager for his clerk, Mr Robert Auld, to have the job.

Mouthful's estate was in Clackmannanshire, and maybe he wanted to hold sway in the county or to do Mr Auld a good turn. For whatever reason, Bruce and Mouthful clashed. Letters flew at dawn to the Keeper of his Majesty's Signet, Sir Gilbert Elliot of Minto. Minto would have to weigh up between the recommendations of the two senators. Was it to be Mr John Jameson or Mr Robert Auld?

In December 1767, dear old Robert Rollo breathed his last, and the cogs of state whirred. On 15 December, JJ was appointed factor to Rollo's estate; on 16 December, he was appointed the interim clerk. On 29 December, John Jameson was named the new Sheriff Clerk of Clackmannan. Mr Auld slunk away, his high hopes dashed.

It was exceptional. Plucked from the bullrushes, this man from nowhere was now at the centre of county business. Sheriffs would come and go, but JJ would remain in his executive post until he dropped. The county court, the price of crops, the collecting of taxes, parliamentary elections, and military recruitment were all in his domain. At twenty-seven years of age, John Jameson had arrived.

At this same time, Bobbing John's grandson, John Francis Erskine, had arrived, too. John Francis had returned to run the Alloa Estate. His path had been very different from that of his contemporary, JJ. Westminster School in London, enrolment at Edinburgh University, and then a bought commission in the army as Captain. Acting now as the Baron of the town, John Francis was able to appoint his own Bailie. He chose the man of the moment, John Jameson.

The feudal duties of Baron Bailie were fast disappearing, although he still held the keys to the town jail. But for JJ, an attraction to the appointment was that Baron Bailie automatically became a trustee for

Alloa Harbour. Navigation might have been dropped for bookkeeping at school, but now JJ could indulge in all things shipping.

Male, twenty-seven years old, good prospects, good-looking, unfamiliar with the affairs of the heart, seeking life partner, female.

The eighteenth-century dating scene was an under-the-radar, misconstrued, and a long-drawn-out wail of desperation. What's new?

The pressure was fierce. It was a flirtatious age of fluttering fans, fainting, and kicks under the table. It could be a painful and confusing time for a quiet, thoughtful young man like JJ. Fathers were the worst. Eager to dump their daughters, they would woo and nudge with large cash incentives. Like Buster Keaton in his film *Seven Chances*, the handsome Sheriff Clerk was in danger of being chased through Alloa by an army of impatient brides.

Penelope Prudence of Edinburgh's *Caledonian Mercury* wrote occasional but extensive columns on attaining happiness in matrimony. She advised against giving large dowries, as husbands would marry the purse, not the person.

JJ had so far avoided trading in his marriage prospects for his career, and now he did not need to trade it in for a fortune, either. Maybe JJ might marry for love.

'*Look Aboot Ye*' goes the Clackmannanshire motto, and obeying the command from Robert the Bruce, JJ did just that. Alloa was a small town, and the young lady who caught JJ's eye was from Alloa, too. A glance at the kirk, a bow as she strolled down Lime Tree Walk with her mother, a raised hat as she rode by with her father, a wave as she trundled along in a jaunting cart with her brothers and sisters. It wouldn't have taken too long for JJ to find out who this striking young lady was, with her natural and flowing poise.

Margaret Haig was a tobacconist's daughter, known affectionately by her family as 'Peggie'. Haigs were all over the place in Alloa. They were the local surgeon, vintners, merchants, and maltsters, managing the coal and the glasshouse.

Peggie's father, John Haig, traded in tobacco. Together with his brother-in-law, George Peirson, he ran a snuff mill. The sailorly named Alloa Pigtail was a celebrated snuff that Haig and Peirson would grind up and spice to be exported and sniffed in London. In addition to his tobacco business, John Haig had recently rented Erskine land on the shore at Alloa. Here John Haig was establishing a new brick and tile works.

Tobacco, bricks, and tiles were all in John Haig's portfolio, but contrary to popular myth, whisky was not. However, John Haig was married to a Stein. Peggie's mother, Margaret Stein, was the daughter of old John Stein, the farmer and distiller at Kennetpans.

Whisky came along with old John Stein, and so, too, did his son James Stein. JJ's former fellow apprentice, Scallywag Jim, was Margaret Stein's brother, and Scallywag Jim was Peggie's uncle.

By today's standards, JJ's interest in Peggie would have slapped him onto the sex offenders list. Peggie was fifteen years old.

Even within the sensibilities of the eighteenth century, Peggie was young, but she was not unlawfully so. JJ's initial approach to John Haig was not, therefore, greeted with shock and horror. There was a bit of an age gap, but that was not too dissimilar from the age gap between John Haig and his wife, Margaret. Margaret and John Haig were an extremely successful match and were still very much in love.

JJ was of an age when he had the means to look after and cherish John Haig's daughter. JJ also had a reputation for being a fair and honest gentleman. Maybe Mr Jameson should take tea with Mrs Haig.

The Haigs lived in the centre of the old town by the marketplace at the Tron of Alloa. Their two-storey house was not overlarge. The doorways were low, but as Mr J entered, Peggie noticed that there was no need for him to stoop as her father did.

Thankfully, Mr J was not as old as the last Sheriff Clerk whom Peggie had seen shaking and shuffling his way through the Alloa streets. But then, Mr J was certainly not the stable boy, either. Mr J did not look as though he could juggle apples whilst taking bites out of them. Nor could Peggie imagine him flipping over a horse's back at full gallop to go under its belly and up the other side as the stable boy could.

Mr J looked towards her; Peggie looked away. Her mother came forward, and Mr J bowed and kissed her hand. Tea was to be served in the parlour.

The small parlour had been specially cleared. There were a few thumps and muffled screams from other parts of the house, but all was strangely hushed.

Margaret Haig gave her daughter the slightest of looks, and Peggie poured the tea.

'Quiet obedience,' thought JJ.

Conversation then made its social way around the business of the town without going anywhere in particular.

Peggie listened and observed.

Mr J's voice was light and rumbly, with a hint of a chuckle. His hair was thick and dark, cheeks high, mouth set stern, eyes deep and serious, with a smile beneath. But Mr J was not the stable boy.

The conversation tottered on as if there was something that needed to be said but couldn't. Peggie wanted to laugh.

The silences became longer.

JJ became aware of a shuffling behind the parlour door.

Occasionally, the door would squeeze open, and a small face would peep and disappear.

"How many children is it that you have now, Mrs Haig?" asked Mr J.

"To be honest Mr Jameson, I was never one for counting," sighed Mrs Haig. "There is Margaret here, of course, then James, Mary, John, George, Ann, Robert, Janet, and baby Caldom."

"That would be nine children that you have, then, Mama," Peggie said, biting her lip to suppress hysteria.

"Yes, nine," agreed her mother.

JJ's reasoning deserted him.

"Nine! That is a wondrous number indeed. It must be a mystery, Madam, as to how so great a number came about?"

Peggie erupted, spitting her tea across the room.

As if cued to do so, the parlour door burst open and in crashed and tumbled and yelled an uncontainable avalanche of Haig offspring. Mother and daughter moved as one. They threw poise to the wind, kicked, pushed, shouted, shoved, and commanded, and the roomful of seven children and a wailing nursemaid vanished within seconds. JJ was confused as to what had just happened. Mrs Haig calmly took her seat as Peggie resumed her role.

"Would you care for more tea, Sir?" smiled Peggie.

From then on, JJ's visits to the Haigs were a new awakening. The household was tripping over with children, and compared with the solitary nature of his childhood, it was a culture shock. But it was also a question of: 'If you like me, then like my family.'

After the initial stilted manners of a first meeting, Peggie took a closer look at Mr J. Conversation became surprisingly easy with this Sheriff Clerk. He certainly wasn't the stable boy, but he was different from the other men in her life. There was none of her Uncle Jim's swagger nor her father's high-strung nature. Mr J never exaggerated as Uncle Jim did nor blew up like Papa. Mr J was calm and listened, an unusual quality in a man.

As JJ listened, he learnt from this young maybe bride. Whilst he might inform her wisely on many matters, she would in return enlighten him on the latest of good reads that he had not had time for. She would also gently challenge his pedantic lawyer behaviour, which made him chuckle and admit to it.

Gradually, too, JJ began to enjoy the company of the fledgling, lively brood that surrounded Peggie and her mother. The brood in turn looked forward to JJ's visits. He would respect the elder brothers and sisters as young adults. The younger children he would playfully scare away with his sudden growls, after which they would quickly and annoyingly return for more.

Entertainment was all home produced with the likes of harpsichord, violin, flute, and singing. A very pleasant afternoon could be spent at the Haigs.

'*A man should love from reason, a woman from passion,*' so wrote the *Mercury*'s Penelope Prudence. When agreeing to marry Mr J, much reasoning came from Peggie but with passion yet to arrive.

Of Mr J, she liked much; indeed, behind Mr J's posture of seriousness, he had a surprising sense of fun. Of Mr J, her mother and father approved; of Mr J, her brothers and sisters approved; but Mr J was not the stable boy. But then again, love in the hayloft had significant limitations. With Mr J, Peggie could be the mistress of her own house.

The wedding was to come along sooner than later. Margaret and John Haig might be bereft of their precious firstborn child and a precious pair of helping hands, but Peggie had her own mind. The house was getting cramped. Once the decision had been made, why wait? She would, after all, be just down the road from all those she loved the most in the world.

'*Marry in September's shrine; your living will be rich and fine.*' So counselled a popular wedding rhyme. The month of September lent itself to a celebration with the last of the summer sun, harvests gathered, and their fruits ready to be consumed.

Weddings, in those days, could be three-day affairs or more. The Penny Bridals were legendary, and their rowdiness caused them eventually to be outlawed. For those who could survive, they were huge fun. They were a hen party, stag do, and a wedding breakfast, all smashed into one. Entire communities chipped in.

The bride's feet were washed, and the groom was chucked in the tub, covered in grease and soot, and scrubbed. The frolicking and the rollicking carried on relentlessly and suggestively until the rather intrusive tradition of 'Bedding the Bride'. Here the wedding guests from hell followed the bride into the bridal chamber, where they continued to drink and fight over one of the bride's stockings.

In contrast, as the Bailie of Alloa, JJ's wedding would be lawful and relatively restrained, with carriages before dawn.

The Alloa Parish registry recorded the following:

> 'Mr John Jameson Sheriff Clerk of Clackmannan Shire and Miss Peggie Haig eldest daughter to Mr John Haig Tobacconist at the Tron of Alloa, gave up their names the 10th of Septr and were married the 12ᵗʰ.'

The 12 September 1768, was on a Monday.

'*Monday for wealth*' went another back page ditty, and wealth was indeed on display for the day. The worsteds were dumped, wigs were shaken free of fleas, and everyone wore their finery. Dresses of embroidered silk taffeta were tipped with sleeves ruffled with lace. They swished haughtily as they vied for attention. Trim-brocaded waistcoats sparkled, lace cuffs flourished, and silk breeches and stockings clung to male thighs and calves. Tartans and plaids took their bow, too, defying any suggested restriction from the post-Jacobite 'Dress Act'.

JJ stood at the kirk door. He had scrubbed up well and dressed in a skirted coat, meticulously sewn waistcoat, buckled shoes, and with his thick dark hair fashionably covered by a short white powdered wig.

Up the path to the kirk came the Haig children, excitedly scattering flower petals.

Peggie followed, as a mirage, lightly stepping onto her freshly scented carpet. Her natural hair was curled high and tumbled. Her silk dress, delicately layered and trimmed with bows, flowed into her every move.

JJ went weak at his silk-stockinged knees.

Within St Mungo's, the vows were made, never to be broken. The wedding was sealed.

The party moved on for the feasting. Variety abounded with broths, barley skink, loaves, oat cakes, and cheeses; meats of beef, mutton, and local game; fish of herring and salmon; puddings of fruit tarts, bannocks, brose, and cream. Ale was poured, and whisky was drunk as punch.

For JJ, it was not the most relaxing of events. He had to ensure that his mother and father were enjoying themselves and not too overwhelmed.

Haigs and Steins had to be indulged, too. Many he knew already from his business, but now they were becoming family.

Of the Steins, old John Stein the distiller had morphed into Grandpa John, Scallywag Jim had morphed into Uncle Jim, and Jim's three brothers morphed into Uncle Robert, Uncle Andrew, and Uncle John.

The Steins were the dominant family, and pushy. With the nuptials fresh, they were not afraid to talk business immediately with their new in-law. Distillers, merchants, and ship owners all cornered poor JJ.

"Mr Jameson, we must congratulate you," smiled Grandpa John. "You will soon be attending meetings as a trustee of the Alloa Harbour. An advantageous position indeed for our family."

The groom's heart sank. JJ did not relish the thought of an in-depth discussion on developments down at the harbour, nor did he look forward to a Stein knocking at his door every other day. JJ might have wondered if this whole business of marriage was worth it. But then he had only to look across the room at his bride.

Peggie was whooping it up, surrounded by brothers, sisters, aunts, uncles, and cousins. She was the princess of the day.

The music played, and the dancing swept the floor and out onto the green.

As dawn threatened, Peggie and JJ were chaperoned to the Sheriff Clerk's modest house. JJ whisked his bride up and over the threshold; shortbread was broken; jollity sang, and then they were left alone.

Her nightgown was freshly laundered and laid out; Peggie pulled to unstitch her dress and made herself ready for bed.

Down below in the parlour sat JJ, tired and respectful. The clocks ticked, and Peggie waited. Penelope Prudence from the *Mercury* had no advice as to what should happen next. Clocks chimed from every room. Husband and wife were now onto new territory.

Margaret Jameson by Henry Raeburn
(National Gallery of Ireland)

Peggie stepped into the parlour. In the soft shifting shadows of early morning, JJ was gently snoozing in his chair. Rumpled, wig discarded, his dark hair tousled, there was a hint of a stable boy. Peggie nudged him awake.

"Ach! C'moan ye sleepy auld fool!"

Peggie took JJ's hand and led him off into their future.

Chapter 7

Industry, Distilling, and Tantrums at Dawn

1768–75

Industry gathers pace in Alloa; John Jameson stays clear of mixing family with business; 1769 – Margaret Jameson born; James and John Stein develop the Kilbagie and Kennetpans distilleries; 1771 – Robert Jameson born; 1773 – John Jameson-2 born; John Jameson is at the epicentre of a very unpleasant election; 1775 – A duel between Ralph Abercromby and James Francis Erskine; John Jameson is made factor on the Alloa Mar Estate.

TWO DAYS AFTER THE WEDDING and it was back to work for JJ. On 14 September 1768, John Jameson attended his first meeting of the Alloa Harbour Trust as a trustee and Baron Bailie. The day's business heralded a significant step in the gathering pace of the new Industrial Revolution. The Alloa Harbour Trust Sederunt book recorded:

The Trustees on the Estate of Mar are presently erecting a Wagon Way from the coal, called the Gin Coal of Alloa, to the harbour, and shore there, and are to erect a peer at or near the said shore for unloading the waggons and shipping the said Gin Coal....

This wagonway was a pioneering transport system that ran along a state-of-the-art wooden track. It combined gravity and horsepower to deliver coal directly from the Alloa mines to the harbour. It was no wonder that the Steins had cornered JJ on his wedding day. The wagonway would increase the profitability of the Alloa Coal, and the Steins would welcome a slice of it.

The conveyor belt of coal wagons also fed two other industries down by the shore: John Haig's brick and tile works and the Lady Frances Glass House.

The glass house was another industrial inspiration from Bobbing John. Having visited Bohemia during his exile, he had been impressed by their exquisite glass-making skills. Bobbing John recognised that Alloa lent itself to glass making, too. It had all the natural ingredients at hand, with salt, kelp, sand, and coal.

Bobbing John's daughter Lady Frances Erskine followed in her father's footsteps, and in 1750 she put her dad's ideas into practice.

Down by the Alloa shore, she founded her glassworks, where bottles were manufactured for wine, ale, and whisky.

By 1767, Lady Frances was finding the running of her factory a little tiresome, and together with her son John Francis, they put the Alloa Glass House franchise out to tender. Control was passed over to William Deas, who led a consortium of shareholders, one of whom was John Jameson. The Alloa Glass House Company and its bottles linked John Jameson to whisky for the first time.

As the various industries developed in and around Alloa, and momentum increased, JJ was well-placed to benefit and influence. Calls from the Stein family were frequent, and when the conversation turned to business, there was pressure for JJ to come to some arrangement.

"Ach, mibbie!" JJ would say, and dodge the moment. John Jameson was wary of mixing family with business, and he had to look no further than his father-in-law, John Haig.

John Haig's snuff factory partner, George Peirson, was the husband of his sister Janet. For years, there had been a long-running dispute between George and John concerning the payment of George and Janet's marriage settlement. It involved profits from a coal business and a wrangle over a sought-after seat at the kirk. The dispute was to appear frequently on the rolls of the Clackmannan Sheriff Court. It was not a pleasant affair and threw a shadow over family gatherings. For now, John Jameson would keep family and business well apart.

At Alloa on the 8 June 1769, and thirty-eight weeks after their wedding, Peggie gave birth to a summertime baby girl. Firstborn Margaret Jameson was baptised a day later, suggesting she may have been a trifle premature. For certain, Peggie and JJ had wasted no time. Margaret Jameson thrived and was given many a name of endearment.

The new and delighted Granny Haig was not to be outdone, so six weeks later, Peggie's mum gave birth to her tenth child, Andrew.

Keeping up the trend also was Uncle Jim. Jim had left behind some of his scallywag ways by getting married soon after JJ. A birth followed as swiftly, too.

But Uncle Jim remained as ambitious as always.

The Steins had been a part of the continuing agricultural revolution. They had enlarged their rented farms and boosted their yields. Over the next twenty years, Uncle Jim and his three Stein brothers would be leaders in the Scottish Industrial Revolution. From their family distilleries, they would dramatically increase output.

Grandpa John Stein wished to leave his Kennetpans distillery to his youngest son, Uncle John, so Jim built a new distillery upstream at his farm at Kilbagie. Coal was dug nearby to heat the stills, and a dam was built to store water from the Ochil Hills. The dam's water fed the distillery, powered mills for threshing, and filled a new canal.

The canal, a mile long, was cut down to the coast to Kennet-pans and its harbour. Originally built to export coal, the harbour could now be used to import grain and export spirit from the two expanding distilleries.

Jim's industrial enterprise was created from a farmer's perspective. The farm and the distillery were interdependent, with Jim using the spent grain from his distilling to fatten up his cattle and pigs on the premises.

As JJ trotted up to visit Jim's new Kilbagie distillery, it was not the sweet smell of malted barley that filled the air but the stench of animal slurry oozing out from the surroundings.

"James," he would say. "Ah, mist give praise indeed to the quantity of odious muck that gives aff from both ends of yer business and yer ability to profit by it."

JJ had high regard for Jim's productivity but little regard for the product.

In the eighteenth century, one imagines that some things tasted pretty good. Farming was organic, and crops were full of flavour, as were fresh fish, game, eggs, and milk.

On the other hand, the aqua vitae, or whisky, produced by Uncle Jim's distillery from grain would have tasted dire. With the excise men impatient for their payments, there was no time for it to mature for the niceties of whisky societies.

Slugged back like a cowboy, a whisky would send a shiver down the spine, ping the stirrups, and shiver back up again. But that was the point. What whisky gave you was a good thwack up into the skull to remove all the ghastliness of reality.

At his local Poosie Nancie's, Robert Burns drank Jim's whisky and appreciated its rascally ways. Rabbie witnessed how 'Dear Kilbaigie' evaporated misery and bought jollity.

For the poor, it gave relief; for the wounded, it zapped infection; for the sick, it widened the arteries; for farmers, it paid workers to harvest; for national security, it gave armies the courage to rage, slash, and stab their way to victory; for governments, it was liquid opium for the masses and raised an increasingly indispensable source of revenue.

Peggie's uncles were onto a winner.

Whether hot with lemon or disguised in a punch, JJ would swerve a Kilbaigie and stick to the brandy.

At Alloa on 17 June 1771, Peggie gave birth to her second summer-time baby, Robert Jameson. Rob was a new wee brother and a welcome distraction for two-year-old Margaret.

Not to be left out, Peggie's mum had nipped in ahead in March with William as her number ten.

The baby industry was in full swing.

Another two years and along came Peggie's third summertime arrival. At Alloa on 5 August 1773, John Jameson-2 was born. But poor JJ-2 had to fight for attention; that same year, death struck thrice.

Grandpa John Stein was an expected passing, as was JJ's father William Jameson, but no one expected John Haig's heart attack at fif-ty-three. Maybe the stress of business or too many puffs of his tobacco, but it was a sudden and shattering blow for the whole family.

Margaret Haig's grief was legendary. She took to her bed, inconsol-able, and refused to get up. The Sheriff Clerk's office became a crèche as Peggie's nine siblings, from toddlers to teens, sought solace with her as temporary orphans.

According to folk law, recorded in *The House of Haig*, the ghost of Margaret's doughty dead mother materialised before her and told her to pull herself together. Eventually, Margaret heeded the spirit and arose to put her Haig house back in order.

Peggie and JJ heaved a sigh of relief as the Haig gang left and the last of the Haig linen clouts were boiled. Peggie and JJ could now devote their time to their three children – Margaret, Robert, and JJ-2.

At thirty-three, John Jameson was well into the swing of married life in Alloa and was averaging one child every two years. Records show that his feet were firmly under the table as a hard-working commu-nity member. As Baron Bailie of the town in 1773, he was given the impossible task of trying to sort out the seating arrangements in the overcrowded kirk. At the same time, he was assisting his friend Bishop Petrie in establishing a meeting house for the Episcopalians. JJ's church was broad.

It is also recorded that in July 1774, John Jameson joined the Dublin Freemasons at their Convivial Lodge No. 202. As clever as JJ was at multitasking, it would have been a challenging moment in his story. A two-month round trip to join the Freemasons in Ireland would have unnecessarily added to JJ's stress, considering there was already a lodge in Alloa, which he never joined. Fortunately, there were several other John Jamesons available to take his place. Dublin would have to wait.

Whilst Peggie's uncles, the Steins, were making inroads into the distilling business, John Jameson's world-famous signature was having an impact, too. Not on the side of bottles but at the bottom of the county's tax rolls.

As Sheriff Clerk, JJ was also clerk to the Commissioners of supply as their collector. Over the next forty years, JJ was responsible for collecting window tax, servant tax, land tax, inhabited house tax, dog tax, shop tax, male servant tax, female servant tax, horse tax, farm horse tax, cart tax, carriage tax, clock and watch tax, tax returns, game duty, and land tax.

JJ's records for land tax held the information on the rental value of land in the county, which in turn supported a landowner's right to vote. Details were kept in a cess book or on cess rolls.

In eighteenth-century Britain, democracy or any semblance to it was nowhere to be seen. The voting population were those who held the freehold of land with a rental value in Scotland of at least four hundred Scots pounds.

A Sheriff's Clerk could be pivotal in deciding who voted and who didn't. This fact was recognised by Bobbing John's brother, James Erskine of Grange, who wanted the law changed '*To prevent tricks of the Sheriffs and Clerks*'.

In 1774, John Jameson was at the epicentre of a very unpleasant election in Clackmannanshire that would test his diplomacy and end with pistols at dawn.

Two local families were vying against each other to be represented in Parliament, the Erskines and the Abercrombys.

Representing the Erskines was John Francis's younger brother and grandson of Bobbing John, James Francis Erskine of the burgh of Forest.

Representing the Abercrombys was Ralph Abercromby, son of Unionist George of Tullibody. Ralph Abercromby, a former pupil of Mr Syme, was now a professional soldier. Running for Parliament was not Ralph's choice or desire, but Daddy told Ralph he must.

James Francis Erskine was also a sometimes soldier for the East India Company. A volatile firebrand, furious James was determined, at all costs, to win back honour for his Erskine family of Bobbing John.

Beneath the surface was the old war of Jacobite and Unionist families, and John Jameson was betwixt the two. JJ's benefactors John Francis Erskine and Robert Bruce of Kennet were on opposing teams. His current boss, the Sheriff, was Alexander Abercromby, Ralph's brother.

It all kicked off a year before at the 1773 annual Michaelmas Headcount. Here, barons and freeholders of the Shire met to expunge those no longer entitled to vote or to enrol others who had the relevant qualification.

As tradition dictated, JJ was unanimously elected clerk of the meeting. Then the shenanigans began.

One by one, it was revealed that the assembled freeholders had carved up their estates to swell their ranks. They had carefully divided each parcel of land so that their values conveniently just tipped over the four hundred Scots pounds qualifying mark.

In each case, JJ had accepted and condoned the divisions.

Sons, sons-in-law, nephews, and chums were all added to the roll.

Objections erupted from the furious James Francis Erskine. He had a surprisingly good knowledge of each division and disputed every claim put forward by the opposing side.

The Abercromby camp kept their composure for the moment.

By the end of the meeting, all new claims had been sustained. The voting fraternity for the Shire in '73 had increased from sixteen to twenty-seven, with six added to the Abercromby camp and five to the Erskines.

With both sides playing the same game of monopoly, JJ was even-handed with them all.

As the election of '74 drew near, a distinct unevenness of hand began.

Furious James had been in a spot of aristocratic financial bother. For a quick fix, he had disposed of some of his estate. Even so, he was convinced, as was JJ, that he had held onto enough land to retain his freehold rights.

George Abercromby seized on this to have the furious James struck off the roll of freeholders. He was backed up by Robert Bruce of Kennet, who refused to allow JJ to log the changes in the cess book.

Inconsistently, George Abercromby's nephew Sandy was given the green light to restructure his lands in a similar fashion.

With the Erskines' prospective candidate in jeopardy, someone behind the scenes made their views known and the protest against James Francis Erskine was withdrawn. Was it JJ?

A little before midday on 3 November 1774, the freeholders of the county began to arrive for the election in Clackmannan. From the top of her crumbling tower, the Jacobite Katharine Bruce spied through her telescope the twenty-six of 1774, trooping up the steps and into the courthouse.

Before the assembled, the Sheriff, the rakish Alexander Aber-cromby, flourishingly produced the writ of election. With a seductive gentleness, he reminded all of the Act of George II:

'For the more effectual preventing of bribery and corruption.'

Then John Jameson, the Sheriff Clerk of the county, arose and produced the principal books containing the minutes of the last Michaelmas meeting and the last election. With a bow, JJ turned and presented the roll of electors to the previous incumbent James Abercromby of Brucefield.

James of Brucefield, a Carolina plantation owner and enslaver, called for the freeholders to elect their choice of chairman. The vote was unanimous for General John Scott.

Following on, the freeholders were asked for their choice of Clerk. As always, and as tradition dictated, one would have expected JJ to be voted in unanimously.

But that didn't happen.

A writer called William Gibson was put up as an alternative candidate to the Sheriff Clerk.

For this vote, the freeholders had divided into two camps.

The Erskine Jacobite team voted for JJ with ten votes but lost to the Abercromby Unionist supporters who voted in Mr Gibson with a dazzling fifteen votes.

The furious James Francis Erskine was outraged that Mr Jameson had not been voted Clerk and he protested, but to no avail.

Was JJ's impartiality being called into question? Was he being accused of siding with the Jacobite families? Had he spoken out behind the scenes once too often at his unease at particular trickery going on?

Suddenly, JJ no longer had a role to play in the election of 1774. He was free to trot back home and wait for the drama to catch up with him.

The election was now a foregone conclusion.

But furious James Francis Erskine was not going to give way to Ralph Abercromby so easily. The ice-pinching draft in the courthouse was of no consequence. This would not be the swift, gentlemanly affair of past elections.

Furious James set about discrediting the assembled Abercromby freeholders and their fitness to vote.

He began by accusing Colonel Mastertone of being guilty of the grossest bribery and corruption. Mastertone's defence was that the bribery allegations were not connected to the present election.

Furious James then went on to target individually and in detail eleven other freeholders. These included Robert Bruce of Kennet and Ralph Abercromby, who had both, rather carelessly, listed the same park in their separate freehold claims.

Furious James was rocking the boat and exposing an antiquated voting system that was not fit for purpose.

The passion-filled accusations were languidly cast aside one by one by the Sheriff, Alexander Abercromby.

With the Abercromby majority in control, there was no way the challenges would ever be considered, let alone conceded to.

Finally, a roll was taken to elect the Member of Parliament for Clackmannanshire.

The minutes noted that the same fifteen freeholders who voted for Mr William Gibson as Clerk voted for Lieutenant Colonel Abercromby, and the same ten freeholders who voted for Mr Jameson as Clerk voted for James Francis Erskine.

Ralph Abercromby was duly elected to Westminster.

Furious James Francis Erskine was having none of it. Backed up by his brother John Francis, his father, and five others, he protested vehemently. He blamed Robert Bruce for being responsible for this *pretend majority* through *'illegal'* and *'oppressive'* measures. He accused Bruce of ignoring his honourable station as one of the senators of the College of Justice and instead using the most extraordinary and violent means to dispossess him, James Erskine, of his rights of freehold.

Finally, furious James accused Bruce of threatening John Jameson with violence and forcibly taking the cess book from him so that JJ could not enter Erskine's freehold.

Bruce replied that he did not think it necessary for him to make an answer to such an *'uncommon'* protest.

The minutes were signed, and the election of Ralph Abercromby stood, but the footnotes of accusations hung in the air and were left to dry on the page.

Before the election had begun in earnest, Jacobite Katharine Bruce had spied through her telescope Mr Jameson's early departure from the courthouse. She suspected that proceedings were not going her preferred way.

As JJ trotted back to Alloa, was he put out or relieved? He certainly had no regrets. Maybe now was the time to chuck in his lot with the squabbling, small-town Scottish aristocracy. Maybe now was the time to seek a less fusty fortune in America? Maybe now was the time to have a go at the distilling business.

Arriving home, his boots pulled off, JJ settled into his comfy chair to ponder the day's events with pipe and brandy. Margaret and Rob poked their wee heads around the door. Papa growled. They ran away, squealing.

Peggie, holding baby Johnny, came in to seek news from Clackmannan. JJ looked up at her solemnly. He cleared his throat.

"Ah wis voted oot, expelled fae proceedings. Dismissed!" he said.

JJ paused a moment for a thought. The furious James would now be meticulously going through each of his separate protests. Mr Gibson the Clerk, and the rest would have to listen and suffer their chilblains in silence. Mr Jameson, on the other hand, was in the warmth of his home enjoying his young family. JJ took a gulp from his pipe and puffed out the smoke. Then it happened—just a wee cackle at first erupting into a choking, chuckling, coughing, spluttering, brandy-soaked, smoke-filled laugh. Mags and Rob crept in and clambered aboard the shaking, sweet-smelling timbers of the good ship Papa.

"Ye auld fool," smiled Peggie.

At the end of the month, Ralph Abercromby took up his seat at Westminster. It wasn't long, however, before the furious James Francis Erskine set off in hot pursuit. As a result, a committee was set up to settle his complaints.

The first point furious James raised was that Ralph Abercromby should be disqualified as he had no right to be on the roll of the freeholders. When the committee replied that it wasn't their job to decide the qualification of freeholders, they sunk James's whole argument. On the advice of counsel, furious James waived his rights to continue.

Ralph Abercromby's election was confirmed.

A few days later, an anonymous pamphlet was distributed. It forcibly restated the accusations against Robert Bruce of Kennet. Honour was at stake. Bruce, as a Law Lord, was unable to defend himself, so Ralph challenged the furious James Francis Erskine to a duel.

At dawn, somewhere in London, the two protagonists met. There was much expectation. Here were two professional soldiers. Pistols were loaded. The seconds stood by. Surgeons and undertakers held their breath. Blood was to be expected.

On command, the two men marched their ten paces and turned. Ralph fired and missed. Furious James misfired.

The seconds intervened, and in the excited muddle of the moment, furious James Francis Erskine confessed that he was the perpetrator of the pamphlet. For Ralph Abercromby, furious James's admittance was enough, and the duel ceased.

Back in Alloa, once JJ had received the minutes of the election, he had transcribed them into the electors' minute book. The brutal accusations against Robert Bruce of Kennet were copied down faithfully, as were the reported threats of violence towards John Jameson.

What was the truth?

For JJ, he would neither confirm nor deny. As Clerk, he simply reported the minutes.

Election over and pistols fired, in December 1775 John Jameson, Sheriff Clerk of Clackmannanshire, became the Erskines' factor on Bobbing John's old Estate of Mar.

John Jameson had neatly straddled two camps, and another door opened.

Whisky Drinking
(Chronicle /Alamy Stock Photo)

Dear *Kilbaigie*, evaporated misery and bought jollity.

Transporting coal on wooden rails
(INTERPHOTO /Alamy Stock Photo)

The new wagonway was now established and ran from
the coalfields down to the harbour.

Chapter 8

The House at the Shore

1775–81

1775 - Helen Jameson born; Peggie and John Jameson move to a new house at the shore; The agricultural revolution continues; 1777 - William Jameson born; The Haigs move to Gartlands; Peggie's brothers learn to distil; 1779 - Mary Jameson born; John Jameson goes into partnership with the Steins to sell the 'Coals of Alloa'; Uncle Jim has some unwelcome publicity; A New decade dawns; 'No Popery riots' in London; 1781 - James Jameson born; The winter takes its toll on the family at the house at the shore.

ON FRIDAY, 28 JULY 1775, Peggie's fourth summertime baby arrived. Baptised Helen, there were many pet names that JJ and Peggie might have called her. Nell and Nelly were commonly used within the family, but Helen Jameson was often referred to as Ellen. Margaret was thrilled that she now had a wee sister to help boss the smelly boys.

With a new arrival every other summer, JJ's house had its limitations for growing a large family. Conveniently, JJ's new job as the factor on the Estate of Mar came with the perk of a rent-free house.

The house was on Bobbing John's Lime Tree Walk, planted just before his rebellion. This avenue of regimented trees was well into its glory years as it marched down from the town to the harbour. JJ's house was one of the few that faced this intoxicating green-leafed parade. For now, it was referred to as the House at the Shore. In the future, the house would be appropriately called Linden House.

There was no grandeur in this residence. It was a long, single-storey, stone-built building with a steep slated roof. The windows were deep set to protect from the cutting shards of cold flying in from the east. Set back from the avenue, the house was fronted by grass with causey paths of delicately laid pebbles. Near to the sea, it filled many of JJ's childhood dreams.

At right angles to the house, a collection of stocky buildings housed JJ's offices. Adjoining these were a cow byre and a stable. A large garden for vegetables and recreation bordered the property, with a park for grazing that stretched back at the rear to the wagonway.

This was a home to relish for a growing family in the eighteenth century. It had evolved, reflecting the self-sufficiency of the time. There was milk on tap, transport grazed at the back, and an ability to grow the now-expanding choice of vegetables.

A child raised at the House at the Shore would grow up amid a heady mix of rural and industrial. With a hop, skip, and a jump, you were at the harbour to see the ships loading and sailing. By the Craigward ferry crossing, there was the fun of Granny Haig's brick and tile works. Next door was the intrigue of the glassworks. But best of all was the railway that ran beyond the park at the back of the house. The new wagonway was now established and ran from the coalfields down to the harbour.

Being the factor for the Estate of Mar segued neatly into JJ's Sheriff Clerk job and to that of being Bailie of the town of Alloa. The Estate of

Mar encompassed both the town of Alloa and the surrounding countryside, two miles by four. Within its whim were houses, farms, mills,
factories, coalfields, and a harbour. So were the infrastructures of roads,
sea defences, dams, irrigation, churches, and schools.

The estate proprietor was John Francis Erskine, but he and JJ were
answerable to the trustees. Over the years, the estate had been sad-
dled with many debts, so trusts had been set up to ensure their regular
payments. The four trust members kept a beady eye on all revenue
and expenditure.

For JJ, part of the job was more of the same in collecting the land
rent and arrears. He was also the cashier for the Erskine family, doling
out allowances and even purchasing lottery tickets for John Francis.
Added to this was the maintenance and improvements of the estate.

John Francis wished to continue to develop the legacy of his grandfather, Bobbing John. The confiscated title of the Earl of Mar was
attached to the land, and good husbandry of that land would go some
way towards regaining the title. Estate improvements seemed a more
peaceable way to reclaim an earldom than slaughtering an Abercromby.
But the improvements were contentious.

The landscape was slowly transforming. Drystone walls lined with
thorn hedgerows were being built and planted to enclose fields and
woods. This was not done for future picture postcards nor for the benefit of wildlife. The alterations were to increase crop growth, prevent
livestock straying, and ultimately raise rents. It was a universal system
adopted throughout the Kingdoms. Even the Rev. James Frame applied
the practice to his Glebe lands.

But there were casualties. Smallholdings and subsistence farming
had to go. Expired leases on these small farms were not renewed, and
farmhouses beyond repair were razed to the ground.

The new and larger farms thus created were then handed over to a
tenant who could pay for and implement the improvements. This was
done in exchange for a provisionally lower rent.

Some have paralleled these changes in Lowland agriculture to that of the brutal Highland clearances by the Clan Chiefs. There is an element of truth in that the landlords were calling the shots. But in Alloa, it was a slow process, and John Francis was not an absentee landlord.

John Francis argued that he was doing away with the feudal system where smallholders were trapped in serfdom. Rents then were often paid by a spell on the coalfields, and it was obligatory to grind corn at the estate's designated mills.

With the new order, agriculture remained labour intensive, whilst at the same time, the local industry was expanding. The population grew.

Nevertheless, that did not negate the uncertainty and hardship the changes wrought on some. As the factor, it was JJ's job to implement the new order. He was the bogie man who came knocking at the door of a crumbling farmstead. Sympathy was of little use. But JJ was better equipped than many to give the career advice needed to help the shift of the smallholder onto another farm or into the urban world next door.

In the summer of 1777, the House at the Shore was filled with the yelps, screams, and laughter from a growing posse of young children. Peggie was in her element.

At the back of the house, the timothy grass had grown long and was ready to scythe for hay. Robert and JJ-2 would crawl through unseen, their breeches smothered in seeds. They listened for the rumble of wagons, clinked together three to a horse. As the empty wagons returned along the wagonway to the coalfields, the thrill was to leap out from the grass and lob in a stone with a thud. Caught, they would get a good punch from eight-year-old Margaret or, worse, a thwack from Papa. But in the tumble of childhood, the risk of a battering was a part of their carefree abandon. At the House at the Shore, there was space to go wild.

When the hay was scythed, dried, and neatly stacked, William Jameson, the new summertime baby, arrived as ordered on 29 July 1777.

Granny Haig expressed her delight at William's arrival, but it was time for her to move on.

Since John Haig's death, Peggie's mum and Peggie's brother James had together made a success of the brick and tile works. But Margaret Haig was ambitious for all her sons.

Leaving the brick and tile works in charge of their manager, William Pirrie, and selling the half share in the snuff mill to George Peirson, Margaret and her family moved to the parish of Clackmannan. Here lived Margaret's Stein brothers.

Margaret Haig rented an ancient, rambling old house called Gartlands. It was owned by Robert Bruce of Kennet and had previously been occupied by Alexander Cumming. Alexander was famed for inventing the U-bend. This bent pipe was significant in eliminating the smell from drains and enabling the flushing toilet to prosper.

But plumbing was not the primary reason Margaret moved to Gartlands, nor was it brotherly love. Margaret's father, Grandpa Stein, had left a distilling legacy from which her brothers were now reaping the rewards. It was Margaret's turn to take a slice for the benefit of her sons.

At the back of Gartlands, a lane led to Kilbagie. All five Haig brothers were to tread this path to learn the craft and business of distilling from uncles Jim and John.

Meanwhile, at the House at the Shore, the path to the future for JJ's children led up through the avenue of lime trees, into the town, and onto the parish or public school.

Mr Bell, the rector, and Mr Patterson, his doctor, advertised in the *Caledonian Mercury* that they '*taught all ordinary branches of education on the easiest of terms*'. As in JJ's day, the teaching of Latin took pride of place.

Mr Bell also advertised that he had a large commodious house for boarders '*who may depend on every possible attention to their diet, education, and morals*'. This facility for the older scholars of the gentry had the advantage of extra tuition.

The school was always striving for improvement, and in the younger classes, they were soon to take on girls. With assisted places for the poor in their early years, it was still comparatively inclusive.

At the end of each school year, JJ, as Bailie of the town, led the school inspection and examination. Clergy, local dignitaries, and parents would gather to witness the children's progress. They would view examples of their works and be entertained by the children's ability to recite or translate.

For the children's achievements, praise would be given to Mr Bell and his assistant. Announcements in the newspapers followed with endorsements by John Jameson and the Reverend James Frame.

JJ, as a parent and Bailie, had a twice-vested interest. There can be no doubt, therefore, that Mr Bell, the rector, monitored the advancement of Mr Jameson's children with extra care and diligence. It is doubtful whether Mr Jameson's children appreciated Mr Bell's attention.

At Alloa on 11 July 1779, Mary Jameson, the summertime Sunday baby, was born.

'And the child that is born on the Sabbath day,
Is bonny and blithe, and good and gay.'

As the sixth child, Mary was all those things – easy, happy, amiable, and loved by her doting brothers and sisters. At the House at the Shore, Peggie and JJ had everything they could have wished for.

Peggie was also fortunate to have a second in command, Margaret. Margaret, at ten, was there for everyone: rocking Mary; chasing William as he squealed and tripped over his long, grubby toddler's dress; milking the cow; taking the pony for rides along the lanes; and policing the lobbing of stones into coal wagons. As Rob lifted four-year-old Helen, Margaret couldn't help but admire the master shots from her younger sister as the stones spun and hit their targets. The children whooped as one.

But the stones thudding into the wooden wagons swayed off on a journey to places light-years away from the sublime life at the House at the Shore.

The wagonway served two collieries: Alloa pits and Collyland. Children at the collieries didn't lob stones into wagons; they lugged coal on their backs. The children carried the heavy loads of coal from the coalface to the surface, seventy feet above. It was a lot more strenuous than doing a morning paper round, and it was compulsory.

Work in the colliery was a family affair, with the colliers extracting the coal at the coal wall and then the wives and their children carrying it up to the surface as bearers. The coal master would pay each collier on the weight of coal brought up by his family.

Colliers had previously been legally bound to the colliery for life. A recent change in the law had given colliers their freedom but only after they had given at least four years' notice. Not many took up this offer. The collier's life contract came with the perk of a free house, garden, fuel, a daily meal allowance, and schooling for their children. With earnings now above average and in uncertain times, colliers and their families tended to remain in their harsh backbreaking occupation for generations.

At the kinder end of 'the winning of the coal', there was the distribution. In 1779, a rare and highly lucrative opportunity for selling the Great Coals of Alloa came up for grabs.

As the factor on the Estate of Mar, JJ was well placed to put in a bid. Living by the wagonway and harbour, he was well placed geographically, too. But until this time, John Jameson had never been directly involved with any large-scale commercial enterprise. Weight was needed, and JJ finally gave in to the pressure from the in-laws.

James Stein of Kilbagie and his younger brother, John Stein of Kennetpans, knocked at the door of the House at the Shore.

"Well, gentlemen, let us do business together," said JJ, ushering in Peggie's uncles.

Throwing caution to the wind, JJ took a daring leap by mixing family with business. John Jameson, James Stein, and John Stein joined to form a partnership as the Alloa Coal Company.

On 3 September 1779, John Francis Erskine and the estate trustees signed up the trio for a ten-year lease. For its trouble and keeping its hands clean, the Alloa Coal Company took five percent of the sale price of all the Alloa Coal.

Traditionally, the coal was loaded onto ships in Alloa and then sailed down to Leith. There the ship's master would gradually sell off the coal, sometimes at only a ton or two a day. JJ's pragmatism stepped in to speed up the process. His contact with merchants in Leith meant that the entire cargo was offloaded immediately. The ships could then return to Alloa without delay.

JJ added to his coal company dividend by purchasing his own ship. His childhood dreams of sailing the oceans had not quite materialised, but shipping coals to Leith was second best. John Jameson's wealth and his business acumen were growing.

It was December, and the decade was drawing to a close. JJ was confined to the house with a cold and a sore throat. Between sneezing, blowing his nose, and Peggie pulling out his younger offspring from under the bed, he had to correspond with Edinburgh lawyers.

Mr Haig and Mr Deas were going bust. Haig and Deas were JJ's predecessors for the Alloa Coal, and the managers for the Alloa Glass-house. Mr Haig, together with Mr Alexander, was also the cashier of the Harbour Trust. Money had gone missing from all three concerns.

JJ suspected that Haig and Deas had scurried off to Edinburgh to seek refuge at Holyrood. Here, within the precincts of the abbey, a sanctuary for debtors was guaranteed, and imprisonment was avoided.

Immediately after Christmas, JJ travelled to Edinburgh to face the creditors and sort out the mess at the Exchange Coffee House. But this was all in a day's work for JJ. As well as his business acumen, JJ was becoming well-practised at recognising the signs of insolvency and then mopping up the financial debris thereafter.

Following the waywardness of Haig and Deas, JJ now took over as the cashier for the Harbour Trust. Bookkeeping was paying its way.

Hogmanay arrived, and Uncle Jim had some unwelcome publicity. Rumours were being spread that his spirits were poisoning people. As Uncle Jim complained, JJ proffered plenty of sympathy and advice. However, he found it hard to suppress his sentiments.

"Mr Stein," observed JJ, "tae effect poisoning, there needs to be some masking o' taste. As the taste of Kilbagie aqua is so obviously poisonous, one can hardly be accused of killing anyone who is prepared to drink it. A wee brandy, James?"

Uncle Jim retaliated to the rumours with his customary flair. Here was a publicity opportunity. Jim took out two large ads, in the *Edinburgh Advertiser* and the *Caledonian Mercury*, where he announced the slurs to the world. A reward of fifty pounds sterling was offered for anyone bringing the author of the malicious reports to justice.

1780 and a new decade dawned. John Jameson was tantalisingly a long way off from establishing a whiskey. He remained a long way from Dublin, too. The 1780s would, however, be a defining decade for JJ and his Stein and Haig in-laws. The 1780s would be a defining one worldwide, too.

As the American Revolutionary War battled towards its conclusion, The MP for Clackmannan, Ralph Abercromby, kept his pro-American Independence views close to his chest. Not so reticent in his views was the Reverend James Frame of Alloa. The Reverend had expressed his opposition to the recent Papists Act. This act had restored certain civil rights for Catholics, to which James Frame was robustly opposed.

In June 1780, Scottish Presbyterian views were exported to London within the frozen mindset of Lord George Gordon. The 'No Popery' Riots erupted. They were on a scale unseen before and seldom since. The frenzied mobs attacked the Bank of England and set fire to Newgate Prison. The decade was in for a bumpy ride.

At the House at the Shore, JJ had his own mob to rule. Robert was now ten years old and leading the pack. Rob was cast as his father's successor from an early age. What he discovered in the clattering classroom would be instilled by his father at home. The House at the Shore was a hothouse for learning.

Respite from all the harsh realities of growing up for the older children came from the distractions of their younger siblings following behind. Another summer arrived, and the one-page book of *Scottish Baby Names* was flicked through. On 28 August 1781, James Jameson took his bow at the House at the Shore. Sunday Mary leaned over his wooden crib, dribbled, and kissed the wee baby James on the head.

For servants, the family had just one maid, Jean Westland. There was a nurse for the children and a stable boy who looked after the horse and cow. By contrast, up at Alloa Tower, John Francis had up to fifteen servants, from maids to butlers to coachmen to postilion.

At the House at the Shore, accommodation was squeezed. The nurse slept with her charges whilst the maid slept under the kitchen dresser. For the stable boy, the byre was warm. When entertaining a local dignitary, it was all hands on deck. No one cared as the stable boy served the soup garnished with straw.

Another winter arrived with its accompanying coughs, sneezes, and worse. In the eighteenth century, death knocked frequently at the doors of the young. Paediatrics didn't exist. Squeezed woodlice, powdered horse dung, toads, leeches, and the indispensable bloodletting were the type of stock tactics used by local physicians. Where immune systems had yet to build, death lurked in the shadows.

In December 1781, two-year-old Mary grew sick. Peggie and JJ nursed their wee girl through the days and long nights. Fevers drenched her, and seizures shook her tiny limbs limp. Doctor, apothecary, cordials, blankets, prayers, and tears were all expended as Peggie and JJ desperately tried to hold on to their carefree child. Eyes sunk, smile gone, she gradually faded, and Sunday Mary slipped away.

Friday, 7 December 1781, the bell tolled from the tower of St Mungos. Beneath the mort cloth, the shape of Mary's tiny coffin was barely visible as it trundled up between the skeletal lime trees to the kirk. The Reverend James Frame told all those gathered that 'It pleases a holy and wise God to remove Mary from this life to a better.'

Once back at the House at the Shore, JJ heaved with sobs until he thought he might suffocate. No one would ever forget carefree Sunday Mary.

Chapter 9

Volcano With Gin

1782–84

Business with the in-laws continues; James and John Haig begin distilling in Edinburgh; Gin is exported to London; 1783 – Andrew Jameson born; John Jameson requests home improvements; 1784 – John Jameson organises a charity ball in Alloa; Jameson and Stein lease the Alloa Mills; James Haig marries; Riots at Canonmills distillery; George Jameson born.

M IXING BUSINESS WITH FAMILY WAS going well for John Jameson. As the Alloa Coal was exported, so came a second Stein partnership to import wood and iron. Near to his home, and with the help of his clerk on the Shore Alexander Bald, JJ could keep a close eye on all his harbour businesses.

On the quay, the rough dirty stuff of loading and unloading ships was carried out by the loftily called Pow-Lords and Pow-Ladies. JJ would be subjected to and amused by the Lords' and Ladies' banter as he strolled along the quayside. Their language was not for society but held onto the more colourful traditions of the Newhaven Fishwives downstream. It was light relief, and JJ gave as good as he got.

John Jameson's confidence in his partnerships with Peggie's uncles gradually grew. He could not fail to be but impressed by the Steins' unparalleled success of their core business of distilling. The Treasury was impressed by the Steins also and passed new laws that encouraged them further.

In 1779, a new act had come into being that declared that anyone in possession of a still of over two gallons capacity was classed as a commercial distiller. The law required them to paint, in '*durable large, legible, characters*', a sign over their doors declaring such. Mere possession of equipment would subject potential distillers to due rates and duties.

The act's effect was a squeeze on the home distiller, the Highland distiller, and the artisan. Demand increased for the industrial Lowland distiller, and there was rapid expansion.

The Excise Office had kept everything neat and tidy whilst topping up their revenue.

The Stein uncles now had three large distilleries at Kennetpans, Kilbagie, and Kincaple. The Kincaple distillery was found farther north, near St Andrews, and was run by Uncle Jim's eldest brother, Uncle Robert.

Uncle Jim was the mastermind behind it all, and now he wanted to develop further. The time had come for two of his young Haig apprentices to branch out.

Edinburgh was the chosen location. It was becoming a booming city. For James and John Haig, it was now a hip place to live.

Peggie's young brothers chose their sites on the rural outskirts of Edinburgh, to the north at Canonmills and the southwest at Lochrin.

Canonmills was so named because the clergy of Holyrood once owned its mills. Now they were owned by the governors of Herriot's Hospital from whom James Haig leased the surrounding land and the mills. The current six mills were powered by water, channelled from the

Canonmills Loch to the Water of Leith. These mills and their lofts, granaries, and stables eventually fed into the new Haig enterprise.

James Haig built his distillery from scratch on the south side of the Water of Leith and along the Long Haugh of Canonmills. The Canonmills parks and surrounding meadows were used for the accompanying crops and interdependent livestock. It was as if Kilbagie had been transplanted wholesale to Edinburgh.

Younger brother John Haig's distillery at Lochrin was ready-made. Near Fountainbridge and Tollcross, the distillery had been converted from a brewery by Alexander Reid, who then sold it on to John Haig.

Reservoirs of fresh water beneath attracted both brewers and distillers to the area. John Haig took advantage by installing a steam engine to raise this pure water at Lochrin.

Another asset was a rivulet called the Lochrin Ditch, or later more genteelly named the Dalry Burn. Following the lead from others, John Haig was able to empty the distillery's waste into the rivulet.

The two Haig brothers worked closely together. Their Edinburgh distilleries were joint concerns with an added heavy influence and capital from Uncle Jim.

With five distilleries producing an ever-increasing quantity of spirit, Uncle Jim needed another market. London was an obvious choice. But what was happily slugged down at Robert Burn's Poosie Nancie's would be spat out at a London tavern. So, the conjurer of Kilbagie transformed his spirits to suit his chosen market. For London, Jim infused his grain spirit with Juniper berries and other botanicals and rectified it into gin.

Steins and Haigs soon began to export gin to London in earnest.

In 1783, whilst Steins and Haigs were busy developing their distilleries, John Jameson was looking for home improvements. In Edinburgh on the 12th of August, JJ presented to the trustees of the Estate of Mar that the House at the Shore '*was not sufficient to accommodate his family and therefore an addition to it was necessary.*' The trustees obligingly asked JJ to submit plans and an estimate of costs. The trustees clearly appreciated their factor.

As the Old Mar Trust Sederunt books reveal, JJ's management style was one of patience and mutual agreement. A gentle chat with Colonel Ralph Abercromby sorted disputes over shared responsibilities; listening to the facts avoided prosecutions of tenants in the town; taking his time meant claims were eventually settled with minimal distress. John Jameson's management methods worked.

When JJ submitted his home improvement plans to the trustees, he requested adding a whole new upper story for his House at the Shore. JJ's request was granted without question.

It had been nearly two years since Sunday Mary's death, and for Peggie came the bittersweet prospect of a new summertime birth. At Alloa on the 18th of August, 1783, Andrew Jameson, the new summertime baby, arrived. For the family, the birth was a massive boost.

Peggie was now thirty, and there was good cause for celebration. The following April, JJ organised a charity ball at Alloa Tower. The county's gentry and their ladies were adorned in their finery. The hooped ball gowns lent themselves to the curves and sweeps within the ancient tower's walls. As the string quartet played, JJ was full of show as he guided the love of his life for all to see. Peggie was suitably proud of her lovable 'auld fool', too.

As the minuet danced, JJ kept in time with the toffs, but his aspirations were quite different. John Francis Erskine, the Abercrombys, and the other aristos sent off their male offspring to the boarding schools of Eton, Westminster, or the legendary Rugby. At the age of twelve or thirteen, whilst the toffs were scrambling around in the mud trying to shove over a wall, JJ's boys were employed as his clerks and apprentices. Those in trade stole a lead in life from their aristocratic masters.

At thirteen, Robert was already immersed in the ways of a lawyer's office just as JJ had been in old Rollo's time. As for Margaret, at fifteen she was nearly the same age as Peggie when she left home to marry. Peggie would not let her eldest daughter out of her sight quite so easily.

Life ahead bloomed, and John Jameson, the Sheriff Clerk of Clackmannan, was not for going anywhere anytime soon.

On the Alloa Estate came a fresh opportunity. Bobbing John's legacy of the Gartmorn Dam and its various downstream mills had fallen into disrepair. The Alloa Coal Company took up the challenge and took over the lease of the mills.

Once again, JJ had linked up with his in-laws as they created the Alloa Mill Company and, together with the trust, invested heavily in upgrading the whole system. The dam was repaired and heightened; new mills, granaries, kilns, and millers' houses were built; seven mills were meticulously machined and brought online.

When the upgraded Gartmorn sluices opened, the water pushed its way down through lades and pipes to power up the new machinery. Wood was chipped, flax was flayed, water was pumped from coal pits, and coal was lifted to the surface. Wheat, oats, malt, and barley were ground, and fountains played for John Francis and his family. With mud flushed from the harbour, Bobbing John's genius was again in full flow.

In May 1784, Mr James Haig, distiller at Canonmills, and Miss Helen Higgins, daughter of John Higgins of Neuk, gave up their names for 'Proclamation of Banns Matrimonial'. James was the first of Peggie's brothers to be married. There was no way Peggie was going to miss James's Edinburgh wedding. Travel needed organising.

To avoid the road jams of wheels stuck in ruts, a smoother alternative was to sail down the firth. The families of Jameson, Stein, and Haig had a flotilla of vessels to choose from. A fifty-ton barque would suit to sail the twenty-eight miles to Leith.

Leaving the children was hard for Peggie but leaving the dust and noise of the builders bashing another storey on top of her house was not. Peggie, JJ, and the rest of the wedding party set sail, and the Alloa Island of Inch, with its buttercup pastures and curious scaffolds of fishing nets, slipped away.

Sailing down the Forth was a watery safari to witness the wildlife as it gathered to feast.

Beneath the water and swimming in their seasons, were herring, sprats, smelts, whiting, haddock, sea trout, eels, salmon, sturgeon, soles, turbot, cod, gurnet, skate, mackerel, and the Egyptian herring. On the seabed lay a boundless free larder of crustaceans with the choice of oyster, crab, lobster, whelk, or prawn. Whales of many kinds celebrated the fathoms deep menu with gymnastic displays. Flight paths were filled with a hungry cacophony of cormorants, gannets, guillemot, wild duck, eider, goosanders, teals, terns, shags, widgeons, fulmar, gulls, and petrels. Well-fed and nesting on small islands were cuties of burrowing puffins. Below them, on their slippery, rocky lidos, were the basking bathing beauties of blubbered seals.

A trip down the Firth of Forth was a glorious high-definition nose-to-nose encounter with the natural world as it once was. For JJ, it was a life-affirming moment for the future. He thanked his ancestors and God for choosing this paradise to live in.

For Peggie, the soft hushing forwards of the barque swept her away from the everyday ties at home. Her slight feeling of sickness arose not from the shifting horizons but because, once more, she was pregnant with number nine.

For uncles Jim and John Stein, as they looked ahead to the limitless seascape, so their ambitions grew.

Arriving at Leith, the buzz put Alloa Harbour into the shade. Leith was Scotland's busiest port, with ships stacked up in a cosmopolitan mix of masts.

Uncle Jim took charge of parking the barque.

"Na need fur the lassies to clamber over foreign decks to get ashore," he insisted.

Onto the land, the men, with their merchant inquisitive eyes, delayed their departure. On the quayside, they kicked and prodded the bundles and barrels, wishing to know what was arriving and departing their shores. At last, and in a couple of hired chaise, they all headed for the city.

The first stop was the distillery at Canonmills, laid out along the Water of Leith. Next, and above these brand-new works, the party paid a visit to the house that James Haig was acquiring for his bride. Recently built and advertised as:

'Commanding a pleasant and extensive prospect, fit to accommodate a large and genteel family.'

Peggie and her mum gave the dwelling the once-over. Satisfied, they stated their opinions as to which rooms they thought should be painted and which should be fashionably papered.

A stroll on through the extensive gardens of shrubs and bushes and next door to the Canonmills residence was a brewery. Here, James Haig was converting the brewery into a rectifying house. The resulting gin would soon be making its way down to London.

The party resumed their journey, up past the elegant new squares to the foot of the Castle. The Nor Loch was almost drained, but a small marshy area remained by the Church of St Cuthbert. The families assembled at the church for the first instalment of the Haig and Higgins wedding.

The Act of Proscription had recently been repealed, and once again, it was OK to dress in full Highland battle gear. Whatever the dress code, tartan was flashed as the celebrations whooped away and on into the night.

There had been much to toast to, but as the last of the revellers wandered home, a cloud hung heavy. The year before, a huge volcanic eruption at Laki in Iceland had catastrophic repercussions throughout the world. A choking haze had descended over Europe, bringing freak weather. Travel was disrupted not by grounded planes but by plagues and fog-bound ships.

In the West of Scotland, the herring season was wiped out, and there was a famine in the Highlands and Islands. As crops failed, wide-scale food shortages hit elsewhere.

Some say that this one seismic event was a trigger for the French Revolution in 1789. If so, a precursor to the Storming of the Bastille was the storming of James Haig's distillery at Canonmills, Edinburgh, in 1784.

A month past the wedding, on the evening of the 4th of June, a riotous mob gathered at Canonmills. They were convinced that large quantities of crops, including oats, wheat, and root crops, were being consumed by the distillery and pushing up food prices. Outraged, they were determined to do damage and destroy the distillery.

The County Sheriff, Archibald Cockburn, had been tipped off. Aware of the distillery's contribution to the city's coffers, he provided arms to defend the premises.

The protesting rioters surged forward, smashed down the distillery gates, and entered the works. James Haig's workforce confronted the mob. Stones were thrown, and casks smashed. Two of Haig's men fired into the crowd. A rioter was killed on the spot.

A bloody stand-off ensued until Archibald Cockburn arrived with a party of Dragoons. Arresting the two workers, who had fired and killed, Archie persuaded the rioters to disperse. James's two employees were marched off to Edinburgh and locked up in the Tolbooth for the night.

Three days later, a more organised demonstration began at the Grassmarket. William Anderson, a labourer, and James Paul, an apprentice tanner, stole a drum from the city guard. Through the Edinburgh streets, they beat the drum, bawling their battle cry: 'For Canonmills!'

This time, a more numerous and threatening crowd joined them.

The shocked residents of the newly built fashionable squares snapped their shutters tight. Reflected in the tall, haughty windows, the drummed-up rabble rampaged past. Armed with sticks and bludgeons, the volatile mob stormed down from the city towards the Water of Leith.

Through the Canonmills village, the rioters swarmed towards the river. A carriage was spotted as belonging to James Haig, and it was stopped. The blinds were drawn, but Helen Haig, James's new wife, was inside.

By now, the rioters were into high doh and surged around the carriage, rocking it back and forth and then flinging open the door. At the sight of a lady, manners prevailed, and the carriage was allowed to escape to Heriots Hill and away.

The Haig distillery had again been forewarned. Within, there was now a strong military guard from the castle. The soldiers barred access to the works and fired on the approaching rioters. Several of the mob were wounded, whilst the rest retreated in frustrated anger and set fire to some barrels and a haystack.

At the Canonmills bridge, Sheriff Archibald Cockburn had gathered with another detachment of castle troops. Here they confronted more of the mob. Archie read the 'Riot Act'. He announced to the gathering that this time the riot would be met with no mercy. The crowd stopped throwing stones but continued pressing forward and swearing.

The soldiers stood their ground with their muskets loaded and bayonets fixed. The mob were almost picking their noses on the bayonets when the soldiers were ordered to present arms. Muskets were raised and made ready to fire. The mob quickly buttoned their language. Collective wisdom clicked in, and the mob retreated.

The ringleaders were arrested, and the hangman had his day with whippings up and down the High Street. Enforced emigration followed.

It was hardly a Haig public relations coup. The distillery had a case to answer. Were the riots justified? Had the distillery aggravated food shortages? Had they pushed up prices?

In his defence, James Haig published an affidavit. He promised that no other grain but barley, rye, and occasionally damaged wheat was used in the distilling process. He added that '*not a grain of oats, pease, or a particle of oat meal, nor any potatoes, carrots, turnips, or other roots, were used in the manufactory*'.

'*The barley,*' James stated, '*is almost to a trifle imported into Leith from distant places. The distillery's consumption, therefore, does not influence the market price.*'

'*Contrary,*' he claimed, '*the distilleries' imported grain to Scotland has increased the food supply by feeding the refuse to the livestock.*'

It is unlikely that the rioters would have read or even heeded James's testament. So, where had the rumours started, and why was James Haig's distillery targeted?

The riots were certainly not instigated by a couple of men who stole a drum. This view was upheld at a meeting called by the Sheriff. His committee concluded that the rioters were acting out the will of other, covert parties.

James Haig pointed the finger. In his press statement, James alleged:

'*The distillers of London, envious of the Scotch in the same trade, are at the present moment exerting their utmost influence to deprive this country of that valuable branch.*'

A volcano or the English? Maybe, a convenient combination of both. For certain, the London distillers were none too pleased that the Scots had invaded their gin market. It would soon be time for Haigs and Steins to be kilted out in their Highland battle regalia.

As autumn approached, builder Henry Dempster fixed two thousand slates from the Haigs' brick and tile works onto the new roof at JJ's House at the Shore.

At Alloa on 26 October 1784, when the dust had settled from volcanoes, riots, and building works, Peggie gave birth to an autumn baby.

Number nine was royally named George. Sadly, George's reign would not last for long.

Leith Pier and Harbour,1798
(Iconographic Archive /Alamy Stock Photo)

Arriving at Leith, the buzz put Alloa Harbour into the shade.

Canonmills Loch and House
(Artokoloro /Alamy Stock Photo)

Next door to the Canonmills residence was a brewery.

Chapter 10

Let Battle Begin

1785–86

James Stein lobbies Parliament; James Stein is accused of bribery; John Jameson takes the 'Edinburgh Fly' to London; John Jameson presents a petition to Parliament; John Jameson inspects the Front Line of the 'Gin War'.

1 785 IN ALLOA, AND JOHN JAMESON was striding confidently along his forty-fifth year. As the Clackmannan Sheriff Clerk and Baron Bailie of the town, JJ was a long-serving and respected citizen. As the cashier for the Harbour Trust, he attended their regular meetings, and as the factor for the Alloa Estate, his reports were written up in the Old Mar Trust Sederunt Books every March.

In August of 1785, John Jameson made it onto the front page of the *Caledonian Mercury* when it reported that JJ was amongst *a very respectable company of Gentlemen* who attended the annual inspection of the Alloa Public School.

'*The Several classes of English, Latin and French gave very pleasing proofs of substantial progress and improvement in all those different batches of Education,*' concluded JJ.

The Jameson children were in good and steady hands, as annually and publicly confirmed by their father.

Evidence of John Jameson's trusted and settled continuity is also recorded in the yearly tax rolls as he collected the various local duties. The records show JJ respectfully paying via himself his window tax which in 1785 had increased from nine to thirteen windows. In that year also, JJ is seen to pay, rather modestly, the tax for just one horse.

By contrast, Peggie's uncle, James Stein, had a lifestyle that was somewhat less modest.

In 1785, JJ collected a rather exclusive tax of five pounds and five shillings from Uncle Jim. This was the duty on a four-wheeled carriage, a mode of transport that in Clackmannanshire was reserved for just six others, mainly from the aristocracy. Scallywag Jim had arrived and was riding high.

As the pillar of society, John Jameson looked over at his in-law, if not with a pinch of envy, then certainly with much interest. Jim's business model seemed flawless. Whilst being driven through the countryside in his four-wheeler, Uncle Jim was successfully driving a juggernaut of five Stein and Haig distilleries. The rewards were immense.

Ka-ching!

From the five distilleries, the exchequer was quids in, too. America's War of Independence had fleeced the government coffers, so for port connoisseur Chancellor William Pitt, distillery revenues needed to be well tapped.

Different factions within the Kingdoms were juggled, and new excise laws were enacted as frequently as births at the Jameson House at the Shore.

Uncle Jim wanted to be where the decisions were made. So, Jim began to commute to London and lobby. At Westminster, he impressed and received considerable praise for his '*open and candid manner*'. The laws swayed Jim's way.

1783 saw private stills of whatever size totally banned. In 1784 and 1785, discriminatory acts divided the Lowlands and the Highlands.

In the Highlands, duty was less, but the still sizes were restricted. No grain import was permitted, and the distillery output could only be drunk within their Highland regions.

To enforce, tell-tale policing was encouraged by divvying up the fines for offences between the informers and the poor. Many a good malt was strangled at birth for the sake of eighteenth-century social security.

The Highland line divided Clackmannanshire in two by following the foot of the Ochil Hills. It neatly clipped Kilbagie off to the south and Lowlands. Swerving northwards, the line headed up to the River Tay, ensuring that Uncle Robert's Kincaple distillery remained in the Lowland region. Uncle Jim might just as well have been the government cartographer who drew the line between the Highlands and Lowlands. Jim's rascally whisky output was safe from being shamed by a barrel of Glenlivet.

For the moment, the Stein and Haig relationship with the Excise Office was mutually beneficial. They were buddies. So much so that John Bonar, the Solicitor of Excise for Scotland, attended meetings with Uncle Jim as he lobbied Parliament. On one occasion, Jim and Mr Bonar even shared a post-chaise for the sixty-hour journey from London to Edinburgh.

But not quite everything was as Uncle Jim wished it to be.

One big nuisance was the local excise officers, referred to as 'expectants', who snooped and sniffed at will around the family distilleries. If tripping over expectants twenty-four-seven wasn't enough, then there was the sudden unannounced arrival of the fore-hammer men. These excise assistants were so called on account of the hammers slung around their necks. The hammers were used to force doors at any time of day and night and to break open casks and tubs, causing damage to both equipment and the spirits.

Uncle Jim had already prosecuted the Excise for trespass and the overzealous use of the hydrometer. In the resulting court case, Messrs Stein lost on the first count of trespass, but they successfully won on their four remaining points, including the Excise's use of the hydrometer. The Steins collected one shilling in damages.

But now it was planned that yet more excise officers would be dispensed to seek out fraud in the larger distilleries.

For Steins and Haigs, the threat was there for some inexperienced jobsworth with his hammer, damaging or fining or confiscating or worse, stumbling across some creative but dodgy practice.

It was time for Jim to have a chat with his best new buddy, John Bonar, the Solicitor of Excise.

On Friday morning, on 2 September 1785, Uncle Jim invited himself for breakfast at Mr Bonar's house in Edinburgh. Etiquette and formalities were not a part of James Stein's new industrial mode of operation. However, Uncle Jim had a forceful charm, and it was not the first time he had imposed himself on Mr Bonar's hospitality.

On his arrival between nine and ten, with hat and gloves removed and pleasantries exchanged, Mr Stein and Mr Bonar sat down together for breakfast. What was on the menu is uncertain, although hot chocolate and spiced bread were trending at the time.

The chat was relaxed. After all, the two had sat a sixty-hour journey together from London. They had a lot in common, principally on the topic of distilling, although from different perspectives. Mr Bonar was in charge of dishing out prosecutions within that industry, and Uncle Jim was intent on avoiding them. This was despite the efforts of overzealous and, to Jim's mind, inexperienced customs officers with their hammers.

As they sipped and supped, they talked of the English distilleries, the Highland distilleries, and lastly, on that niggle, the increase of customs officers at Jim's distilleries.

Breakfast was cleared, and Uncle Jim took his hat to leave.

Then James Stein made a daft, comical, ridiculous, lethal, blundering move onto Mr Bonar. Mumbling incoherently about his gloves, Jim gripped Bonar's right shoulder whilst thrusting a packet into his right-hand pocket. Before any response or explanation could be made, Uncle Jim had scuttled out of the room.

As the dust settled from the flurry of Jim's exiting cloak, Bonar took and opened the thrust packet. Within, he found five hundred pounds worth of notes. For that money, Mr Bonar could have popped off and bought himself a substantial house in the New Town of Edinburgh. In addition to the money, there was written on the packet a rather tempting note:

'*This to be repeated once a year.*'

University educated, amateur poet, highly respected son of a minister, Mr John Bonar realised he had just been handed a bribe. It was obvious. As Solicitor of Excise, he had the power to stop or squash prosecutions. If he were to be under James Stein's pay, his fidelity would be compromised.

This was not the first time, either.

During the case of the hydrometer, James Stein had similarly, post-breakfast, shoved another wad of notes into his pocket. On that occasion, Bonar immediately returned the sum.

It was clear to Mr Bonar that James Stein was in the habit of inducement. Such behaviour was a felony, and it could not be ignored again.

To the consternation of Peggie, JJ, and the rest of the family, Uncle Jim was to stand trial at the High Court of Edinburgh for bribery.

South of the border, the English distillers rubbed their hands in glee. For many, this was an early sortie into a trade war with Scotland.

Much rested on the case; the reputation of the five great distilleries, the reputation of the family, and the prosperity of many.

John Jameson's upstanding reputation was in danger, too, of being compromised by his close association with the accused. JJ must have heaved a sigh of relief that at least that association did not include distilling.

After a nail-biting year of waiting and as Christmas 1786 approached, '*The trial of J Stein for the attempting to bribe the solicitor of excise*' arrived.

The jury was chosen, and Sir Ilay Campbell, the Lord Advocate, presented the case for the Crown. The incriminating packet with notes of five hundred and one pounds sterling plus inscription was produced in the court. The trusted, honest Solicitor of Excise, Mr Bonar, recounted the events in great detail. The evidence for bribery was damning.

For his defence in his trial, James Stein had the means to hire the best from the pool of esteemed Scottish lawyers. And there could be none better than the Honourable Henry Erskine, the Dean of Faculty.

Harry Erskine went out of his way to take on the most challenging of cases, his most famed being that of Deacon Brodie. In that later case, he lost, and despite Harry's vigorous and eloquent endeavours, Brodie was committed to the gallows.

By comparison, defending Uncle Jim and steering him away from any unpleasantness would be a stroll around George Square for the tall, elegant Harry.

So confident was Harry that when a witness could not positively identify James Stein's handwriting within the said packet, he let it go, as it was of no consequence.

For Harry, his trump card was the accused, James Stein. He drew on Jim's natural persuasive charisma to elaborate on what the jury could see standing before them.

As Harry spoke, his melodious voice pleased, and when he paused, one wanted to hear more.

"Here is the accused," he waved gracefully. "A most extensive distiller, perhaps one of the greatest in Scotland. He is a fair and honest dealer, which no witness has denied. I have never known for any prosecution to be taken by the revenue against him. Indeed, annually, he pays very large sums to the government. But above all, Mr Stein has not, in any of the conversations mentioned, ever solicited for or hinted in the most distant manner that Mr Bonar should do him any favour."

Harry then brought forth the noble, the esteemed, and your everyday to vouch for Uncle Jim's good character. There was aristocrat John Francis Erskine of Mar, banker Sir James Hunter Blair, and baker Mr James Craig. They all concurred as to the honesty, honour, and upright dealing of Uncle Jim.

Finally, Harry drew the jury's attention to Jim's lobbying at Westminster. Mr Bonar had acknowledged that James Stein had joined him on several meetings with other distillers and Scots Members of Parliament.

"The packet was not a bribe," Harry said. "It was a thank you for the trouble that Mr Bonar had given, the assistance that had led to the new distiller Law. It surely could not be imagined that such a large sum had come from Mr Stein alone. This thank you was a gift from all the distillers of Scotland."

Within that day of the court rising, on Monday, 4 December 1776, the jury of county gentlemen and citizens of Edinburgh gave their unanimous verdict.

They found that the delivery of five hundred and one pounds sterling to Mr Bonar was proved.

They did not find the intention of seducing and corrupting the said John Bonar proved.

Phew!

A conspiracy theorist would have had no problem convincing anyone that there was a connection between the riots at Canonmills and Uncle Jim's bribery charge. Peggie's brothers had no problem with believing that connection, either.

Shortly after Uncle Jim was charged in November 1785, James and John Haig and other distillers published complaints in the *Caledonian Mercury* under the banner of '*Distillery of Scotland*'. They wrote that Scottish distillers were being treated in a prejudicial manner:

'The combined distillers of London have without ceasing employed themselves, their influence and their interest, both in public and in private, to ruin and destroy the trade in Scotland, and have left no means untried for that purpose.'

They said this was borne out by the insolent and destructive behaviour of the fore-hammer men, who were now arriving unannounced and with firearms.

The article desired further to inform the public that: *'Seizures have of late actually been made in London, of quantities of goods of different kinds and the only cause assigned was that they came from Scotland.'*

It seemed that there was a war going on, undeclared.

In February of 1786, as James Stein awaited his trial, John Jameson had a unique opportunity to visit the front line.

As the cashier for the Harbour Trust, JJ had been authorised to procure a new Act of Parliament for anchorage duty. The old act had expired, and the harbour needed improvements. Such were the ways of the Union and long distant government: duty could not be collected without a new act and the long haul to London.

It wasn't an ideal time to visit the gilded capital. It was winter, and Peggie was expecting number ten in March. But this was a rare chance to observe the workings of Parliament, to pay a visit to Peggie's sister Mary Mackenzie, and above all, to witness firsthand the business of Steins and Haigs in London.

There were just eighteen days for John Jameson to prepare, travel, and present a petition to Parliament.

The pressure was on for speed. Impresario Mr Palmer's Royal Mail Coach had yet to take a bow. Centre stage, for now, was the Edinburgh Fly. James Boswell had used this new service a couple of weeks before, and it promised breath-taking speeds to London in four days.

Armed with harbour plans, budgets, Acts of Parliament, and a pistol or two, JJ trotted to Edinburgh, where he took a room at the White Horse Inn, Canongate, a popular terminus.

At six o'clock the following morning, well wrapped up in his heavy coat, JJ boarded.

Horns blew, and the Fly took off.

Spoked wheels animated into life, the ice cracked, and stones spat.

Up front, multiple hooves chopped forward, hitting, missing, and skipping the beat.

Within, the forced companions were swayed, squashed, and upholstered together.

Horns blew the more whilst from the roadside, up top, and inside, there was a runaway excitement as adventure began.

The lacquered Fly slammed down into the dark border lands towards Kelso.

Every fourteen miles or so, horses were changed, and there was a brief opportunity to stretch limbs and take a leak. Inns were the raison d'être for travel. At every 'stage', they provided a rolling supply of meals and pots of ale. It was a rugby team's dream away day.

For the forty-five-year-old JJ, the journey gradually became a test of endurance filled with apprehension. With no advanced traffic reports, there were potential hazards around every corner. Armed hold-ups, floods, drownings, drunks, smashes, and tip-ups were all probable. Horses were also unpredictable and had their individual issues.

But the Fly was confident as it reached and followed the Tweed along to Coldstream. Victorious, it clattered over the bridge into England.

The carriage conversation was well thought through and styled to the age. But for the most part, it bored, and when polite to do so, JJ took out his well-thumbed copy of *Gulliver's Travels*. As JJ read, he couldn't contain his amusement at the absurdities within his novel. Loud, chesty chuckles burst out, startling his neighbours.

Later, following a full luncheon of border ale and Cheviot mutton, the carriage dozed off as one. JJ dreamed of Lilliputians swarming over him and pinning his hair to the ground. Shaking awake, he watched as fleas hopped along the fuzzy heads of his fellow passengers.

It was advertised that it took a day for the Fly to travel to Newcastle. But winter prevailed, and the day was long, drifting into night. A postilion was placed on the lead horse.

JJ looked out into the dark Northumbrian desolation, where lurked the fear of robbers or worse. His habit of paying his way meant that JJ carried large amounts of money tucked deep into his great coat. Some budding Dick Turpin could easily shatter plans at the point of a flintlock. Anxiety mercifully left him with the bright arrival at Mr Brodie's Turk's Head and the overnight in Newcastle.

The sleep between stale sheets was short. The relentless journey continued on to York. In the heart of Englishness, JJ slept in the shadows of the massive Minster.

A Yorkshire breakfast and down through England, the Fly flew. On and on until conversation could not be born, and bones were shaken and blanched by a billion stones to lose all sensation.

Then, at last, pent up for four days, relief came with one final, travel-weary, deafening fart as the Fly arrived at the top of Highgate Hill. London was revealed to disappear off into the smoky horizon.

Jet-lagged, travel weary, disoriented, JJ clambered down from the Fly at the White Swann Inn at Holborn Bridge. Here he slept the sleep of travellers.

JJ's contact in London was solicitor Mr John Spottiswoode. Mr Spottiswoode was an occasional visitor to Edinburgh and a sometimes colleague and dining companion to James Boswell. Together, Jameson and Spottiswoode prepared a petition for Parliament.

On Wednesday, the 22 February 1776, John Jameson arrived at the ancient Thames-side ramble of buildings and fire hazards that were the Palace of Westminster.

The House of Commons was boxed inside the old gothic medieval chapel of St Stevens. Luckily it was winter, and the smelly Thames had not added to the Commons' odour of the male locker room.

For the roll that day, there were up to forty petitions, bills, motions, reports, and addresses dealing with land enclosures, fisheries, American trade, the army, the navy, turnpike roads, shops, pawnbrokers, the bounty on Spanish ships, widening streets, and disputed elections.

After various lock-ins, cavorting around with the Mace and sifting out members' names from five crystal glasses, the day's business got underway.

Up in the gallery, JJ looked down onto the land of Lilliput, where the bewigged Speaker, Charlie Cornwall, kept his boredom at bay with a pint of porter.

Following a bill for repairing a road in Dunstable, JJ finally got his name check. His crafted petition for Alloa Harbour was read. It wasn't exactly a showstopper, but it was swiftly referred to a committee of Scottish Members. Charlie ordered another pint of porter.

At nine the following day, the Alloa Harbour committee met.

Sir Thomas Dundas, who was to later commission the nation's first steamboat, presided. Ironically, Dundas also presided over the new Forth and Clyde Canal that would eventually cripple the Alloa Harbour.

John Jameson and Mr Spottiswoode were summoned, together with accounts, plans, and records. After presenting the case, Jameson and Spottiswoode retired to Westminster's Bellamy restaurant.

"Well, Mr Spottiswoode, at least we persuaded their eyes to remain open," observed JJ.

A luncheon of chops and fine wine from the Bellamy cellars followed.

The next day, Dundas and his committee reported back to the Commons, where leave was given to bring in a bill. The old act was brought out, dusted, and polished to suit requirements. JJ's bill began its journey through the Commons and to the Lords. There was nothing more to do but wait.

There was time now for JJ to take a trip downriver from Westminster to the East End and to pay a visit to Peggie's sister Mary Mackenzie.

Just beyond the Tower of London was the gin-swilling, unruly, boisterous neighbourhood of Rosemary Lane. Famed for its rag fair, the population was a rich mix of migrants, the poor, the well-to-do, shopkeepers, sailors, and merchants. Here, fortunes were made at every level, from rags to riches.

In Rosemary Lane lived Mary and Andrew Mackenzie.

It was a relief for JJ to be away from the uptown carriage society and to now relax with family. But it wasn't just for the home comforts and Mary's dinner of haggis, neeps, and tatties that JJ visited. Here off Rosemary Lane, he could get a perspective into the largest Scottish invasion of London ever.

The beachhead was nearby, stretching along a series of wharves lining the river. Unchallenged, Stein and Haig sloops and brigantines sailed up the river to land their cargos of gin and rectified spirit. The barrels were hauled ashore, and it was over the top and tapping into the market as speedily as possible.

The East End lieutenants commanding the campaign were the agents. For the Steins, Sandieman and Graham of John Street; and for the Haigs, their brother-in-law Andrew Mackenzie of Rosemary Lane.

The foe was the large, powerful, and opulent body of London distillers. The ammunition on both sides was the price. So far, the Scottish side was gaining ground, helped by cheaper fuel and labour. But the war was hotting up. The London distillers were wealthy and were all for driving out the Scottish pilferers by continually lowering their prices.

In retaliation, a letter had recently appeared in the *Caledonian Mercury* signed '*Ultimatum*'. It was a call to battle that likened the MP, and a spokesman for the London distillers, Henry Beaufoy, to the Earl of Surrey at the Battle of Flodden.

The battle cry went up:

> *'We have faced the English crossbows and her spears; and why not her gold, of which, part, by the by, is our own?'*

Uncle Jim's courtroom champion, banker James Hunter Blair, provided the artillery to undermine that English gold. With his partner William

Forbes, he serviced transactions for James Stein in London and gave the business much credit.

This was of particular interest to JJ and caused him much concern. He observed large sums of money, bills, and credit notes circulating on a merry-go-round at Uncle Jim's behest.

For JJ's old-fashioned school accountancy ways, borrowing from Peter to pay Paul did not sit well.

But for now, business was thriving. London was carousing on cheap gin whilst Uncle Jim's jangling carousel spun. He was winning his war. Far back from within the cobwebs of time came the faint "Hurrah" from Bobbing John.

On a more peaceful note, news arrived at Rosemary Lane that Peggie had given birth to a wee girl in Alloa on 20 of March. The Christening would wait until JJ's longed-for return. In Rosemary Lane, a toast of brandy was drunk whilst Mary Mackenzie dabbed away a tear.

Before his travels home, JJ took a tourist stroll down Oxford Street. This luxuriously paved half-mile thoroughfare was candy for shopaholics. Late night shopping until ten p.m. was every day, except for the Lord's.

It was said that there were more lamps on Oxford Street than in the whole of Paris. Their double rows lit a glittering, brash, eighteenth-century Las Vegas.

Tall, stylish windows transmitted the crafted products of the newly industrialised towns and cities to the world. Silver, brass, crystal, and gold gleamed on silk and reflected the extremes of wealth.

There were mesmerising displays of clocks, cutlery, china, furniture, and the latest in polished coaches and lacquered carriages.

The exotica of figs, grapes, oranges, and pyramids of pineapples were there to pick. The revered skills of the confectioner were laid out to tempt and win the last penny.

Of particular interest to JJ was the sale of spirits.

In Rosemary Lane, it was the price that sold the gin. Along Oxford Street, spirits were sold from spirit booths and were individually lit to attract. The light was shot through liquids of every colour to entice from within. Crystal flasks and bottles shimmered to show off the shapes to come. Here was a foretaste of future branding; spirits were given appeal that transcended mere intoxication.

JJ took note.

For a gentleman from Alloa, to shop along Oxford Street was to disrupt his Presbyterian-trained mind severely. Maybe he should buy a mother of pearl and laced fan for Peggie; perhaps he would choose comfits and sugarplums to share amongst the children; for fifteen-year-old Robert, there was a very appropriate pewter snuffbox complete with a hunting scene.

But one thing he decided for sure to buy was a London-made gold pocket watch to add to his collection. The whole family would appreciate and wonder at the advanced intricate mechanisms. It would also satisfy JJ's stricture for timekeeping; plus, it would hold its worth well beyond the paper swirl from Uncle Jim's fairground antics.

On 29 March 1786, the House of Lords passed JJ's harbour bill.

One last luncheon at Bellamy's and JJ dug deep into his coat and paid Mr Spottiswoode one hundred and ninety three pounds, eleven shillings, and ten pence.

Five more days followed of shuddering shocks to the spine, and JJ arrived home at the House at the Shore. He was tired but happy to be back where he belonged.

Peggie had missed the 'auld fool'.

The booty from London's Oxford Street was laid out for all to see. Faces were flushed, and gasps came with delight as gifts were shared.

A few days later, Peggie and JJ's new baby daughter, Anne Jameson, was baptised at Alloa on 11 April 1786.

For his troubles, travel, and seven weeks' absence from home, the Harbour Trust paid JJ seventy guineas.

But JJ's trip to London had also given him an invaluable insight into his in-law's distilling business. He could now see that the

Steins and Haigs were following certain strategies that were verging on recklessness.

Like Lemuel Gulliver, John Jameson's eyes had been opened. Maybe one day, he would travel and adventure again.

House of Commons in session during the reign of George II
(North Wind Picture Archives /Alamy Stock Photo

Up in the gallery, JJ looked down onto the land of Lilliput.

The Thames and the Tower of London
(IanDagnall Computing /Alamy Stock Photo)

Unchallenged, Stein and Haig sloops and brigantines sailed up the
river to land their cargos of gin and rectified spirit.

Chapter 11

Reckless

1786–88

1786 – Another new distillery act; Distillery output increases;
1787 – Young William and James Jameson take an Edinburgh
whisky tour; John Haig's wedding; Carrying on a losing trade;
1788 – Parliament debates; The Ceres drops anchor in the
Thames; The collapse of the Stein and Haig distilleries.

S INCE HIS TRIP TO LONDON, John Jameson kept a wary eye on the
fortunes of Stein and Haig distilling. He had no direct involvement
with the distilling, but his Stein partnerships in the Alloa Coal, the
Alloa Mills, and the Alloa wood and iron company meant that he was
not immune from any turbulence.

In July 1786, the Scottish newspapers announced the birth of
another new distillery act. This was the new distiller law that was central to Harry Erskine's defence and had come into being four months

before James Stein's bribery trial. Uncle Jim's breakfasts were plastered all over it.

As a fellow Westminster lobbyist, James Haig also had his words heeded. The fore-hammer men's days were numbered. The expensive, oppressive, and embarrassing method of levying duty onto a distillery's output had been done away with. Instead, a neater, snoop-free, annual licence fee per still was to be paid.

But there was a nasty tail with a sting that was nailed onto the act and fixed by the English foe. A duty of two shillings per gallon was to be added onto all Scottish spirits landed in England; so much for the Union and the free trade advocates.

The London distillers sniggered and waited for Scottish gin to run dry. But it didn't. Instead, the output from the Famous Five distilleries was ramped up.

Uncle Jim's tactic was to view the new licensing law as a window of opportunity.

The licence fee on each still was paid on the still's capacity. The fee was computed on the still's capacity being discharged once every twenty-four hours. However, if the still was worked and discharged twice a day, that licence fee would, in effect, be halved. So, the Stein and Haig distillers used their ingenuity to speed up the process.

Glasgow coppersmith Stephen Maxwell was hired to make extensive alterations to the stills. By making the stills flatter and shallower, the fermented wash could be brought to a boil in a shorter time. Beneath, the heat from cheap, home-grown coal accelerated the evaporation and distillation.

Distillery workers were like soldiers firing off artillery. Drilled, they charged and discharged stills at a rate of six or seven times a day instead of the one. Home consumption in Scotland was almost duty-free. Home consumption subsidised the London War. What a pleasant way to do battle.

The three months before the new act saw two hundred and forty-five thousand gallons exported from Scotland to England. Three months after the new act, it had jumped to nine hundred thousand gallons of mainly Stein and Haig spirit. Even JJ couldn't contain his chuckles at the English distillers' shock and outrage. It was ka-ching, ka-ching, to Scotland and null points to England.

1787 arrived, and Uncle Jim's bribery trial had been kicked into the past. Distillery production continued to be ramped up. Jim's Kilbagie distillery alone was not only producing a yearly output of three thousand tons of spirit, but over seven thousand cattle and two thousand pigs.

But the English were as dogged as their invaders and determined to drive out the enemy at all costs. It was those costs John Jameson feared that James Stein would be unable to keep pace with.

May 1787, and all were wealthy. Optimism shone, and there was cause for celebration.

John Haig's Lochrin distillery was now in full intoxicating flow, and John Haig was about to take the plunge and be married.

Peggie, JJ, and all the family journeyed to Edinburgh for the nuptials. Peggie chose to stay at her brother James Haig's large, twelve-room house at Canonmills, with its glorious views up to the castle and down to the Forth. They descended onto James and Helen's one-child home with their brood of eight.

For the Jameson young, a visit to an uncle or relation so often had the added excitement of seeing a new distillery and its workings. It was natural for them to think that this manufacture of liquor was what all cousins did.

Nine-year-old William Jameson was at an age and of a temperament where he wanted to discover the minutest details. On arrival, Will set out to explore with his wee brother James in tow.

Leaving the house, the boys skirted around the Canonmills Loch and the deep lades that led to the mills.

"Dinna ye slip, wee Jimmy," cautioned Will. "A blootert fell in the lade last week. The mill wheel smashed his skull to bits. They found his brains in the tummy of a herring in Newhaven."

Carefully, William and James made their way to the river and the distillery.

Through the distillery gates, the yard was crammed with yet more hazards of heavy hooves, trundling carts, rolling barrels, sweat, and celebratory language. William guided his small brother.

"Never git behind the hooves of a horsey, Jimmy," advised Will. "A wifie had her jaw kicked aff, and they had to feed her through a nook in her neck."

To greet the boys was their tour guide, Uncle Bobby Haig.

Distiller Robert Haig worked for his elder brothers between their two Edinburgh distilleries. Today, he was about to be given a run for his money by his Jameson nephews on this, the Canonmills Whisky Tour.

William had already watched and knew off by heart every stage of the mystical changes that turned fields of barley into whisky.

In Alloa, Will had seen the vast floors of the malt houses where the barley was teased up to the point of germination. He had been tempted to taste the resulting sweet, nutty malt as it dried in the kilns. He had watched water-powered mills or the Kennetpans' steam engine grinding the malt to grist.

Now, inside the hotness of the Canonmills distillery, William and James inspected the mash tuns where warm water dissolved the sugars from the grist to create the wort.

They looked in awe at the enormous wooden fermenting tanks where they were told that men made dizzy with fumes had fallen in and drowned. Within the tanks, nature worked her will as wort mixed with yeast turned to wash.

At this stage, bounding along, in true whisky tour fashion, came Uncle Bobby's old joke.

"Here we could stop!" he would say. "Just add a few hops, and we might make a very presentable pint of ale."

"But that would be crazy, Sir," said William. "You're a distiller!"

"Exactly, young Will." And Uncle Bobby would lead the way through to the burnished kingdom of copper stills.

The boys felt the fierce heat of the Alloa coal executing its eastern alchemy. Unable to see inside the stills, they had to believe as the wash boiled up and vaporised. Out of sight, the spirit condensed and was heated up again to coil down to earth through copper worms. The gentle fields of barley had turned into hot raw spirit.

Checked by the hydrometer, and the sacred liquid was hammered into casques and rolled away.

For William and wee James, exploring the distillery was the high point of their visit to Edinburgh, but the primary purpose was to celebrate their Uncle John Haig's wedding.

Peggie's brother was marrying Christian Jameson, no near relation but the daughter of a Leith timber merchant.

On Tuesday, 22 May 1787, the rough, unshaven furze of Edinburgh's Arthur's Seat dazzled in sweet yellow. Down below by the coast, the families gathered in their finery and hand-me-downs to attend the nuptials. At Our Lady Kirk of Leith, they witnessed as John Haig and Christian Jameson's marriage was signed off in heaven.

The wedding bells rang.

Out came the young Leith ragamuffins to greet the happy couple at the Kirk Gate. There was money to be made. John and his brother James scattered handfuls of silver and coppers, and the traditional 'scramble' began. The wedding party was now off to a shouting, cheering, laughing good start.

Gathering at Leith Assembly Hall, the floors were a melee of intertwined families. Aged aunts squinted over their fans and puzzled over who was who to whom? The family's baptismal template of names was limited even with their variants – Margaret to Peggie, Helen to Nell, John to Jack, William to Bill, Robert to Bob, James to Jim. The list was short and conventional and cried out for a 'Peaches' or a 'Wigbert'.

Peggie and JJ looked on with pride as their young asserted themselves and engaged with those around them. Like their father, they could banter with the best, from the Pow-Lords and Pow-Ladies down at the harbour to the county set, up at the tower.

At eighteen, Margaret always kept an eye on her younger siblings as her mother was keeping an eye on her. Later she would sing, and people would nod and approve and wonder if she was a soon-to-be bride.

Laughter erupted as fifteen-year-old Robert, full of tittle-tattle and skilfully taking snuff, was wonderfully indiscreet as he entertained those gathered around him. In a few months, Rob would be fully fledged as a writer, and already he was stepping firmly into his father's footprints.

Thirteen-year-old JJ-2 was competitive at the heels of his elder brother and sneaked a nicotine hit from Rob's snuff box. Johnny, like Robert, was learning his father's trade at law but looking less towards the Clackmannanshire county set and more towards Edinburgh.

Eleven-year-old Helen, hair and dress flying, charged and threw herself into every reel and dance going.

William, at nine, charmed everyone and carefully ushered off wee James and Andrew with their nursemaid before the revelries turned to falling over.

Cousins jostled and flirted; fiddles thrilled and twisted; feet whisked up the rhythms; reels swirled in an ensemble. With arms raised high, romance was out in the open. The excitement increased at the thought of catching a glance or a squeeze from a hand as you passed.

Pulses raced faster with one unashamedly, unsubtle, and most suggestive of dances: 'Bab at the Bowster'. A boy would dance with a cushion, then placed it before a girl who knelt on it before they danced off together with the cushion between them. All the unmarried took part in this sport of matchmaking. It caused much hilarity and chin-wagging.

Peggie tipped her fan and watched with interest as one arrogant cousin, eighteen-year-old John Stein from Kilbagie, was tempted to try his luck with Margaret. The boy was not a favourite amongst his peers. His father's wealth, it seemed, had gone to his head, and he exuded an entitlement way beyond his years. As he approached with his cushion, Margaret gave him a withering JJ look. Not wishing to risk a cushion kicked in his face, Mr Stein retreated and danced on foolishly, alone with his cushion. Mags grabbed her young brother Will, and to cheers, the small and the tall danced comically around the floor.

With the celebrations in full swing, there was now the opportunity for the families to mull over business affairs. Uncle Jim, the Don Corleone, was buoyed up by his continued success at outmanoeuvring the London distillers. He held forth, spreading bonhomie and assurances that all was going well on the battlefront.

"By rights, the London market will be ours in nay time!" Jim declared.

JJ was not so convinced. He was aware that Jim's fiscal tactics in his war were questionable, but he kept his cold counsel to himself.

"Where to next?" asked Jim. "Ireland?"

Ireland was the second largest market amongst the Kingdoms, and for James Stein, it was sitting waiting to be tapped. To introduce large-scale Stein-styled industrial distilleries there was an all too tempting opportunity to be missed.

"Aye, a wee bitty far away, mibbie?" mulled Jim. "But over there wid be the chance fur the youngsters tae test their metal!"

"James," said JJ, sniffing his brandy. "Ah hear the Irish have a secret weapon that the English don't have; it's called a sense o' taste."

Peggie's mum snapped her fan shut, closing down any criticism of her Stein family.

JJ bowed, conceding to his mother-in-law. He dared not let her know what he knew and the fears he had for the Stein and Haig fortunes.

The musicians struck up a Strathspey, and gently JJ and Peggie took to the floor. Peggie noticed JJ's quiet, thoughtful mood. But she knew something, too. As they circled together, Peggie whispered to JJ.

"Thir's mibbie a bairn on the way?"

JJ brightened up, doing an extra hop and tickling Peggie's hand.

"Ye auld fool," she said, giving him a wee kick.

Long after Peggie and JJ had left, the night swirled on to a crescendo. The distiller's wedding spilt out into the streets, where the shared jollity pranced off as far as Leith Links to dance, then dodge the golf balls at dawn.

As the year progressed, the Stein and Haig ingenuity of shallower stills began to lose ground. London distillers, with their gold, retaliated by lowering their prices further. The raiders' reliance on the circulation of bills increased.

JJ was not the only one to suspect James Stein's unsustainable reckless behaviour. Towards the end of 1787, Sir James Hunter Blair's banking partner, Sir William Forbes, began to grow uneasy, too. In his memoirs, Forbes was to write that he became aware that the Steins had been *'indulged with a degree of credit much beyond the bounds of prudence'*.

Their banking house had advanced Uncle Jim and Co., by today's values, over fifty million pounds. It was time for the banking house to reduce the extent of their engagements.

On the surface, no one was any the wiser, whilst Steins and Haigs continued spending. The houses at Kilbagie and Kennetpans were enlarged, new furniture bought, and new ships commissioned. With his ship the *Neptune*, Uncle Jim was even planning a spot of fishing off Greenland.

Confidence boomed.

Uncle Jim shuffled his eighteenth-century credit cards as he bounced bills from one trader to the next. The carousel swirled whilst oblivious to it all in Alloa, at the House at the Shore, baby Janet Jameson arrived on 27 December 1787.

1788 and the New Year brought the English Corn distillers hammering at the doors of Parliament. They drew attention to the fact that Uncle Jim's masterly lobbied Distillery Act of 1786 was obtained through falsification. It was a lie when the Scots had stated that their stills, on which the new duty was levied, could only be worked once in every twenty-four hours. Of course, Uncle Jim could raise his hands in all innocence and declare that the statement had been made before his stills had been altered for multiple daily operations.

Then another bombshell exploded. Not only had the Scots' output increased, but with the smaller-capacity stills, the revenue had plummeted. Chancellor William Pitt gulped and slugged down another bottle of port.

When it comes to alcohol, Westminster always takes a particular interest. Tuesday, 5 February 1788, the entire House of Commons formed itself into a committee to debate the matter urgently.

The following day, Prime Minister, Chancellor, Port connoisseur, and jakey of all trades, William Pitt, put forward a proposition *founded in impartial justice*. He said: "*The circumstances operating to the disadvantage of the English distillers had so clearly been made out as to call for an immediate remedy.*"

Mr Pitt moved that an additional duty of sixpence be added to every gallon of 'Scotch' spirit.

Sir James Johnstone for Dumfries, a man who had chosen Presbyterianism as 'the least expensive road to heaven', boomed: "Robbery!"

Sir William Cunynghame for Linlithgow arose to passionately point out *the hardships it would expose*. He argued: "*I conceive it peculiarly hard to the people of Scotland, that their markets be open and loaded from England, while the markets from England are shut to the Scotch.*"

But the Union's playing field sloped steeply to favour England. The ingenuity of its smaller neighbour was perceived as cheating, and the majority voted to cut short Uncle Jim's two-year act and slapped on an additional sixpence to all spirits brought to London from Scotland.

While Scotland's premier industry was debated at Westminster, two hundred and seventy six barrels of Kennetpans and Kilbagie spirit were swung aboard John Stein's new sloop, the *Ceres*.

As the readings of the new distillery bill were navigated through Parliament, the *Ceres*, captained by Thomas Jameson, sailed down the east coast towards London to beat the new tax.

On Thursday 21 February, the new bill passed through the House of Lords and received royal assent. On that same day, the *Ceres* dropped anchor in the Thames.

David Sandieman, Stein's London agent, was relieved at the sight of the sloop. Uncle Jim's creative accounting system had stretched Sandieman and Graham's finances to the limit. They depended on landing the two thousand gallons of spirit to clear a Stein-led overdraft of thirty thousand pounds.

Mr Sandieman rowed across the mucky waters to the *Ceres* with his bills of lading and a pay packet for Captain Tam and his crew.

Captain Tam gratefully took the wages, but as Mr Sandieman handed over the bills of lading, Tam noticed at once that they had not been endorsed. It seemed banker Sir William Forbes's squeeze on credit was taking effect. Without the endorsement, Mr Sandieman could not take possession of the spirits on which his solvency depended.

The wind dropped, and the swirl of paper credit fluttered to the ground.

Sandieman and Graham went bust, triggering company carnage. The great distilleries of Kilbagie, Kennetpans, Kincaple, Canonmills, and Lochrin crashed spectacularly, one after the other.

The collapse, for Lowland Scotland, was seismic. The Big Five were dominant in the newly emerging industrial landscape. The distilleries of Kilbagie and Kennetpans had alone produced more excise duty than Scotland's entire land tax revenue.

Livelihoods were lost, businesses were destroyed, rents were reduced, and estates were neutered. All were affected.

The ash of destruction billowed down and snuffed out the light. From his Alloa grave, Bobbing John coughed and cursed.

The Old Tolbooth, High Street Edinburgh
(history docu photo /Alamy Stock Photo)

Uncle Jim, with brother John Stein and their nephews James Haig
and John Haig, passed the empty stage and gibbet with a feeling of
chill, not thrill.

Chapter 12

Picking Up the Pieces

1788–1793

1788 – Steins and Haigs face their creditors; Family assets are seized; John Jameson rescues the Alloa Coal; 1789 – John Jameson buys the Lochrin distillery; Francis Erskine Jameson born; 1791 – John Francis Erskine purchases Kennetpans for John Stein; Action is brought against the Lochrin distillery; Uncle Jim flees to Russia; The five distilleries gradually resume their work.

JOHN JAMESON, IN HIS CAPACITY as Sheriff Clerk and as a notary public, had presided as an undertaker over the corpses of many a one-time flourishing company. But the distillery collapse of 1788 was like no other, and JJ would be stretched to the limit in administering to the bereaved.

For now, JJ's advice to his in-laws was not to scamper away and seek protection within Holyrood Abbey but to meet directly with their debtors in Edinburgh.

The ecclesiastical, legal, and commercial heart of eighteenth-century Edinburgh was at the top of the High Street by St Giles, Cathedral. Over the road from the cathedral was the Royal Exchange, where merchants would meet and negotiate. Newly built, it was stuck on top of and merged into old alleyways and houses, one being the ghostly Mary King's Close.

Separating the Royal Exchange from St Giles, Cathedral was a row of buildings and tenements built inconveniently down the centre of the High Street. They created a permanent bottleneck.

At the Exchange end were the Luckenbooths housing traders, colourful artisans, and book publishers.

At the other end was the Old Tolbooth and prison, together with a stage that would have been the envy of today's Edinburgh Festival Fringe performers. So would the crowds that this theatrical structure drew for its public executions.

Monday, 3 March 1788, ten days after the *Ceres* had fatefully dropped anchor, Uncle Jim, with brother John Stein and their nephews James Haig and John Haig, passed the empty stage and gibbet with a feeling of chill, not thrill.

Down the Luckenbooths, they negotiated their way through the congealed congestion of carriages, horses, pedlars, beggars, and sewage. Writers' Court then led them up the side of the Exchange building, where they entered the smoky interior of Charles Walker's Tavern.

At Walker's Tavern, the Stein and Haig brothers faced their principal creditors.

Presiding was banker and philanthropist Sir William Forbes.

'*A man*,' so wrote his friend James Boswell, '*of whom too much good cannot be said.*'

True to form, even though his banking house had been brought to near collapse by those gathered before him, Forbes showed no antipathy, and calmness prevailed.

Attending the meeting also was another principal creditor of quite a different character. David Steuart was an ex-Edinburgh provost, property developer, antiquarian book collector, and corn merchant. He had been supplying the distilleries with mountains of imported barley and was determined to ease his losses by whatever means.

The meeting's first consideration was to elicit the facts from the distillers and hopefully minimise the catastrophic fallout to their creditors by acting quickly.

First, it was revealed that a large number of livestock was to be fed at three of the distilleries. There was grain on hand for feed, but that needed processing through the distilling. Kilbagie, Kennetpans, and Canonmills distilleries would continue production for a couple of months to feed the cattle off the residues, or 'draff', until they were sold.

Uncle Jim's fishing trip to Greenland was also considered, and it was decided to keep it afloat. Jim was ordered to equip his ship, the *Neptune*, with fishing lines and beer so that it could be sold as an ongoing concern later in the month.

Pragmatic deliberation was then given to the brothers. Their assistance and expertise as distillers were needed in the early days. Protection from irate creditors was provided, and allowances would be paid in the short term.

Following this pleasant interim meeting at Walker's Tavern, the harsh truth struck.

Sequestrations were pronounced on the five bankrupt distilleries and assets seized. Five committees were formed for the five estates, and trustees were appointed to look after those assets. David Steuart became the principal factor and was at the heart of all the winding up and selling off.

The optimism at John Haig's wedding of a year ago had vanished.

The number of creditors grew daily from bankers to merchants, to tailors, to fleshers. Bit by bit, the personal effects of the five brothers were exposed before the committees. They were raked through, and inventories made. All but the pants the brothers sat in would be put up before the creditors to consider and their trifles extracted.

As the long, arduous business of unravelling began, JJ's hands were already full. As trustee for the Alloa Glasshouse, JJ was in the process of selling it off together with all its woes. With unashamed nepotism, JJ's sixteen-year-old son Robert was given the responsibility as the clerk of the roup for an auction.

On 20 March 1788, Rob and JJ sold the glassworks for four thousand, six hundred pounds to Archibald Geddes of the Leith Glasshouse and Thomas Elder, the Lord Provost of Edinburgh. It would be another one hundred and thirty years before Jameson and Son would be reunited with bottles.

With the deal done, JJ could now concentrate on putting his own house in order.

It was extremely fortunate that John Jameson had no direct connection to the Stein and Haig distilling. But he needed to urgently address his Stein partnerships in Alloa Coal, the Alloa Mills, and the Alloa wood and iron company.

JJ acted swiftly and sent a memorial to the creditors' committee. Counsel agreed that the insolvency of James and John Stein had dissolved the Alloa Coal Company. The creditors, therefore, had no claim on any future profits from Alloa Coal. JJ and John Francis heaved a sigh of relief.

A new coal contract was then entered into between John Jameson and the Alloa Estate. JJ's banter with the Pow-Lords and Pow-Ladies at Alloa would continue, due in part to the benevolence of John Francis Erskine.

A similar arrangement was made regarding the Alloa Mills Company. With the company dissolved, JJ continued to manage the mills and invested in further improvements.

When it came to the Alloa wood and iron company, the creditors' committee ordered it to be wound up, goods sold, and debts collected. JJ was relieved. This company was becoming a rather messy business with a Stein residue of a threatened prosecution over a shortfall in the payment on import duty.

JJ turned to tackle the family carnage.

Across all the families, the events were humiliating. Traders, bailiffs, and government officers, some of whom were from JJ's own Clackmannanshire Sheriff's office, called on the various family homes unannounced, seized goods, and demanded payments. Whilst houses and their contents were put up for sale, strangers would wander in, rummaging through wardrobes and drawers, trying on shoes and dresses for size and style. The discomfort spread far and wide amongst the family from Clackmannanshire to Edinburgh and down to the Mackenzie's in London's Rosemary Lane.

Uncle Jim, however, seemed to be immune to all the humiliation. With his house up for auction and his goods and shackles sold around him, James Stein continued to wheel and deal. He even attended various creditors meetings, suggesting that his son John Stein take on the cattle and distillery at Canonmills. Despite his bankruptcy, Jim's charm and persuasion had not left him, and his suggestion was considered.

Peggie's mum was not as resilient as her Stein brother. For a few years now, she had been running and receiving the income from the Alloa brick and tile works, but it was legally inherited and owned by her bankrupt son James. When Margaret Haig wrote to the creditors' committee and asked that she retain the lease, they naturally refused her and ordered the works to be put up for sale. Family tension increased as JJ brokered the deal and sold the works to his agent on the Shore, Alexander Bald.

For widow Haig, gone was her pride in her family and her certainty of a year ago.

Peggie gave JJ a nudge.

Autumn arrived, and JJ, at the behest of Peggie, paid a visit to her brother John Haig's Lochrin distillery in Edinburgh. Behind the heavy stone walls, all was quiet. Leaves filled drainage channels and slimed the slippery cobbles. With the workhorses sold, the stench of animals that permeated a busy factory had gone. The stores were emptied of grain, rye, and barley together with the casks of juniper berries. Gone were the rats.

Inside the buildings, JJ walked through the echoed halls of drained mash tubs and cold stills. Stale soot hung in the rafters, and a taste of bleeding copper caught in his throat.

Taking a nosey and a kick around the works also was a merchant banker and Glasgow coppersmith, Stephen Maxwell. Maxwell, in between exporting rum stills to the West Indies, had been manufacturing and adapting stills for the Haigs. He was now one of their principal creditors, and he aimed, as others, to make good his losses.

Maxwell was checking out an October sale of old copper and waste tin. Like JJ, he was also sizing up the distillery for an auction in December.

A metal man, Maxwell knew the value of the scrap on hand. He had been responsible for cutting much of it away when adapting the stills for the gin wars. He alone could take full advantage of it, so in October, he snapped it all up for five hundred pounds.

JJ and Maxwell now looked to the December auction of the Lochrin distillery itself. Their objectives were different. Maxwell aimed to recover debts, and JJ aimed to help Peggie's brothers return to business.

What they did have in common was that neither were distillers and that both were keen to work together. By joining forces, purchasing power would increase, and risk would be diluted.

The Lochrin distillery and parkland had a reserve, or upset, price of two thousand, five hundred pounds. JJ knew that with the supply of distilleries far exceeding their demand, there was no way Lochrin could fetch that price. As he predicted, JJ and Maxwell bided their time, and Lochrin was withdrawn from the market until April of the following year.

JJ and Maxwell now had the upper hand in a buyer's market. JJ conveyed to the creditor's factor David Steuart that they were unhappy with the next upset price of one thousand, five hundred and fifty pounds. David Steuart again delayed the auction whilst the creditors' committee lowered the price once more.

Wednesday, 29 April 1789, at the Royal Exchange Coffee House, James Gibson, Writer to the Signet, offered on behalf of John Jameson and Stephen Maxwell the upset price of 1,200 pounds.

Friday, 15 May, in Edinburgh, JJ risked a dunk from a chamber pot as he rummaged amongst the toys on sale along the narrow Krames down by the Luckenbooths. Any day now, Peggie was expecting number twelve, and he was on the lookout for distractions for the younger children. He purchased a couple of colourful wooden dolls for daughters Janet and Anne, and then walked across from St Giles, to the Royal Exchange.

In the coffee house, with his dolls stuffed in his pocket, JJ stood and addressed the committee for the creditors of John Haig.

"Gentlemen," he announced, "you should be in no ways concerned, but we shall be deviating from the articles of purchase."

JJ then outlined his planned purchase of the Lochrin distillery. He especially desired that he and Mr Maxwell should grant separate bonds to bind each to their respective proportions of the price with separate cautioners to guarantee.

From now on, John Jameson would only vouch for his own solvency.

JJ chose John White of Penicuik as his cautioner, a cotton mill owner married to Peggie's sister Ann. The brother-in-law's responsibilities would be brief, as JJ offered to pay up his portion of the price immediately.

One-third of the price was to be paid by JJ and two-thirds by Maxwell. The committee agreed to the deal, with the purchase declared from Pentecost, on 7 June 1789.

At the age of forty-eight, John Jameson entered the distilling business with his first distillery not in Dublin but at Lochrin in Edinburgh. The deal shaped and brokered by JJ was a model for the future. The risk was spread, and bonds were singular and clean, with none of the entanglement that had happened between Haigs and Steins.

The running of the distillery was to be left to the expertise of John and James Haig. JJ was to be an 'anonymous' partner. John Jameson had ensured that the Haigs would distil on another day. Margaret Haig could now give a nod of acknowledgement to her son-in-law and have a little less pessimism for the future.

JJ arrived home, the proud part owner of a distillery.

The younger children cared not a jot for that and were more interested in the Luckenbooths' Cherokee-dressed celebrity Indian Peter.

"Papa, Papa, did you see th' Indian?" they asked.

"Ach Aye," joked JJ. "He was sitting there in the coffee hoose, his feathers all colours, fae his heid tae the flair."

The children were hooked.

"Papa, did he tell ye his tales?"

"Ach aye, he tellt me his tales, smoking his peace pipe he was and blowing smoke rings tae the ruif."

JJ continued to humour his younger children as, puffing away at his pipe, he told the legendary tales of Peter Williamson and his capture by the Cherokee Indians. He narrated the stories in reverse, with Williamson as an enslaved child in America having been "snatched aff the quay at Aberdeen!"

The children ran away, squealing.

The stage was now clear for John Jameson to update the elder members of his family on the deal that was shaping all their futures.

Nine days later, Anne and Janet were gifted their colourful new dolls. Peggie had given birth to a son. On 17 June 1789, Francis Erskine Jameson was baptised in Alloa.

To honour your boss by giving his name to your son, one would assume that a considerable debt was owed and that friendship carried far.

JJ was indeed grateful to John Francis for the many opportunities he had put his way, not least the renewal of the Alloa Coal contract. JJ's son's baptism would also help keep his boss sweet for the future.

When the Stein and Haig distilleries had hit the rocks, corn merchant and the creditors' factor David Steuart wrote to his nephew Charles:

'I shall lose some money but thank God it will neither bend nor break me, but it will however give me much labour of body and vexation.'

They were accurate words for creditors and debtors over a long eight-year slog.

Courts of Session also laboured as they tried to untangle the claims and counterclaims made between the creditors' committees of the five distillery estates.

Gradually, cattle, horses, pigs, mill wheels, steam engines, houses, furniture, saddles, ships, vast stocks of spirit, plus a seat at the sell-out Alloa Kirk were sold off.

At Lochrin, JJ had created a template that enabled a distillery to begin functioning again under the direction of the bankrupt distillers, even before all the debts were cleared.

At Kennetpans in 1791, John Francis Erskine and Thomas Steamboat Dundas wished to reinstate Uncle John Stein similarly. Unfortunately, the creditors' factor David Steuart had nipped in before them and bought the works to sell it on at a profit for himself.

John Francis was unhappy with what he perceived as Steuart's *'Art & Duplicity.'*

Joining forces with Bruce of Kennet, he threatened to cut off the water supplies from the Kilbagie Canal to David Steuart's new purchase. Steuart was left with no alternative but to sell the works at cost price to John Francis and Dundas.

For John Francis, his reinstating of John Stein was hardly altruistic. Credit came from a trust fund belonging to John Stein's children, and when he wrote of his plans to Thomas Dundas, he concluded:

'I have little Idea of the possibility of one or the other of us being the poorer for it.'

Profits were to be made, but it required faith, organisation, and, most likely, persuasion from JJ.

At Canonmills, the creditors' factor David Steuart had more luck than he had at Kennetpans. The Canonmills House and its adjacent former brewery were sold to Edinburgh brewer James Eyre. Steuart then bought the distillery, granting Uncle Jim his wish by installing Jim's son John Stein to run it. John Stein later took over the ownership.

At Lochrin, the Haigs were the first to be up and running when, in 1791, the distillery hit the headlines. John Jameson, as proprietor, was dragged into an environmental issue.

Certain persons, including a washerwoman, the Erin Brockovich of her day, complained that the distillery was making the Water of Leith unfit for man or beast. The Lochrin burn, prosaically named the Lochrin Ditch, already had the reputation as a usable sewer. It wandered through various neighbourhoods of Edinburgh to enter and pollute the Water of Leith at Roseburn. On its way, it received the 'offscouring' of houses and trades from as far away as George Square.

The Lochrin had been a stinker for many years, so maybe there was an unfairness to pile all the blame for the fouling of the Water of Leith onto the distillery alone.

The dispute eventually reached an appeal in the House of Lords, where they did not think the distillery's practices needed to be *'abated'*. If the Lochrin was a common sewer, it could be likened to the Fleet Ditch in London, where all kinds of effluent were allowed. Public health and hygiene had not arrived in London, nor had it arrived in Edinburgh. An unsavoury practice in London benefited a Jameson and Haig business in Edinburgh.

By 1792, Canonmills was at work again, and Uncle John Stein had begun to distil at Kennetpans.

Uncle Jim was nowhere to be seen.

Whilst everyone else had been playing by the rules, James Stein, of course, had not. Old habits die hard, and he played fast and loose as usual. Many suspected him of not being scrupulously honest and revealing all. Writs were pursuing him and sticking like confetti at a wet wedding.

By 1790, Uncle Jim was obliged to flee to the Continent. Here he contacted an old chum, Sir Charles Gascoigne, a former director of the local Carron Iron and Canon Works.

Sir Charles was now in Russia at the invitation of Catherine the Great. He was helping her build her heavy artillery. Having been in similar plights to those of Uncle Jim, Sir Charles offered him sanctuary in St Petersburg.

With financial help from Sir Charles, Uncle Jim conjured up and produced vodka for the Russians in St Petersburg. Jim's distilleries in Russia created yet another fortune for him.

Jim never returned to Scotland, but many years after his death, in 1811, James Stein's name returned to the Court of Session in Edinburgh. Here his bills for thirty-eight thousand roubles were sued for and won by Sir Charles Gascoigne's daughter, Lady Haddington. Jim's methods for paying off debts had remained as convoluted and bouncy as ever, and were instrumental in bringing down his son's banking business.

Battered and bruised, all five distilleries slowly eased their way back into production. From their dramatic collapse, John Jameson had learnt much and had taken his first steps into distilling.

The English taxes increased further, and the Stein boom days were over forever.

Uncle Jim had led them all in a merry dance towards inevitable insolvency. But JJ would miss James Stein, the rascally likeable conjurer of Kilbagie and the genius of Scotland's distilling industry.

John Francis Erskine by Ciaran Murphy

JJ was indeed grateful to John Francis for the many
opportunities he had put his way.

Chapter 13

To Ireland

1792–95

1792 – John Jameson's family continues to grow. 1793 – John Jameson is given the freedom of Perth; John Jameson has a row with the Sheriff at the Sheriff's Court. 1794 – Robert Haig builds a distillery in Ireland. Colliery accountant James Allan goes bust. 1795 – John Jameson buys the Alloa Dry Dock; Journey to Portpatrick and over to Ireland.

D ISTILLERY OUTPUTS MAY HAVE FALLEN, but Peggie and JJ's production line of children at the House at the Shore wasn't easing up. With no family planning and improved survival rates, large families were the vogue of the day; but Peggie and JJ's output was exceptional.

In Alloa, following on from Francis Erskine, Elizabeth Jameson was born in 1791, Henry Jameson in 1792, Mary Jameson-2 in 1794, and Alison Jameson (at number sixteen) in 1797.

With this bounty came much grief. Out of sixteen children, only nine went on to survive into adulthood. Every child's death was as keenly felt as that first loss of Sunday Mary.

By 1792, the House at the Shore had more than doubled in size, with two storeys and children of all ages running everywhere. Yells, screams, shouting, and laughter spilt out of a Peter Pan land filled with endless childhoods.

From across the park came another exciting, high-pitched, but unearthly sound from the future. The wagonway had recently been fixed with new wooden rails topped off with bars of 'malleable iron'. Over these squeaked and scraped the cast iron wheels of the wagons. Metal now ran on metal.

The wagonway was the pride of Alloa and boasted as being the most complete railway in Britain. For the children, it continued as a rite of passage to leap out from the grass and lob in a stone as the wagons passed.

Alongside the house, the offices had also increased in size and were busier than ever. The business of the estate, the town, the county, the coal, the ships, the mills, the Lochrin distillery, and the local legal affairs prevailed.

At nineteen, Rob had been admitted procurator to the Clackmannan Sheriff's court. Now he was as indispensable to his father as Margaret was to her mother.

JJ-2 was off to Edinburgh to work as a writer in law. There, Johnny would be near his Haig uncles, the Lochrin distillery, and maybe doing the odd bit of business for the enemy at the Excise Office.

A new clerk was working at the House at the Shore, William Jameson. Will, at fourteen, was as amiable as ever; not even the furious James Francis Erskine could faze him. William's fellow clerk was Robert Bald, the son of Alexander Bald, JJ's agent on the Shore. Within JJ's hothouse of learning, the two teenagers had much to discuss as the Age of Enlightenment continued.

The French Revolution had shaken the world; *Rights of Man* by Thomas Paine had just been written; 'The Society of the Friends of the People' for parliamentary reform had been founded. In Scotland, many, including John Francis Erskine, Robert Burns, Uncle Jim's lawyer Harry Erskine, and his brother Thomas all supported these reforming movements to a greater or lesser extent. Even the now General Ralph Abercromby voiced his belief that:

'Unless the opinions of a young man of twenty had a tinge of republicanism, he would be sure to be a corrupt man at forty.'

A breeze was lifting the dead leaves.

During these formative years, William Jameson and Robert Bald had much to discuss and argue over. As Scotland's leading mining engineer, Robert would become an outspoken reformer, condemning the practice of using women and children as coal bearers. He was also critical of the damaging effect of whisky on workers and would try to introduce reforms here, too. The banter between the two young clerks would have been fierce. William would grow up with a strong sense of social responsibility, maybe influenced in part by Robert Bald.

JJ's opinions were seldom voiced. He was a pillar of the status quo. His actions, however, occasionally revealed his sentiments.

An entertaining series of commercials for Jameson Whiskey once portrayed John Jameson as a heroic figure willing to sacrifice all to rescue an overboard barrel of whiskey. But the actual John Jameson was a man of quieter heroics and greater humanity. A true tale of a John Jameson rescue did involve the sea and maybe is the stuff of a Christmas commercial for the future.

The winter of 1792 was bitter, with exceptionally violent storms that disrupted the coal supply along the east coast of Scotland. Scarcity sent coal prices rocketing and the poor wanting. Perth was particularly hard hit, with ships unwilling to brave the North Sea and then navigate up the River Tay to the town. Christmas and New Year were looking bleak. John Jameson was concerned and wrote to the Provost of Perth, saying:

'Sir, In the present scarcity of Coal, I had resolved to send a Cargo to your care for the use of the poor of Perth.'

With *all his heart*, JJ had set about finding a ship willing to make the Journey.

But *'shipmasters govern themselves,'* he conceded.

Even the master of a ship he owned refused to navigate the Tay. Eventually, on 22 December 1792, JJ managed to persuade Captain John Brown of a sloop, the *Nelly* of Kincardine, to ship sixty tons of coal as a gift to the poor of Perth.

The storms were raging again, and it wasn't until Christmas Day that Captain Brown set sail from Alloa. For JJ, there was an anxious wait. Coal was a hazardous, shifting cargo for a sailing vessel, and when no news came of the ship's arrival, JJ wondered if poor Captain Brown had sunk to the bottom.

Fortunately, the *Nelly* and her cargo arrived just before Hogmanay, when JJ's gift of coal was immediately distributed to the households of seven hundred and sixty needful persons.

This news was delayed to JJ due to John Caw, the provost, taking to his bed after New Year. Maybe the celebrations had gone too well for him.

When eventually the provost arose, thanks were publicly given to JJ for his generosity, and he was conferred with the 'Freedom of the Town of Perth'. John Jameson could now march, drum, or drive a flock of sheep through the streets of Perth unhindered. Author John Buchan and statesman Winston Churchill would likewise be honoured by Perth towards the end of their careers.

But JJ, at fifty-two, had yet to fulfil his destiny and set foot in Ireland.

Unlike his trip to London or his Perthshire honour, I have yet to discover a record or ticket stub from JJ's first or any Irish excursion.

For the first fifty years of his life, all documentation places John Jameson's activities and business enterprises firmly in Scotland. However, jumping ahead and looking at JJ's will, a large proportion of his estate was by then vested in Ireland.

John Jameson was a cautious and canny character regarding his business deals. Whilst he would instruct others to carry out elements of his affairs, he preferred to show up in person to seal the deal. This was demonstrated during the purchase of the Lochrin distillery in Edinburgh.

JJ's notes and letters show him to be sociable, too. He wrote to his surveyor of taxes, James Watson, who lived twenty miles away in Linlithgow, that he had no doubt to the *exactness* of his *summings* for the county's taxes, but adds:

"I expect soon to be your way and will do myself the pleasure of giving you a call."

It is unlikely that John Jameson did not do himself the pleasure of giving Ireland several calls, too. The questions would be: when and why?

John Jameson and Son of Bow Street once produced a small book illustrated in wonderful flowing whimsy by the artist Harry Clarke. Titled *The History of a Great House*, it touches on the truth when it says of JJ:

Desiring to secure the future of his sons he visited Ireland...'

JJ took his family responsibilities and their futures seriously. Eldest son Robert was now well on the way to succeeding his father in all he did. The future for JJ's other sons wasn't quite so clear-cut or secure.

With cousins and uncles in distilling and JJ investing in Lochrin, it would seem natural that some of his boys would follow into that trade. William especially had a passion for it.

But competition in Scotland was fierce, and already it was becoming crammed with aspiring young Stein and Haig distillers. The government wasn't helping, either.

Peggie's third brother, Robert Haig, began looking seriously at the possibility of distilling in Ireland. Naturally, JJ followed suit and looked at Ireland's opportunities, too.

Like Scotland, Ireland had its gripes with London but, on the face of it, was halfway to independence with its own Parliament and legislative freedom. Unfortunately, their Parliament was full of bribery, corruption, and Protestants only.

A hair's breadth away was Theobald Wolfe Tone and his United Irishmen with a dream of a secular, independent Ireland. This forward-thinking group of Protestants and Catholics had a key for sorting Ireland's woes that would never arise again. Through their lobbying and the Catholic Relief Act of 1793, they managed to achieve the right for certain Catholics in Ireland to vote.

The United Irishmen's ambitions continued, but they ill-advisedly included the word 'Republic' in their manifesto. This gave the snobby grandees in the Parliament the boke. With the war with the revolutionary Republic of France declared, the United Irishmen were outlawed and forced underground.

Ireland in 1793 was not all rainbows.

In 1793, JJ's life in Alloa, Scotland, was not all purple heather and Brigadoon, either.

JJ's day job and attendance at the Sheriff's court continued regularly.

The Clackmannan Tolbooth had cracked and crumbled so severely that court days were now conveniently held in Alloa. With a job for life and near home, who could complain?

Nonetheless, permanent jobs can have their downside when trapped with certain work colleagues, and so it was with John Jameson.

As Sheriff Clerk, JJ was to serve eight different Sheriffs. These Sheriffs would frequently appoint substitutes, and it seems that JJ managed to rub along with them all until along came James Waddell.

Appointed as Sheriff Substitute by Sheriff William Tait, Mr Waddell appeared to be a nit-picking jobsworth. JJ disliked James Waddell intensely, as he always seemed to be poking his nose into those areas that were JJ's domain.

Having been in the job for twenty-five years, a few things could have been better run. But no one had ever doubted JJ's honesty and fairness until Waddell.

One area where Mr Waddell started to rummage was the clerk's collection of fees.

When *causes* came before a judge, that case had to be enrolled by the clerk, for which a fee was paid. If the case was called in the absence of the representing lawyer, then the case had to be called again, and another payment was made to the clerk.

Unscrupulous clerks could make a tidy sum on the side. By calling cases at inopportune moments, when they knew the representing lawyer was absent, they could go on to collect a second or maybe a third fee.

Some judges joined in with their clerks and together enjoyed much profitable fun, with the judge taking his seat unexpectedly during mealtimes or in the middle of a toilet break.

This practice was referred to as *riding the clerk*.

Maybe it was JJ's refusal to indulge in such practices, but whatever it was, Waddell's relationship with this clerk soured.

Mr Waddell's private life was not to JJ's liking, either.

Unable to ride his clerk, the Sheriff was, however, riding a young lady of Alloa, Katherine Brown. Through these out-of-court activities, Katherine became pregnant, and a child was born. The Alloa Kirk was alerted, and enquiries were made into the Sheriff Substitute's alleged fornication. James Waddell's haughty written reply to the Rev. James Frame was without apology:

> *"I have ordered the girl to be taken into care and will do every Justice to the Child. I presume this will satisfy you."*

There was little to like about Mr Waddell.

A spat with JJ was on the cards; eventually, it snapped out into the open court.

The issue concerned a judgement Mr Waddell had given in a previous case and centred on the clerk accepting petitions and fees during vacations.

The handwritten recordings of JJ's voice in the Alloa Sheriff Court Book resonate down a two hundred and thirty-year-long sound corridor.

"*My Lord,*" JJ is calmly heard to say, "*a determination given by the Sheriff in one case is not a rule for him to follow it in another. I shall still continue to receive petitions which are lodged during vacation till such time as the regulations are repealed.*"

"*Mr Jameson,*" Waddell petulantly and squeakily replied, "*I gave a determination. You are prohibited from receiving petitions in vacation, so therefore, return the fees.*"

"*So, my Lord.*" JJ paused and cleared his throat. "*You are ordering me to return fees I have never received?*"

"*Sir, hold your peace in Court,*" Waddell's voice scraped, his stomach churned breath wafting across to JJ.

"*My Lord!*" challenged JJ. "*I believe your judgement has proceeded from spleen. You have no right to interfere with my fees.*"

John Jameson enraged Waddell. His judgement had been called into question, and he had been accused of acting out of spite.

In the cramped courtroom, Waddell spat and scratched whilst JJ held his ground.

Waddell ordered JJ to minute what he had just said.

JJ refused to minute anything until he had gone through his roll for the day. He also refused to hand over the Court Book for the Sheriff to minute himself.

The roll finished; seven witness statements were taken, with Waddell adding his own.

He wrote:

'I have been Grossly insulted and much injured by the behaviour of the clerk of the court.'

Down through the centuries-long sound corridor, JJ's growl echoes as he reportedly said:

'I have met with more abuse than any Gentleman could have expected from another.'

John Jameson's nasty spat on that chilly Tuesday morning of 12 November 1793 was yet another reminder that the wee county of Clackmannan, with its cosy wee courtroom, was becoming a little bit too wee for JJ and his growing family.

On the 15th of January, 1794, Peggie's brother, Robert Haig, took a lease on four acres of land outside Dublin. Here he planned to build the family's first Irish distillery. For JJ, it was timely to flick through his diary to see when he could squeeze in a trip to Green Erin.

In October 1794, any travel arrangements would have had to be put on hold. JJ's colliery accountant, James Allan, had fiddled the books. Money had been filtered from the Estate of Mar for Mr Allan's personal use. On the discovery and orders to pay up, Mr Allan had gone bankrupt. JJ was to be kept busy for months, but luckily, he had help on hand from his son Robert. The bankrupt's creditors nominated Robert Jameson as factor and trustee, with his father as his cautioner. JJ's training and faith in his children were paying off.

As always, JJ cast an entrepreneurial eye over the bankrupt's goods and shackles. There was a ship and a well-stocked timber yard, but the most valuable of assets was Mr Allan's Dry Dock at Alloa for ship repairs.

The dry dock appealed to JJ. It was a magnificent piece of engineering with two large, watertight gates. Ships were floated in or out or up or down on the tide, and the dock could berth vessels of up to eight hundred tons. JJ's contacts with ship owners would ensure the dry dock's continual use and profitability. JJ also had the advantage of living near the dock itself. To put in a bid was a no-brainer.

By March 1795, there was finally space in John Jameson's diary to take a trip to Ireland. 1795 was timely for JJ's first visit. Seven years had passed since the catastrophic collapse of Scotland's distilling, and the family had recovered. Brother-in-law Bobby was already establishing himself in Ireland, with uncle-in-law John Stein looking to establish himself, too.

On 24 March, John Jameson had just one last item on his to-do list before any undocumented trip abroad – 'Buy Alloa Dry Dock'.

At noon, at the house of Mrs Haig Vintner, those interested in purchasing the Alloa Dry Dock gathered.

Outside, the horses of a post-chaise stamped and snorted irritably.

Inside, Robert Jameson hovered nervously.

Lieutenant Drysdale, judge of the roup, announced the upset price and asked for bids over £800.

Rob set up the sand glass, turned it over, and it began to run.

George Colvin, a bleacher, placed the first bid at £805.

Following George close behind and raising the bids at £5 a time were William Geddes from the Glass House and David Spottiswood, Writer to the Signet.

The bidding progressed to £925 when John Jameson, Sheriff Clerk, entered the bidding at £930.

Excitement rose as bleacher George Colvin tipped the bids over into four figures at £1000.

Upwards battled George and JJ to the vertigo-inducing price of £1065.

Then a dark horse entered the fray; James Clerk from Airth walloped in with an offer of £1075.

But James from Airth only had the stomach for one more bid at £1080, as Mr Jameson gave in the highest offer at £1085.

John Jameson was now the proud owner of the Alloa Dry Dock.

To loud cheers and thumping, JJ bounded out to his waiting post-chaise.

The door slammed. The jockeyed post-boy geed up, and the fractious pair of horses was let loose. The chaise rocked and jumped the Alloa ruts, and they were off on the first leg of the journey to Ireland and Dublin.

For the thirty-two miles to Glasgow, JJ was on familiar roads. Out by Tullibody and on and over the Forth at Stirling, his memories from childhood came back to haunt him as he travelled.

The sight of Stirling Castle evoked the shattering sounds of cannon fire rebounding across to Alloa in 1746.

Chillingly, at St Ninians, the lonely tower stood, severed from its church by the axis-knocking Jacobite explosion of a powder magazine during their retreat.

Crossing the burn of Bannock, JJ relived that battle through the trembling voice of his teacher Mr Moir, recounting the glorious victory of Robert the Bruce over one hundred thousand Englishmen in 1314.

Over the rushing River Caron, the horses sweated and strained and pulled JJ through to the modern world.

Intersecting their road came that recent marvel of human ingenuity, the Great Canal, that joined the estuaries of the Forth and Clyde.

At the Cumbernauld Inn, the horses were changed, and JJ stretched. There were twelve more miles of half-sleep as dusk crept over the flat damp lands.

Three miles from the journey's end came a clue as to their near arrival; the drawbridge over the Monkland coaling canal. Soon the post-chaise was clattering down the High Street of the pretty town of Glasgow with its towers, steeples, and ancient cathedral.

Turning into the Gallowgate, the horses snorted to a stop before the pretentious and faded Saracen's Head. Liveried servants with powdered hair bustled the weary Sheriff Clerk inside.

What a delight it was! Travel tired and weary, JJ could indulge. On offer was a meal of mutton and 'Oceans of Claret'. JJ took what satisfied, retired, and slept in a bed, clean and free from bugs.

The next day, JJ arose, breakfasted, and took the Royal Mail Coach to Ayr at nine o'clock.

Setting out from the Saracen's Head, raggedy children ran to chase the carriage out of town, down Gallowgate, Saltmarket, Bridgegate, and over the Clyde to the spinning village of Gorbals.

The day before, JJ had been alone in his hired post-chaise; now, he had the entertainment of his fellow travellers. As they passed the Govan coal works, opinions were triggered about the colliers' low life, laziness, and drunkenness. JJ listened as his fellow passengers debated and, when asked for his sentiments, replied:

"Sir, the colliers' labours keep one's toes warm in winter."

A lady with a pug dog objected.

"I care not a jot for those filthy fellows! I have a plentiful supply of logs ready chopped to keep myself and wee Porgy warm through several winters."

"Madam," answered JJ. "It is coal that will drive the future on which our nation depends. A few years from now, you will be transported to Kilmarnock at twice our present speed, powered through the intense heat of coal."

"Mr Jameson, I am quite content with the speed at which we are already travelling. I do not wish to arrive before my supper is ready."

JJ chuckled, and so they rumbled on over the fertile Ayrshire plain.

At Kilmarnock, they stopped for a change of passengers and conversation.

Travelling on down towards the west coast, they caught their first sight of the Irish Sea just beyond Monkton. Passing Prestwick along the Sands of Ayr and on into the town of Ayr itself, they arrived at the King's Arms Inn by midafternoon.

Time to relax, stroll, and sup at six before the next day's travel onslaught.

JJ took his seat at seven o'clock the next morning on the *Diligence* for the sixty-three miles to Portpatrick.

The first stage of the journey was fast and flat until they reached the fairground ride at the Brig o' Doon. His fellow traveller, a Belfast minister, jumped in surprise at JJ's involuntary "Whoop!" as they flew up and over the Doon's 'Rialto'.

Breakfast was taken at the village inn of Kirkoswald, where there was time for the minister to take a stroll up the hill to view the church.

With horses changed, the *Diligence* made its way down to the coast to hug the Irish Sea to Girvan and then on to Ballantrae.

Offshore at nine miles, the strange rock of Ailsa appeared to float and follow, keeping them mysterious company.

From Ballantrae, newly equipped with its fourth fleet of horses, the *Diligence* entered Glen Napp. A grim, deep, extensive landscape of hills, cascading waterfalls, sheep, goats, and the occasional farmhouse gave the feel of a deserted journey to nowhere.

Twelve miles and the waters of Loch Ryan came into view. Downwards to the village of Cairn, the stagecoach staggered to inn and dinner.

JJ tucked into fresh herring, and tender roasted Galloway mutton, washed down with a very presentable wine.

With the fleet of horses changed for the last time, the *Diligence* thundered along Loch Ryan to Stranraer.

Then, for the final six miles, the coach bumped, swayed, and twisted down a dark, rocky road to Portpatrick. As they jolted, the minister informed his travelling companion that this road was well known to be the worst in Scotland. JJ's lumbar winced.

At seven-thirty, the flickering light from a sea-flavoured inn greeted JJ to Portpatrick.

His greatcoat cast off, it was time for a modest supper of kippered salmon and port in the parlour. JJ engaged with the company of 'travellers-all' for a short while.

But the day's motion continued as the parlour floor sunk and rose as if he was at sea already.

Before he became garbled, JJ clambered the stairs to bed.

Sleep was fitful and not helped by the continuous herding of imported cattle and horses beneath his window. The trampling took him to dream of his childhood and the worry of those endless lines of armies straggling through Alloa.

Morning and the night of a thousand hooves had gone.

JJ looked along to the pier with its lighthouse tucked below the rocky hills. The packet boat was making ready. There was still time for a leisurely breakfast before boarding.

The inn's table was filled to cheer and tempt. Fresh salmon, cold ham and eggs, honey, stirred oats, marmalade, preserved fruit, tea, and coffee.

JJ ate lightly. He had sailed many times on the Forth and German Ocean, but this was a new sea, and the quirks and motions of one sea were unlike another.

Four government packets sailed the twenty-mile passage between Portpatrick and Donaghadee. They were described as elegant, safe, and commodious.

JJ took great pleasure as he walked along the harbour and quay, examining the vessel from every angle. It was indeed long and elegant, with its two tall masts and bowsprit shooting forward. There was nothing that man could do to improve this streamlined skimmer of the seas.

JJ jumped down onto the deck and felt the sea's kick of youth. Confidently and steadily, he walked the planks of Baltic pine.

The agents advertised that they provided 'small apartments with beds or entertainment'. They also promised that no cattle would be carried. JJ dipped his head to take a look below.

More offensive than the presence of cattle was the wailing of passengers. A party in one of the small apartments shrieked that they would drown. JJ sighed; the vessel was still tied to the harbour wall. He wished for Peggie.

"Madams," she would say, "yer upsetting the sailors. On account of yer bawling, they will be unable to determine where the waves skelp the rocks. The shore is but a step away, so please depart now or haud your peace fur the safety of us all."

JJ chuckled at the thought of Peggie taking command.

Farther down in another compartment, a raucous party were bolstering their bravado with bottles of porter. Their sentiments on Popery and Oliver Cromwell were not to JJ's liking.

He returned to the deck as ropes were cast off.

With the precision and artistry of a circus act, the sailors whistled, hauled, and leapt as slowly sails rose and caught the wind. Powering forward, the vessel navigated through the narrow rocky harbour entrance and slapped into the sea.

From below came screams from the doom-mongers and nervous guffaws from the Cromwellians.

JJ stood firm and exhilarated, imagining himself as 'Master' commanding the ship's certain course through the trickeries of wind and waves.

The voyage was boisterous.

Down below, breakfasts were predictably returned, together with the carrots from the night before.

Above on deck, JJ was levitated to a new heaven, away from the confinements of stagecoach travel. Here he tasted freedom second only to that of sea birds.

The twenty-mile passage was unpredictable. On the Irish Sea, ships could be delayed by storms; becalmed, with passengers half-starved; swept past harbours by tides; beached on islands or sometimes horrifically wrecked or sunk. Overall, the packets to Donaghadee were reliable, with passages taking from two to four hours on average.

JJ arrived well-salted and would have been quite willing to go back and return for more, as one day he would. John Jameson stepped ashore, for the first time in Ireland, at the small market town of Donaghadee.

Settled into rooms, JJ enjoyed an evening of open-armed Irish hospitality and a famed Irish supper. Neither he nor the carefree chatty company cared a jot for his gradual incoherence until he swam to bed happily.

Allan's Dry Dock.
(Brian Jameson)

John Jameson was now the proud owner of the Alloa Dry Dock.

Map of JJ's journey from Alloa to Dublin by Helen Cann.

Map of JJ's Journey, Alloa to Dublin

Chapter 14

Dublin

1795

A stop at Castlebellingham; arrival in Dublin; A Jingle to Ringsend; A visit to Robert Haig's Dodderbank Distillery; Marrowbone Lane and Bow Street; Cruising on the Grand Canal; John Stein and Roscrea.

T HE DUBLIN MAIL COACH SET off from Donaghadee at six o'clock in the morning to arrive at six o'clock the following morning. To take this twenty-four-hour overnighter would have meant that JJ could have completed his journey from Alloa to Dublin in five days. But JJ decided to take a more leisurely pace.

With many letters of introduction, he could have the pleasure of calling in on several people whilst he travelled the ninety-two miles through Belfast, south to Hillsborough, Newry, Dundalk, Drogheda, and Dublin. There was also one particular place that JJ was curious to stop at en route.

Thirty-four miles north of Dublin was the post town and village of Castlebellingham. It was famed for having one of Ireland's finest and largest spreading Elm trees. But surpassing Castlebellingham's Elm tree in reputation and age was its ale. Through a poetic 'Good Beer Guide' of Ireland, written a thousand years before in the 'Poem of Cano', this County Louth ale was one of fourteen recommended quaffing from a horn. It even had the royal approval of the local King:

'To Findia is served up sumptuously
The Ale of Muirthemne'

Carrying the mantle forward and maintaining the reputation of this ancient ale was the family of Bellingham. The Bellingham family had arrived with Oliver Cromwell and had later galloped around for King Billy. The continuation of an excellent Irish brew had made amends for their dodgy past and the presumption of the village's name. The brewery was now one of the foremost in Ireland, and for JJ, this was a choice place for a convenient stopover.

When JJ sat down in the Bellingham Inn for dinner, he was not to be disappointed. At the table was served a tender, delicate, and highly flavoured chicken with spring onions, cabbage, and buttered in the soil, Irish potato. From a barrel was poured into a tankard the deliciously brewed and strong Bellingham ale. JJ savoured his drink slowly. It was refreshing, thick, and rich with a rounded sweetness from the deeply roasted barley of County Louth.

As he relished his drink, JJ reflected how he shook and trembled when tasting one of his in-law's whiskies, also made from barley. He decided that the brewer, Mr O'Brien Bellingham, required a visit.

JJ's presence as Sheriff Clerk of Clackmannan had travelled ahead of him. O'Brien Bellingham was only too willing to host. There was much as a merchant JJ wanted to ask. How were consistencies maintained, the barley sourced, and what was the secret of the very successful sales? Bellingham ale was now bottled and exported. It was a brand to count with Whitbread, Burton, and Ringwood ales. It had entered the English market.

Sales may have had an extra fillip from O'Brien's younger brother, William. William Bellingham happened to be an MP and a private secretary to William Pitt. He had now been appointed Commissioner for victualing the Royal Navy. No sailor would object to the odd bottle of Bellingham while waiting for the French to appear around the corner.

But there was more to this beer than opportunist marketing. The secret to the success of Bellingham's one-thousand-year-plus ale lay in the sustained quality of its ingredients, locally grown in the surrounding countryside. County Louth barley was the key to an ancient ale and maybe the key to a new whiskey.

JJ had learnt much. He would return for another pint and his family, too. Castlebellingham would become an excellent and enjoyable stopover and more.

Travelling on, a brief stop was made at Drogheda, where every second person would offer a trip to King Billy's river Boyne battlefield. JJ sidestepped King Billy and took the heavy coach to Dublin.

Nine miles out of Dublin, the coachman suggested that JJ come aloft to view his first-time approach to God's City. Pausing by the medieval round tower at Swords, JJ clambered up top.

"There you go, yer Honour," welcomed the coachman. "You're as high and mighty as the conquering Caesar entering Rome."

The coachman was right. The culmination of seven days of travel had bestowed the spirit of the conqueror. Perched high and above, JJ surveyed the lands of his arrival keenly. As the coach climbed the hills, he caught glimpses of what surrounded him. The Howth Peninsular bending around protectively to the north of the enormous Dublin Bay. It embraced a sea white-flicked and studded with ships. Far away to the south, he could see the faint blue fringe of the Wicklow Mountains. Here was the source of much of the water that quenched Dublin's thirst and gave character to its brewing and distilling.

Nearing the city, wealth fertilised the roadside with thick lawns, stately villas, trees fit for cathedrals, and honeysuckle cottages. Ahead, towers, domes, and steeples lured until Dublin's immense and developing city arrived.

From Drumcondra, JJ processed down Dorset Street, passing the half-built squares of tall, flat-packed houses. The new-builds of Edinburgh came to mind, but these latest additions, with their cascades of brick, gave a lighter, quick step touch. Along Great Britain Street and they were heralded by the Doric façade and tower of the Lying-in Hospital, Dublin's temple for maternity care. High on his triumphant chariot, JJ rode on down Sackville Street, a breathtakingly wide mall lined with the Palladian palaces of viscounts, earls, and political toffs.

Graciously, the barely built Carlisle Bridge carried him up and over the city's shortcut to the oceans, the River Liffey. Stretched out along the quays lay the copular-crowned Custom House. This was a city built for commerce and aching for its coffers to be filled. John Jameson had arrived in Dublin.

Clambering down near the quiet parks of Trinity College, JJ found rooms for his stay.

'Dear Dublin' was how John Francis Erskine had described the city to JJ, and he soon felt that this was a place he could also grow fond of. With all its outward grandeur, it had a closeness and easy-going welcome. Doors opened quickly and generously. Gone was the frugal Scottish hospitality to be replaced by an Irish thrift of 'serving champagne to preserve one's best Claret'.

An affability and philosophical wit were everywhere, from the top to the bottom of society. The familiar salutation of 'Your Honour' elevated commoners and popped lords in their place. Had the Republic arrived already?

What was certain was that the old religion from Rome ran through the city's veins and throughout the land, and no amount of cruelty and bloodletting could bleed that dry.

The questions for JJ were: Was Dublin a place where he could do business? Was it somewhere his sons could settle happily and flourish?

To help him to answer those questions, number one on JJ's agenda was to seek out those areas that were best suited for distilling.

Dublin was peppered with small distilleries. The smallest were those that served the dram shops, where the spirits were practically raw and of the quality to be found in a school chemistry lab. Licenced at forty pounds apiece, there were neighbourhoods where every other house was a dram shop. They caused much outrage. A contemporary travel writer, John Carr, wrote: '*The Government might as well impose a tax upon coffins and inoculate all its subjects with the plague.*'

Like in Scotland a decade before, there were calls for the government to outlaw the smaller, ropier establishments and bring in a more regulated system.

Whilst intoxication was the primary selling point, some establishments prided in the quality of their spirit distilled from barley. In 1795, Roe, Power, and Teeling were names already in Dublin to be heard of in the future of today. But they were small establishments that changed location frequently and often switched from distilling to brewing and back at the drop of an excise.

To begin, JJ took a trip to visit the new kid on the block, Peggie's brother Robert Haig. Bobby's distillery was being built out of town on the River Dodder. To travel there, the Dublin transport system gave JJ a variety of colourful contraptions to choose from.

The Noddy was a battered old chaise with a seat for the driver on the shafts. The driver's nose was uncomfortably close to the horse's tail. As they trotted, the driver bobbed up and down, and nodded his nose away from the rear.

Then there was the open vis-à-vis. This was a jaunting car with a coachman and one horse that could transport six passengers. Mounted on two small wheels, the passengers sat on a bench, back-to-back. The locals referred to this as the Irish vis-à-vis or, more poetically, the cul-a-cul or arse-to-arse.

The Jingle was another favourite. Mounted on four slender wheels, it resembled a coach with the sides and the doors blown out. This covered sprung cart could carry six to eight passengers, and as it progressed, it rattled and jingled, hence its name.

JJ decided to take the Jingle from nearby Baggot Street. The fare was sixpence, and it set off at the driver's convenience when it was full to his satisfaction. Most passengers were travelling to the Pidgeon House at the South Wall for the packet to Holyhead. JJ got off at Ringsend, where the River Dodder met the Liffey.

At Ringsend, JJ witnessed Dublin's disgrace of poverty that oozed out from every crevice in the city. Many of these horrors were to be recorded by the reverend James Whitelaw in his survey of Dublin in 1798.

Back in Edinburgh, sewage was chucked from windows with a courteous warning before landing in the street below. Gravity would then continue the cleansing on down through the steep wynds, with assistance from the frequent rains. Dublin was flatter. In the poor, densely populated parts, sewage and every other bit of refuse were often deposited into small backyards. Here the putrid gunge would climb slowly up to first-floor windows. The stench was so thick you could slice it up and post it through the letterbox.

JJ covered his nose and walked swiftly on.

In under half a mile, the toxic rags of Ringsend were forgotten as the Dodder flowed fresh and fast from the Wicklow Mountains. Round a bend, where the river took a plunge, Robert Haig was building his new distillery.

Bobby had taken a lease on four acres of land belonging to the mega landowner, Viscount Fitzwilliam. The Viscount's nearby brickworks also supplied the fabric for the distillery's construction. Bobby had bucked the Dublin trend of building his distillery near the city centre, and he mirrored much on the location and style to that of his brother's distillery at Canonmills in Edinburgh. To distribute his output, he bought a brown-bricked warehouse in the central and rumbustious red-light district of Temple Bar.

What impressed JJ was how quickly Bobby had adapted to and integrated himself into the life and business of Dublin. Only a few years before, he had been working for his brothers in Edinburgh, where he was caught up in the collapse of their distilleries. Now he was very much part of the Dublin scene and involving himself with the politics of Irish distilling.

Bobby met up at the Eagle Tavern on Eustace Street with his fellow distillers. There they would collectively tackle the quality of malt, the high price of coal, and the occasional need for moratoriums during scarcities. The Eagle Tavern, whether by design or accident, also just happened to be the location for the setting up and the founding of the United Irishmen.

Bobby's Dodderbank distillery had much going for it. It was close to transport links, had a good supply of Wicklow water, and was just downriver from Donnybrook with its famed fair. If nothing else, Dodderbank could provide an excellent springboard into Dublin's distilling for William Jameson.

From Dodderbank, JJ then surveyed the possibilities of a distillery within the city. Near the heart of Dublin was the historic Liberties area, with traditions of distilling, textiles, and brewing. A lure to the area was again its impeccable Wicklow Mountains water. This arrived via an old reservoir known as the City Basin and was distributed via the Grand Canal.

Arthur Guinness was already consuming large quantities of this local water, which he exported at great profit to London in the form of his rich black porter. Around the corner from Arthur's James Street brewery was Marrowbone Lane. Here there were other breweries and several distilleries, including that of John Teeling.

Serving Marrowbone Lane was the Grand Canal, an advanced, lengthening, liquid highway. The Grand Canal ran to the centre of Ireland and was now well on the way to the River Shannon, Limerick, and the West Coast. A suburban spur was soon to be completed, taking it around Dublin to the River Liffey and to connect to the open sea. Marrowbone Lane was a prime area for JJ to keep an eye on.

To the north of the Liffey, there was another district to consider. In the parish of St Michan was found the old street of Loughboy. Now called Bow Street, it ran parallel to the marketplace of Smithfield. The neighbourhood was established, busy, and central. Transport links were good, too. You could roll a barrel down Bow Street, and with the help of the odd kick, it would plop into the river Liffey within two minutes.

Curiously, backing onto Bow Street was the Church of St Michan. St Michan was well known for having been used by George Frederick Handel as a rehearsal studio before he premiered the *Messiah* on Fishamble Street. The church was also famed for its crypt beneath. Here, the bodies of past Dublin citizens tumbled from their rotting coffins to appear miraculously preserved.

The quality of the vaults of St Michan encouraged the neighbours to sink vaults and cellarage for keeping beers, wines, and spirits. Similarly, others built underground cisterns to store the fresh spring water that fed the neighbourhood.

Taking advantage of these subterranean facilities were small distilleries and breweries. In 1795, Mr Michael Dodd was distilling at No. 1 Bow Street, and in Smithfield, John Swan was switching from distilling to brewing.

For JJ, the disadvantage of the area was that, unlike Marrowbone Lane, space was limited. But that was about to change.

A large, enticing slab of land was on the market that stretched back from Bow Street along Carters Lane to Smithfield. For the present, it was filled with tenements, smallholdings, and greens. But the *Dublin Evening Post* informed its readers that sixteen properties on this land would be '*out of lease*' in five or six years and would '*become extremely valuable*'. It was a property developer's long-term dream.

For John Jameson, the moment had not arrived to buy into Bow Street. In his usual fashion, JJ would bide his time and let others do the bidding.

Before returning home, JJ had just one last observation to make. Peggie's uncle, John Stein of Kennetpans, was soon to be discharged from all his debts. He was now following Robert Haig's lead to Ireland, but Dublin was not his choice of location. Curiously, John Stein was looking to build a distillery at Roscrea in County Tipperary. For JJ, it would be a pleasant divergence to discover: why Roscrea?

The first half of JJ's journey was taken on the Grand Canal from Dublin to Monasterevin. To be transported along a canal was the ultimate in travel; here, bone sockets and nerve ends would find relief from the continuous body-battering of road travel; here was calm and freedom from the agonising uncertainty of the sea; here was total reliability from the time of departure to the time of arrival.

The canal boats were about thirty five feet in length and slender. On board, passengers were accommodated in a raised cabin. Within this room were windows with cushioned seats on each side of a long dining table. On top was a deck for taking the air.

The journey was not without excitement. Cascades of water would flush down to raise the boat wondrously up through the dark masonry locks to the surprise and light of the countryside above. Then quietness as the horse gently towed the boat along the canal at four miles an hour. Passengers relaxed and reclined on their cushions to watch the fields, towns, and villages of County Kildare slowly unwrap around them.

From a kitchen in steerage, meals were served by the crew. According to travel writer John Car, JJ could expect '*a leg of boiled mutton, turkey, ham, vegetables, porter and a pint of wine at four shillings and ten pence a head*'.

No wonder travellers often spoke wistfully of how they could become cruisers on the Grand Canal of Ireland for the rest of their lives.

At Monasterevin, JJ had to leave luxury and travel on to Roscrea in a more traditional way: by carriage.

He journeyed on through the flatlands to the central plain of Ireland. Dotted here and there were square watchtowers and picturesque thatched cabins. Some of these cabins were little more than mud, stones, weeds, and straw. They had a transience about them, where they might be flung up overnight to be kicked down by a disgruntled landlord in the morning.

Skirting by the Slieve Bloom Mountains, JJ crossed into County Tipperary and arrived at Roscrea. Roscrea was an ancient market town with much to please an antiquarian with a castle, monastery, and an eighth-century version of the gospels, the Book of Dimma.

The town and surrounds were owned by the Dawson/Damer family, who had the reputation in Dorset of removing an entire village when it disrupted the views from their mansion. In Roscrea, they didn't seem overly upset by the plans for John Stein's brand-new distillery.

Roscrea was in the middle of nowhere, at the crossroads to everywhere but no place in particular. It seemed rather odd that John Stein had chosen this locality for his first venture into distilling in Ireland. So why Roscrea?

Stein distilling had always been interdependent on farming. County Tipperary was a good barley-growing area and suitable for black cattle, in which the Steins specialised. There was another good reason, too. Ireland did not have an overabundance of coal. The Steins were used to shovelling it up for free from their back garden.

On the other hand, Ireland did have vast supplies of peat for fuel. It might be a little damp, but it could be found for next to nothing close by to Roscrea in the Bog of Corbally. Roscrea fitted the Stein template, but whether it would work in practice was another matter.

For JJ, Roscrea was pleasant enough but very far from the sea. Due to its remoteness, it was a non-starter.

Dublin was the place where John Jameson knew he could do business. It was also a place he felt at home in, and he believed his sons would, too.

JJ departed for Alloa to consider and choose his moment. That moment might have to wait. Events in Ireland were about to become rather nasty.

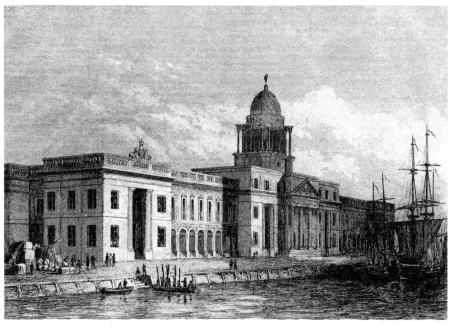

Custom House in Dublin, Ireland, 19th century
(FALKENSTEINFOTO /Alamy Stock Photo)

Stretched out along the quays lay the copular
crowned Custom House.

Chapter 15

Nastiness Then Opportunity

1795–1800

1795 – The Battle of the Diamond; 1796 – The Alloa Election; Toff Tantrums; Bantry Bay; 1797 – General Ralph Abercromby takes command of the army in Ireland; 1798 – General Ralph Abercromby resigns; Open Irish Rebellion; Death of Wolfe Tone; The Stein Roscrea distillery is bankrupt; 1799 – John Jameson hands in his notice as the factor on the Estate of Mar; 1800 – William Jameson goes into partnership at Marrowbone Lane.

O N HIS RETURN TO ALLOA and on 16 May 1795, John Jameson attended a final meeting of Commissioners *'For raising men for his Majesty's service in the navy.'*

The burgeoning war against revolutionary France required the ports around the Kingdoms to provide a quota of recruits. In his absence in March, JJ had been elected as an Alloa Commissioner. Thankfully, now all business had been completed, and there was no need for JJ to march around the Shire waving a flag.

Ninety-five jolly tars had been drummed up from within the vicinity of Alloa and Stirling. For the pleasures of the likelihood of a lashing, the loss of a limb or two, or a drowning, a twenty-guinea bounty was given to all recruits.

Robert Jameson had been appointed Clerk to the Commissioners, but he later lost the job together with the bounty of two shillings and sixpence per recruit. The Commissioners reported that:

'Robert Jameson had it not in his power to favour us with the due attendance judged necessary.'

Rob, it appears, thought that his duty lay with his father's business and not with the King's.

JJ looked over his shoulder to Ireland, where the rumblings of conflict could also be heard.

In September 1795, an event happened near Loughgall, County Armagh that would eventually push Ireland towards open rebellion. The Battle of the Diamond was fought between two vigilante groups, the Catholic Defenders and the Protestant Peep o' Day Boys. What followed became a lawless and indiscriminate hounding and slaughtering of Catholics.

Soon after this catalytic event, Wolfe Tone, from his exile in Philadelphia, journeyed to Paris to seek support for his United Irishmen and their dream of a secular republic. The French were particularly partial to the idea.

At Alloa, a less serious slappy-slap-slap squabble of toffs was brewing. JJ gave a deep, grumbly sigh. It was that old chestnut, the parliamentary elections.

John Francis Erskine had ambitions to put himself forward as an MP for the elections of June 1796. Family honour plus a few brownie points towards that elusive earldom were his incentives.

John Francis sought support from Thomas 'Steamship' Dundas. Dundas responded by advising John Francis that he might enhance his prospects more if he wiped out the Erskine family protests of 1774. These were the protests and accusations made by his brother, the furious James Francis Erskine, which triggered the duel with Ralph Abercromby.

John Francis took no notice of Dundas's advice and did nothing. The protests remained festering in John Jameson's transcribed minutes of that infamous election.

For the June 1796 election, it was déjà vu. John Francis was running against that old adversary, Ralph Abercromby. As usual, Ralph was an unwilling candidate, having been pushed forward by his family and his now ancient father, George. Luckily for General Ralph, he was absent during the ensuing shenanigans as he was away soldiering and fighting the French in the West Indies. JJ was once again in the middle of the two warring families. Thankfully, although there was a lot of spitting and threatening and double-dealing, by the time the election arrived in June, all was sorted and dusted.

At Alloa on 21 June 1796, JJ was customarily and unanimously voted in as Clerk for the freeholders, and the roll was called. Out of a possible list of twelve freeholders, four were present. The four unanimously elected Major General Sir Ralph Abercromby to represent the Shire for the second time.

The result was declared; the furious James Francis Erskine joined the freeholders. A motion had been called to expunge his protest of 1774. The minute book was open on the offending pages. It was as accusatory and defamatory as it had been twenty-one years before. But James Francis Erskine was having none of it. The furious James refused his consent to have the protest expunged. There was no choice but to withdraw the motion and for the Erskine protest to remain.

Then, irrationally and, to JJ's horror, the furious James seized the electors' book. In one deft move, he ripped out the two offending pages. The furious James Francis Erskine had expunged his protest but in his particular volatile way. Poor JJ was left with a torn and defaced electors' book. Such were the tantrums of toffs.

JJ looked longingly over the sea to the greener, toff-free grass of Ireland.

That November, 1796, came another incentive for JJ to cross the Irish Sea. John Jameson's contract for the sale of Alloa Coal was due for renewal, and John Francis informed JJ that he did not wish for the agreement to remain in JJ's hands. Maybe there was an element of slight from John Francis over the election, or perhaps John Francis felt JJ had been too trusting of the bankrupt colliery accountant, James Allan.

Whatever was felt, JJ bowed out gracefully to John Francis's wishes. As he did so, he rather sweetly wrote his testimonial to be delivered to himself:

'I believe Mr Erskine and his trustees will do me the justice to express their satisfaction that I have faithfully discharged every obligation incumbent on me by the lease which I held.'

A void appeared in JJ's portfolio. He looked again to Ireland, but in Ireland, events were about to spiral out of control.

In December of 1796, the defence of the Kingdoms by the navy was shaken to the hems of their Jolly Tar's bell-bottoms. At Wolfe Tone's behest, fifty French ships carrying fifteen thousand crack troops sailed for Bantry Bay. It was a plausible plan that might have saved much future angst and given John Jameson an earlier shot from a Pernod Ricard investment.

Unfortunately, December was not a choice month for rowing ashore to view the beauties of Bantry Bay. The turbulent Atlantic gave off its full westerly force, the likes of which had not been seen for decades. Havoc was wreaked onto the French fleet, with no landings made and thousands lost at sea.

A dream was gone, and retribution was swift.

The Dublin government goaded the country towards total rebellion through a rule of terror. The United Irishmen and their followers were to be rooted out by whatever means. Magistrates were given free rein to declare Martial Law on a whim. The army was made available to administer justice through house burnings, pitch capping, half-hangings, and other imaginative tortures. There was a policy of divide and rule, where Protestants and Catholics were coerced to turn against each other. Babies replaced stirred oats and honey for breakfast.

Into this mayhem rode John Jameson's new Member of Parliament for Clackmannanshire, General Sir Ralph Abercromby, the bête noir of the furious James Francis Erskine. Ralph had, as usual, no regard for his recent election. Soldiering was Ralph's passion, and in December 1797, he was appointed Commander-in-Chief of the army in Ireland.

Ralph felt it was his duty to get the army up to scratch to deal with further French invasions, but not to beat up the locals. However, when he arrived, as Ralph was to write later, he was shocked by: '*The cruelty and tyranny practiced by a vindictive Government and a licentious army.*'

Ralph set about restoring discipline, regulating conduct, and bringing to task any lawlessness amongst his troops.

The corrupt advisers within the government immediately went into overdrive to rid themselves of this Alloa man. They plotted to induce the House of Commons to pass a resolution that Ralph had shown to be an enemy of his country. They conspired to proceed immediately to impeachment.

Ralph was soon to find his position untenable. After only four months on the job, he was forced to offer his resignation.

Unsurprisingly, with Ralph gone, rebellion burst forth in May 1798.

Deep hurt, frustration, and anger erupted. All over Ireland, smithies beat out locally fashioned pikestaffs to prick the swollen bellies of heartless rule. Feelings were fierce and shared, but luckily for the authorities, they were uncoordinated. Defences were quickly raised, and martial lawlessness was established in Dublin and elsewhere. The elegant bridges JJ had crossed so recently were now horribly adorned with the corpses of United Irishmen.

In Wexford, fury at the government's terror campaigns was intense. Rage overwhelmed the government forces on many occasions. But the

United Irishmen were poorly equipped. Near Enniscorthy, the insurgence was crushingly defeated at the Battle of Vinegar Hill. Retribution was ghastly, accompanied by rape, plunder, and murder. The heads of rebel leaders were cut off and displayed on their pikes as trophies.

The rebellion was all but over until August 1798, when a thousand French troops came ashore in Mayo. Here there was significant local support from Irish pikemen. The British scampered away at the 'Races of Castlebar'. The Irish Republic was declared but short-lived. The defeat came at the battle of Ballinamuck, where, as usual, the French were treated as prisoners of war, and the Irish were hung.

Finally, another French force surrendered to the navy in Lough Swilly in October. Wolfe Tone was on board the ship *Hoche*, and he was captured. Tried and sentenced to death in Dublin, Wolfe Tone requested to be shot. His request was denied, so to avoid a public hanging and give a cheap thrill to the Dublin toffs, he cut his own throat. Wolfe Tone died a few days later, on 19 November, and so died the rebellion of 1798. But Wolfe Tone's message remained:

> *"I have laboured to abolish the infernal spirit of religious persecution."*

John Jameson's MP, General Sir Ralph Abercromby, would have conferred with many of Wolfe Tone's sentiments. As a former pupil of the Jacobite Mr Moir, Unionist Ralph had a wisdom and a more comprehensive view, unusual in men of his profession. Ralph wrote:

> *'Ireland's misfortunes, and the evils with which she is threatened, proceed from the illiberal, the unjust, and the unwise conduct of England and the wretched system of English domination.'*

Those were harsh words from a general and a soldier of the King.

Since JJ's visit in 1795, Ireland had been to the dark ages and back. It didn't seem like the place or the time to embark on any new and risky venture. But then, JJ was forever the one to pick up the pieces after the disaster had struck.

For now, the rebellion had run out of steam, and it was also the end of the line for a failed and corrupt government. A more proper solution would not come for at least one hundred and twenty years, but a clear-out was scheduled.

In Dublin, Bobby Haig was continuing to work his distillery at Dodderbank.

Unfortunately, Uncle John Stein's distillery failed in Roscrea before it had even begun. In December 1798, *'the assignees of John Stein bankrupt'* advertised the sale of the distillery, malthouse, and seven acres in the *Dublin Evening Post*. Brand new and unused, the distillery had been bankrupted and on the market for over a year. The rebellion, damp peat, and Stein's debts in Scotland on unpaid duty would have all added to the pressure that led to the distillery's failure.

Undeterred, on the 1st of December, 1798, Uncle John's son, John Stein Junior, signed a lease with Dublin merchants Chalmers, Smith, and Edgar for a small concern in Marrowbone Lane.

In a very short time, this venture looked decidedly shaky, too.

Then, in 1799, John Jameson handed in his notice as the factor on the Estate of Mar and took the credit that he was owed from the Alloa Mills. Cash in hand, JJ was free to pursue all things whiskey. It was a timely move.

JJ's son William Jameson was now an accomplished distiller. Apprenticeships and opportunities had come from uncles and cousins in Clackmannanshire and Edinburgh. He likely also spent time with his Uncle Bobby at Dodderbank. At twenty-two, William was raring to go into business on his own.

Early in 1800, father and son looked together at the prospects available in Dublin.

Dublin distilling was not in the best of shape. The business was not helped by catastrophic harvests and almost no imported grain due to the Napoleonic Wars. Dublin distillers, led by the government, had introduced a prohibition on all distilling from grain.

For JJ and Will, it was a buyer's market.

Marrowbone Lane had a buzz that William liked. The Liberties area of Dublin abounded with artisans of all kinds and a mixture of Catholics, Protestants, and Huguenot immigrants. As everywhere in Dublin, there was extensive poverty, and it was a melting pot for uprisings of all kinds.

Some years before, the women of Marrowbone Lane had rebelled against the misogyny engrained into Irish society. In the act of extreme domestic violence, a man had cruelly beaten his wife with a cabbage stalk. His wife was so enraged that she assembled a group of women to retaliate. Armed with their cabbage stalks, they fell upon the husband with such severity that he died of cabbage stalk wounds the next day.

Volatile Marrowbone Lane was a fertile area with orchards and market gardens, as demonstrated by the availability of cabbage stalks. However, JJ and William could see that the old Stein model for distilleries and their interdependence on farming was not their way forward. Distilling in Dublin would be very different from what had gone on before.

When JJ and Will looked along Marrowbone Lane, there were various possibilities to consider.

John Teeling had ceased trading at one end, and his premises were up for sale. Nearby, the old brewery of Atkinson and Reilly was now being converted to a distillery by Nicolas Roe. Down at the other end, at No. 50 Marrowbone Lane, were the faltering works of Stein and Edgar.

At present, No. 50 was a minor concern, comprising an old brewhouse and a still, with only the brew house in use. But at No. 50, there was an opportunity for expansion up to the banks of the Grand Canal. No. 50 also had a ready-made partner in Will's cousin John Stein Junior.

JJ took a leap of faith in his twenty-two-year-old son, William, and came up with the dosh.

On 20 November 1800, William Jameson and John Stein Junior bought and signed a lease for the now-expanded Marrowbone Lane distillery, with two dwelling houses, gardens, stores, utensils, a steam engine, brew house, and a malt house up by the Grand Canal. Stein, Chalmers, Smith, and Edgar were replaced by Jameson and Stein.

William Jameson had arrived in 1800 to spearhead John Jameson's Dublin ambitions finally.

Ralph Abercromby
(Old Paper Studios /Alamy Stock Photo)

Into this mayhem rode John Jameson's new Member of Parliament
for Clackmannanshire, General Sir Ralph Abercromby.

Robert Emmet's execution in front of St. Catherine's Church
(De Luan /Alamy Stock Photo)

For William Jameson, evensong at St Catherine's could
never be quite the same again.

Chapter 16

Bow Street

1801–05

The aristocrats and the beginning of the Bow Street distillery story;1801 – Margaret Jameson marries William Robertson; John Jameson-2 distils at Tulliallan; 1802 – In Dublin, distilling from grain is resumed; A Dublin panto; John Stein takes over Dodd's distillery; John Jameson-2 marries Isabella Stein; 1803 – Robert Emmet's rebellion and execution; 1804 – Bow Street distillery for sale. 1805 – The Bow Street distillery is purchased.

O N 1 JANUARY 1801, IRELAND was politically glued to England. The Irish Parliament was abolished, and Catholic emancipation was promised but quickly forgotten.

The toffs of Sackville Street started to move out, and their palaces were turned into hotels.

A new order was emerging of merchants and bankers.

At Marrowbone Lane, John Jameson had his foot in the door. It was a small beginning, but JJ was there for the long haul.

For another group of investors in Dublin, it was anything but small beginnings.

From 1796, the long-term opportunities of Bow Street had started to be taken up, and so began the story of the Jamesons' Bow Street distillery.

Dublin brewers and brothers Edmond, John, and Richard George Grange were gradually buying up those advertised slabs of land and property between Bow Street and Smithfield that lay along Carters Lane, Duck Lane, and New Church Street.

Their ambitions were large-scale, extensive, and expensive. Breweries, distilleries, malt houses, and mills were all a part of their grand scheme. The Bow Street site was first earmarked as a brewery with distilleries on John Street, James Street, and Francis Street, and another brewery on Usher Street.

The Granges' ambitions for their enterprise would have pushed John Jameson and Arthur Guinness into selling Shillelaghs. But money was needed.

The Grange brothers were well connected but in a dilapidated, moth-eaten, aristocratic way. Their mother, Mary Rochfort, was related to the Earl of Drogheda and the nearly extinct Earls of Belvedere. Although there was no immediate family wealth, their Rochfort aunts, Harriet and Diana, had aristocratically tapped into large amounts of dosh through their marriages.

Harriet married Essex man John Sperling, who had mountains of inherited and self-made wealth. He liked to spend and had recently commissioned Benjamin Henry Latrobe, later the architect of Capitol Hill, to build him a hunting lodge.

Diana married Sir John Hadley D'Oyly, an ex-pageboy and an occasional Member of Parliament. He had made a large sum of money out in India from the East India Company.

Harriet and Lady Diana were persuasive with their husbands. They advised their spouses that insider information had it that brewing and distilling were in for a renaissance in Ireland. Family fortunes could thus be trebled, crumbling turrets restored, and children's futures secured for a lifetime trimmed with ermine.

John Sperling and then Sir John Hadley D'Oyly poured their money into the Granges' enterprise.

By 1799, and as the *Dublin Evening Post* promised, much of the property between Bow Street and Smithfield was coming out of their leases and freeing up. The various bought premises that included tenements, dwelling houses, two inns, a vault, greens, a drying kiln, and a foundry were now consolidated into one concern.

On 10 April 1799, the Grange brothers, John Sperling, and Sir John Hadley D'Oyly resolved to build a large capital distillery on the Bow Street to Smithfield site. Twenty-three thousand pounds was then spent on two large stills plus apparatus, new offices, extensive storehouses, and a malthouse capable of malting twenty thousand barrels per year.

It was estimated that the profits from Bow Street could annually achieve twenty thousand pounds. There was a slight problem in that the Dublin distillers' prohibition was continuing. All the money was sinking one way with no sign of it bubbling back up again anytime soon. By 1801, another investor was needed.

Mary, Harriet, and Diana Rochfort had a cousin, Gustavus Rochfort. Gusty was one of those aristos who was full of entitlement but entitled to nothing. Previously, he had laid claim to his maternal grandfather's estate of Castle Hume, but the Irish House of Lords had rejected this.

Having a large family to support in a manner proper, Gusty was continuously on the lookout for ways to improve his circumstances. By a stroke of providence, Gusty's cousins, the Rochfort sisters, came up with the investment opportunity of a lifetime. With no ready cash, Gusty borrowed money at a high interest and sunk it into the Grange enterprise.

John Jameson, William Jameson, Robert Haig, and others looked on and wondered: What next?

At Alloa, what next came a wedding and a milestone for the Jameson family.

Peggie and JJ had to face up to it that they couldn't cling to their children forever. With William now in Ireland, it was their eldest child Margaret's turn to sail away. For her, it would be to sail down the east coast of Scotland.

On 24 February 1801, Margaret Jameson was married at Alloa to William Robertson from Eyemouth.

Eyemouth is a small Berwickshire market town with a harbour. Although a good two days sail away from Alloa, it was not hard to see how it came about that Margaret had caught the attention of Mr Robertson or vice versa. Eyemouth specialised in grain export, and its ships would frequently sail up to Leith and on to Alloa. William Robertson was an indispensable collaborator with the distiller, the corn merchant.

Maggie's departure was hard to contemplate.

For Peggie, Margaret had been by her side for two-thirds of her life. For the rest of the family, Margaret had been there as their big sister always. Peggie had to keep reminding herself that she was not presiding over a wake but a wedding.

At the ceremony, one would have understood why JJ's eyes were also welling up.

On the stroke of 'I do', JJ gave away a hefty dowry of eight hundred pounds a year. This executive's yearly salary was to be provided throughout Margaret's lifetime and for those of her children.

JJ's love shone through whilst his wealth revealed that the 'auld fool' couldn't have been doing too badly.

In the assembly rooms above the Parish School in Bedford Street, the families gathered for the celebrations. It was catch-up time to see how all John Jameson's children were faring.

Twenty-eight-year-old JJ-2 talked earnestly to his father while trying to keep his pipe alight. Johnny had recently caught the distilling bug from his younger brother William. Happily for Peggie, he had remained nearer to home. As William had set up shop in Dublin, John Jameson-2 had gone into partnership with his uncle Andrew Haig at a small distillery at Tulliallan. Down the Forth from Alloa, JJ-2 was cutting his distiller's teeth.

Thirty-year-old Robert Jameson lorded it like the local squire whilst being as indiscreet and hilarious as ever. Rob was now the factor on the Estate of Mar as successor to his father.

A few months into the job and Rob had had a baptism of fire. The Erskines' house at Alloa had burnt to the ground, and only Alloa Tower had survived. Silver snuffbox in hand, Rob dramatised last August's events for the benefit of his aunts.

"I was alerted by a crescendo of bells and drums," he declared. "The French have invaded, I thought. Hurriedly, I arrived at the house to discover the ladies clambering perilously from a window in their night-gowns. Behind them were the horrors of flames, leaping up to destroy the entire mansion in moments."

Rob dramatically snapped his snuffbox shut and whispered, "The ancient curse of Alloa Tower has been reawakened!"

His aunts gasped.

From a cloud of his best Virginian came JJ's chuckle. "Sir, the only curse reawakened wis that modern curse o' candles, curtains, and care-less lassies," snorted JJ.

William Jameson, to everyone's delight, had arrived from Dublin. Will, at twenty-three, was as charming, attentive, and now as Irish as ever.

James Jameson, at twenty, teased William for his new Irish lilt. Stu-dious and bookish, Jimmy shared his opinions on his latest reads with anyone who would listen.

Andrew Jameson, at eighteen, was the idol of every young female cousin and the latest fledgling lawyer.

Peggie squinted over her fan protectively at fifteen-year-old Anne Jameson and fourteen-year-old Janet Jameson. There would be enough time to save for their dowries and protect them throughout their lives.

'Bab at the Bowster' struck up. The ladies' fans fluttered in anticipation as the unmarried men took turns with the cushion to place it before their desire.

Forbidden sexuality, yearnings, or revulsion were all masked through the curious burlesque of the dance. That was until a fight broke out as two young girls battled for Andrew's cushion. Helen intervened with fists flying, punching both girls one way and the cushion the other.

As his turn arrived, JJ-2 put down his failed attempts at pipe smoking and took up the cushion.

The fluttering of fans slowed down in anticipation. Johnny danced, then placed his cushion before his cousin Isabella Stein. The Greek chorus of fluttering fans built to a crescendo.

The startled seventeen-year-old Isabella looked at the cushion and then ran from the room.

Fans clicked shut, and glances were shared. The distiller from Tulliallan picked up his smouldering pipe, shrugged, and thought:

'Try and do better next time.'

The wedding was jam-packed and full of hullabaloo. When winter had become endless, it was a welcome excuse for the whole town to go bang.

As the whoops and yelps continued, Peggie and JJ took their leave. With lantern held high, the Constable led the way down between the frosted lime trees to the Shore. Peggie had been Empress for the day, but now she could not help but think of all her children gone and never to return. JJ hugged her close, and she breathed in the comforting scent of tobacco. The auld fool chuckled as Peggie snugged in.

Throughout 1801, the Napoleonic Wars were gathering momentum, and the prohibition on distilling in Dublin continued. John Jameson's advice was to take advantage of such events. At Marrowbone Lane, William Jameson and his cousin John Stein Junior put their house in good order and explored the markets in anticipation of when business resumed.

William went out to tread the streets and learn the Dublin 'Knowledge'. Acting as his own agent he got to know the various landlords and the city itself. He discovered the eccentricities and wit of a city born out of the harsh resourcefulness of extreme poverty. Rags of every colour and substance were patched into garments that cocked a snoot at fashion. Begging was as indispensable a part of the city's commercial life as banking. The contemporary travel writer John Carr recorded the wit of one such beggar as he followed a limping, gouty, irritable, old gentleman:

> *"Ah, Plaze yer honour's honour, I wish God had made your heart as tender as your toes."*

Young Will's heart was with his city of Dublin and the people.

In January 1802, a new pantomime arrived in Dublin, playing at the Amphitheatre Royal on Peter Street. It wasn't 'Cinderella' or 'Dick Whittington' but 'The Death of Abercromby'. Not your seasonal outing for the kiddies.

Since Ralph Abercromby's less-than-successful visit to Ireland four years ago, he had now become a national hero. The sixty-seven-year-old had led the troops to victory at the Battle of Alexandria and had routed the French from Egypt. Unfortunately, where the furious James Francis Erskine had failed, the French had succeeded. Amid the fray of cutting and slashing, a spent musket ball had lodged in Ralph's thigh. A week later, in March 1801, General Ralph Abercromby of Tullibody was dead.

To see a re-enactment of the death of his former neighbour, William Jameson, would have been in for a long evening.

The curtain rose precisely at seven to begin another pantomime, 'The Castle of Blackenberg'. This was followed by a seven-year-old doing rope dancing, a young equestrian leaping over two garters and through a balloon, and a female equilibrist performing exercises on the slack wire. Finally, after various comic medleys, pony racing, and poems and whilst many were leaving to catch the last jingle to Blackrock, the band struck up for the Grand Military Egyptian Pantomime.

The climactic death scene goes unrecorded, but *Saunders's News-Letter* ecstatically reported:

> *'To see the horses belonging to the Light Cavalry at the moment of Victory, in the highest pitch of animation, the spectator can scarcely believe his eyes!'*

It was hardly a prequel to 'Riverdance', but it did provide a spot of good low-brow jingoism.

By 1802, William Jameson had little time for flag waving of whatever hue. Recently, Dublin Castle had made a proclamation that permitted the malting from grain that was followed by the authorisation of the distilling of whiskey from the 1 January. The Dublin distilleries, which had survived the prohibition, were ramping up. The opportunity had arrived for Marrowbone Lane to prove its worth. The Napoleonic Wars created not only a shortage of corn but also a shortage of French brandy. With JJ's favourite tipple in short supply, it was up to William to provide him with a decent substitute.

JJ waited patiently and looked over to the other side of the River Liffey to where the Bow Street story continued. In June of 1801, the aristocratic combo boosted the distillery's value by renewing the lease for a dynastic nine hundred and ninety-seven years. They then disposed of their other distilleries in John Street, James Street, and Francis Street, and pushed all they had left into Bow Street. The brand-new capital distillery was gearing up for production. Lending the aristos an advisory hand was JJ's brother-in-law Robert Haig. Bobby would be JJ's informant from the inside.

Up at the other end of Bow Street, Dodd's smaller distillery at No. 1 had been a casualty of the prohibition. Opportunely, a new but older kid had arrived on the block to buy up Dodd's lease.

John Stein Senior was back in Ireland, in business and going into partnership with John Kennedy in February 1802. As Kennedy was a non-active partner, Stein Senior required Stein Junior to lend a hand. William Jameson was now virtually running the Marrowbone Lane distillery on his own.

Back in Scotland in Tulliallan, JJ-2 was not enjoying the same autonomy as his younger brother Will.

Uncle Andrew Haig was not the easiest of men to work with. He certainly did not share the view of quality over quantity. Occasionally, too, and much to JJ's raised eyebrows, Uncle Andrew had failed to keep his breeches buttoned. That led to run-ins with the kirk.

But for JJ-2, Tulliallan had one important factor going for it: its proximity to Kennetpans.

Just a two-mile trot and Johnny could pick up from where he had left off with the dropped cushion. Whilst Stein Senior was in Ireland, romance blossomed with Cousin Isabella.

Down the coast at Eyemouth, Margaret kept up the family tradition of summertime babies. On 15 May 1802, Peggie and JJ's first grandchild, Robert Robertson, was born.

Autumn came, and the hankies were out, as on 3 October 1802, Isabella Stein and John Jameson-2 were married in the town of Clackmannan.

Uncle John Stein would have to dig deep into his pockets for the dowry or any loose change. His second venture into distilling in Ireland would soon cost more than he had bargained for.

1803 and the modern world was advancing and shrinking. Thomas 'Steamboat' Dundas had finally met his fame. His commissioned steamboat, *The Charlotte Dundas*, powered itself up his canal from the Forth to the Clyde. A steam packet across the Irish Sea was only a decade away.

Alloa was to have a modern touch, too.

Robert Jameson, like his father, seventeen years before, took a trip to London. There, he obtained a bill for further harbour improvements.

This time, Rob had tacked onto the parliamentary bill, '*cleansing, paving and lighting for the Town of Alloa*'.

In Dublin, the dark ages were returning.

In July, dining at his house in Marrowbone Lane, William Jameson heard the horrible screams, gunfire, and commotion of a rising in nearby Thomas Street.

It was to be expected.

The promise of Catholic emancipation had never happened. This was owing in part to the psychiatric condition of George III and his hate for Catholics. William Pitt resigned over the matter, but it wasn't long before rebellion erupted.

Robert Emmet was an idealistic, poetic, Protestant leader from the last remnants of the United Irishmen. On 23 July 1803, Emmet organised a disorganised and miss-timed rebellious march onto Dublin Castle. In Thomas Street, events rocketed out of his control due to the actions of a boozed-up rabble. Alarmed at their violent behaviour, Emmet called off the rebellion. But the rabble went on the rampage, dragging toffs from their coaches and soldiers off their horses and hacking them to death.

The authorities rushed in with ugly slaughter, and the rebellion was left with seventy dead and hell for a hangover.

Unfortunately, the primal behaviour didn't end there. Robert Emmet was arrested, and after his trial, he was publicly hung outside Will's parish church of St Catherine's. Once hung, with his body still warm, Emmet's head was sliced off and raised above a horrified crowd. Resentment was driven deep. Emmet's cause and the eloquence from his trial lived on:

'*When my country takes her place amongst the Nations of the Earth, then and not till then, let my epitaph be written.*'

For William Jameson, evensong at St Catherine's could never be quite the same again.

1804 arrived, and the Bow Street story continued. Two events happened along this street almost simultaneously.

Uncle John Stein, true to form, was having problems with the creditors of his distillery at No. 1 Bow Street. As a result, his partner, John Kennedy, was unhappy and wanted out. The partnership was dissolved.

Uncle John Stein was now on his own and needed help to survive.

At the same time, and farther up Bow Street, the bankers were rattling the gates of the aristocrats' new and more extensive distillery. The co-partners of Edmond and Richard Grange & Co, decided enough was enough and put their brand-new Bow Street distillery onto the market.

JJ had waited for the right moment, but now he had a conundrum. He had a choice between two Bow Street distilleries. Would he throw a lifeline to Uncle John Stein's small distillery, or would he bid for a top-of-the-range, large, modern distillery and hang Peggie's uncle out to dry?

JJ felt a tug of duty towards John Stein. He was Peggie's uncle, JJ-2's father-in-law, and he was the maternal grandfather to JJ's new grandson, born that January.

But there were also the futures of JJ's sons. Not only did JJ-2 want out of Tulliallan, but there were James and Andrew following on behind.

JJ's decision had to be based on sound business for everyone's sake. To invest in John Stein's distillery looked like throwing good money after bad. To purchase the aristocrats' distillery was a more expensive option, but it was a bargain considering the money that had been sunk into it.

The aristocrats wanted out double quick to settle debts and avoid the soaring interest on loans. JJ would have the upper hand for any deal. As JJ deliberated, Peggie told the 'softy auld fool' to get on with it.

At the end of the year, JJ-2, Isabella, and baby JJ-3 travelled through to Dublin and moved into rooms in Sackville Street.

JJ brokered and pushed forward funds to meet the purchase price of sixteen thousand, four hundred and thirty-one pounds, nineteen shillings, and twopence.

On 28 March 1805, whiskey history was made as John Jameson purchased the Bow Street Smithfield distillery from Grange, Sperling, Sir D'Oyly, and Rochfort in the names of William Jameson, John Stein Junior, and John Jameson-2.

Uncle John Stein Senior's habitual bankruptcy was followed by the indignity of his possessions being examined by all. Plate, china, glass, bedding, and 'an excellent piano forte' were put on the market together with the distillery at No. 1 Bow Street.

Uncle John Stein could not have been too harsh on JJ's decision. His son and his daughter would benefit, and so would his grandson.

More importantly, for the Irish nation, the Jameson family were in charge of their two Dublin distilleries and were on the way to producing a decent whiskey.

A prospect of the city of Dublin from Phoenix Park. After a work by James Mason. (Classic Image /Alamy Stock Photo)

Chapter 17

A Whiskey in Its Youth

1805–15

Margaret Jameson dies; The benchmarks are set for John Jameson Whiskey; The Jameson brothers settle into Dublin Life; 1810 – Andrew Jameson marries; John Stein junior moves to Limerick; 1812 – The Jameson brothers negotiate the nuptials for Janet's wedding to John Woolsey; 1815 – Peggie dies; James Jameson marries.

1805 WAS THE YEAR THAT John Jameson and his sons bought their Bow Street distillery from the aristocrats. From my schoolboy cramming, it was likewise the year of the Battle of Trafalgar and the death of Nelson. But for Peggie and JJ, it was sadly the year their first-born child and much-loved daughter Margaret died at thirty-six.

It was summer in the small Berwickshire harbour town of Eye-mouth, where Margaret and her husband were raising their two small boys. Robert was three, and John Jameson Robertson was one. At the end of July, Margaret gave birth to a third boy, William. A week later, Margaret passed away. Motherhood's high-wire act had taken its toll.

Within the Alloa Kirkyard, near the fast-deteriorating St Mungo, Margaret was laid to rest.

The family were shattered. Margaret had been so much a part of everyone's lives.

Peggie would never fully recover.

Heartbreaking, but action was required. Margaret's three very young boys had to be taken care of, so grandparents, aunts, and uncles rallied round, with Alloa and Dublin becoming the boys' second and third homes after Eyemouth.

Tragedy united, and the bond of family was strengthened.

Across the divide of the Irish Sea, all four younger Jameson brothers gradually filtered through to Ireland.

From the beginning, Jameson Whiskey in Ireland was a Jameson affair, with father and sons combining their different strengths in building the foundations of a whiskey brand that was to develop, survive, and flourish for over two centuries.

They owed much at the start to Peggie's Stein uncles in Scotland, from whom they had learnt the basics of distilling. They were also fortunate in coming in off the back of the Steins' early pioneering industrialisation.

The differences between the two families and the reasons for their successes and failures were that the Steins were farmers first, and the Jamesons were lawyers first.

JJ was the bedrock of the Dublin enterprises by providing the initial purchasing power and guidance. His lifetime experience had taught that success and survival rested on sustainable, strong capital fed by profits. In the short term, the strong capital enabled buying the best ingredients, equipment, and skills. In the long term, strong capital was biblical in enabling expansion in the prosperous years and tying over the works during the lean times. You can't create a good whiskey if you go bust after four years. Establishing a fine whiskey can take tens to hundreds of years and the expertise of many.

JJ's mantra held for generations and enabled success. Whilst other well-meaning enterprises were forever going to the wall, Jameson survived.

JJ also set the benchmark in his son's quest to craft the perfect nip. Sixty-five years later, in the book *Truths About Whisky*, a Jameson whiskey was described as '*a carefully brewed glass of toddy that when friends are met together round the fireside, enlivens talk and quickens fancy. It conduces to quiet and dreamless slumber, to awake refreshed, with a cool palate and an easy head.*'

The ancient Irish Usquebaugh, made by monks, was very aromatic and flavoured by adding all kinds of seeds and spices to the mash when distilling. This created a reputation for Irish whiskey being less fiery and milder than its Scottish counterpart.

Ancient was a long way back for William and John Jameson-2 to go, but they gave the nod to those old monks and their Water of Life. They aimed to produce an Irish whiskey that was smooth and wholesome.

The sacks of juniper berries that the aristocrats had left behind in Bow Street would not be needed. Instead, the flavours were to come initially from the grain. So, the sourcing of good-quality barley was a priority. Taking the lead from their father, William and JJ-2 strengthened their contact with the Castlebellingham brewery to resource their barley from County Louth.

In the past, a constant moan from the distillers in Dublin had been the poor quality of malt on the market. The newly industrialised distilling of William and JJ-2 meant they took control of their malting. They had pride in announcing that their early whiskey was '*Real Malt Whiskey*', and they advertised it as '*Made solely from Malt of the finest quality, without any mixture of other corn whatever*'.

The enhancement of whiskey by ageing it in a cask was well known. The traditional 'Old Irish Whiskey' origins were said to have come from burying illicit whiskey to hide it from the customs and then digging it up a few years later.

However, most whiskey, even probably Old Irish, was sold young. This had much to do with the licensing laws. Once the duty was paid on the spirit, the incentive was to sell the whiskey to recoup the expenditure. If stored, a proportion of that duty would evaporate and waft away for the enjoyment of angels.

In 1804, a form of duty-free warehousing was introduced in Dublin. It wasn't perfect, but gradually the 'In Bond' system came about. Bow Street began to take advantage of the vaults and cellarage beneath. The brothers experimented, and the quality of their whiskey in the ageing process leapt forward. Within sixteen years, '*Jameson & Co – Three-Year-Old Whiskey*' had entered the market.

The variations in creating a whiskey are infinite; experimentation was continuous for the brothers. Joined by younger siblings, James and Andrew, opinions were shared, and notes were taken with precision. Slowly the four lawyers built their cases for the perfect tipple with JJ as their judge.

John Jameson's interests were now split between Alloa and Dublin. JJ fulfilled his life job as the Sheriff Clerk of Clackmannan faithfully. But his eldest son and heir, Rob, was more than capable of running the office without him when needed. At those times, JJ could depart to indulge in and enjoy his Kingdom of distilleries in Ireland.

The family base in Dublin was 33 Prussia Street. Here JJ-2 and Isabella lived, and for Peggie and JJ, it was a welcome change from the muddle-built House by the Shore. Prussia Street was a classic eighteenth-century townhouse with spacious grounds and gardens. Nearby was rural Phoenix Park, and a gentle half-hour stroll away was the Bow Street distillery.

During the summer, Peggie and JJ might stay for three to four months at a time, with travel taken over a leisurely ten days. Once settled into Prussia Street, JJ could potter down to Bow Street, where the old man could stick his nose into everything.

JJ's four sons were making Dublin their home. While JJ-2 and Isabella raised their family in Prussia Street, William moved to Merrion Square, and James and Andrew took houses at 19 and 24 Harcourt Street.

For worship, the brothers had an eclectic religious background of Scottish Presbyterianism, Episcopalian, and Secessionism. On their first arrival in Dublin, they felt at home amongst the Presbyterian dissenters' congregation of Eustace Street; later, this congregation was to adopt the more liberal-minded Church of Unitarianism.

At the same time, William and James joined their local Church of Ireland at St Catherine's, Thomas Street. St Catherine's was run by a leading Dublin cleric, the statistician and philanthropist James Whitelaw.

James Whitelaw was a man who did not look the other way. He researched, visited, and documented the appalling conditions under which the Dublin poor lived. Two of his parishioners, William and James Jameson, did not look the other way, either. With no state welfare, philanthropy was a necessity. All the brothers went on to make it their business to contribute to the many charities, from free schools to fever hospitals to poor relief.

Politically, the brothers backed Catholic emancipation, were regular signatories for their civil rights, and would later support Daniel O'Connell's Catholic Association.

In 1810, Andrew Jameson was the first in the family to be married in Ireland. Catherine Jameson, an army surgeon's daughter, was no near relation but having the same surname proved to be a handy chat-up line for both. The marriage was solemnised, and Andrew and Catherine settled down in Harcourt Street to raise their 'Made in Ireland' children.

The Marrowbone Lane and the Bow Street distilleries had also been bought in their cousin John Stein Junior's name. Cousin John was a restless soul and a country boy at heart. Later, he would move to Dorset to lead the life of a country squire, breed cattle, and become Sheriff for a year. For now, not long after the Bow Street signing and the collapse of his father's distillery, John Stein Junior collected his dividends and trotted west to Limerick.

In Limerick, with a business partner John Brown, he founded the Thomond Gate distillery, where the Stein model of distilling and farming was applied. Farms were bought nearby, and cheap fuel in peat was transported by canal from a bog at Portcrusha. What the Steins had aimed to achieve in Roscrea, they began to accomplish in Limerick.

By 1811, Uncle John Stein Senior's Irish debts were sold off, and with the help of JJ-2, a flour mill and bakery were bought at Marlfield near Clonmel. It was out with the cakes and in with the whiskey as the mill was converted to another Stein distillery but with Jameson backing. Away from Dublin and in the countryside, the Steins prospered for a while.

For John Jameson, the highlight of the long haul from Alloa to Dublin remained the stopover at Castlebellingham for a decent pint. Beneath the greenery of the ancient elm tree, JJ stepped down from his carriage and on into the glowing gloom of the inn. A new brewery manager had now arrived to bid him welcome, Mr Woolsey.

John Woolsey was the local vicar's son, a Bellingham nephew, and ambitious. His Bellingham ale had remained, as travel writer John Carr reported, '*remarkably good*' and, for JJ, as delicious as ever.

Wiping the foam from his lips, JJ turned to his host.

"Mr Woolsey," he said. "Your ale tempts me to stay and continue no further. Mibbie there's a way forward to some future partnership and there to share with us the secrets of your perfections."

Mr Woolsey took up the idea of a partnership but perhaps in a different manner than JJ had in mind. At one family stopover, JJ's youngest daughter Janet caught Woolsey's eye. For Janet, Mr Woolsey was quite pleasing, too, and a romance began to brew and blossom.

JJ was not averse to the idea of a wedding between Mr Woolsey and his daughter. He approved of Mr Woolsey, and he approved of his father, the Rev. William Woolsey, who had supported a Catholic bid for freedom.

Peggie had her doubts. She was about to lose another daughter and needed to ensure that her youngest was well cared for. JJ put forward a proposal of a dowry for his daughter of three thousand pounds. Peggie and JJ agreed that this would be solely for Janet Jameson's use.

In 1812, when the marriage was due to take place, the ambitious John Woolsey was preparing for the deal of his lifetime. He was poised to take complete control of the Bellingham brewery with his cousin William Cairnes. Woolsey needed cash. He looked to Janet's dowry and his future in-laws for some assistance.

"It is of great good fortune to the lawyer," observed JJ, "how frequently the romance o' wedding bells becomes entangled with the ropes o' business."

JJ cannily placed his sons JJ-2 and William in command of the pre-nuptial agreement. Entrusted with Janet's dowry, the lawyer brothers advanced Mr Woolsey two thousand pounds but attached a settlement on the Woolsey estate to this loan.

At Castlebellingham on 30 March 1812, with his lands at Priorland and Haggardstown now assigned to Janet Jameson, the Rev. William Woolsey solemnised the deal and married Janet and John.

'Good boys,' thought JJ.

At the celebrations, the Scottish contingent was allowed the hilarity of 'Bab at the Bowster'. The Irish mob speedily grasped the idea. By the time James Jameson had danced with his cushion and placed it before a girl, there was no holding her back. It was a case of a sister swap. Elizabeth Woolsey and Jimmy danced around the hall with the cushion between them and on into a marriage proposal.

The Jameson–Woolsey shared interest in malting and in barley strengthened. William Jameson and John Woolsey soon formed a partnership for a new distillery at nearby Drogheda. Romance and business prospered, and the flavour of a Jameson whiskey continued to improve.

For visiting the grandchildren, travelling to weddings, or checking in with the distilleries, the rollercoaster journey to Dublin for Peggie and JJ was beginning to lose its charm. Recovery time was taking longer.

By his seventy-third year, eighteenth-century life was playing havoc with JJ's limbs. Lent on by horses, rattled by carts, swollen by dampness, inflamed by gout, age called for a more sedentary life.

For a short time in 1813, JJ had to deputise part of his duty as Sheriff Clerk owing to his inability to travel far. For the Irish clan, it was now their turn to travel to Alloa, report their progress, and deliver their biannual remittance.

In January 1815, the brothers and their sister Janet defied storms to travel to the House at the Shore for another reason. Both Peggie and JJ were unwell.

JJ pulled through, but at sixty-two years of age, exhaustion had set in for Peggie. Sixteen pregnancies, their births, and many losses had made her vulnerable. During the killing winter months that had taken so many of her younger children, Peggie finally also succumbed.

The 'auld fool' was with her until the end.

At the outset of their journey together, there could have been no notion of what would come. Then, Peggie provided the switchback ride of a lifetime through her Stein uncles and her Haig brothers. Holding on tight, it all came very right for them in the end. Their devotion to each other grew, with Peggie often leading the way through their forty-seven years of marriage. The proof of the pudding was in the successes of their surviving offspring.

The House at the Shore, once so full to bursting, now echoed empty.

JJ felt bereft and alone, but he was not. Daughter Helen was there to boss away melancholy, Robert to fill in on all the gossip, and Anne to maybe sing of an evening.

In June came the Battle of Waterloo, and in August, JJ presided over yet another election.

In September 1815, there was good reason for one last mighty effort to visit Ireland. James Jameson was marrying Elizabeth Woolsey in Castlebellingham.

Without a doubt, the marriage was a love match. But for James, business was at the centre of everything he did, which may have made him a little annoying to some. James's model was Arthur Guinness II, whom he monitored and mirrored. James stalked Arthur into various useful and career-enhancing organisations. He was elected to the 'Dublin Society' of arty do-gooders, became a member of the society of the 'Ouzel Gallery', and then became a director of the 'Corn Exchange Buildings Company'. But most useful for James was following Arthur's footsteps towards banking.

Conveniently, his bride Elizabeth was related to the Palmer family of vicars and bankers. So, it wouldn't be long before distiller James Jameson, like his idol Arthur Guinness, would become a director of the Bank of Ireland. Access to capital would be assured.

At the nuptials, as the Rev. Papa Woolsey brokered the heavenly bit, JJ could look around and see that his dynasty in Ireland was well set up and provided for. In 1815, William Jameson continued to run the Marrowbone Lane distillery partnered by his youngest brother Andrew; John Jameson-2 continued to run the Bow Street distillery partnered by his brother James and under the banner of Jameson and Co.

In Castlebellingham, daughter Janet would soon take over Milestown House with her brewer husband, Mr Woolsey. Ivy-clad and chimneyed, their new home sat gracefully by the leafy banks of the River Glyde. JJ may well have sneaked a peek. It was here, one hundred and fifty years later, that I would meet JJ and Peggie for the first time.

The wedding was over, and in October 1815, JJ returned to Scotland through the colour fest of autumn and into the gloaming of his life.

Newhaven Pier, Firth of Forth
(Stephen Dorey Bygone Images /Alamy Stock Photo)

Paddle steamers were beginning to proliferate up and down
the Forth.

Chapter 18

The Gloaming

1816–23

Alloa in 1816; Forth Paddle steamers; A visit to John Francis;1817 – Andrew Jameson takes over his distillery in Wexford; 1818 – James Jameson goes into partnership with George Roe; 1822 – Anne Jameson marries Captain Stupart; King George IV visits Dublin; William Jameson dies; 1823 – John Jameson-2 is taken to court; The Booterstown Casanova; John Jameson breathes his last.

OVER JJ'S SEVEN DECADES, ALLOA had changed much. Its industry had developed dramatically. But despite the copper works, the glassworks, the breweries, and the spinning mills, much of the rural feel of the town remained. The cocks crowed in the morning, the day's pace was leisurely, and everyone went peaceably to bed at night when the sun dimmed.

The Mar mansion had yet to be rebuilt, but the ancient Alloa Tower stood within the pleasure grounds, sheltered by a sea of trees.

The purity of this Mar landscape and its waters had recently been threatened by none other than Andrew Haig. He was intent on building a new distillery just upstream. John Francis Erskine was forced to take legal action and put a stop to this Haig enterprise and its dross polluting his estate. Thankfully, JJ-2 had left and was well away in Dublin before this uncomfortable spat.

The old, dilapidated kirk of St Mungo was slowly being demolished, and a new St Mungo was arising on Bedford Place. Along this road, modern-styled villas were popping up and farther down was found the recently built Grange distillery.

Andrew Stein of Loanside ran this enterprise. Robert Jameson had joined in with his Stein relative and another cousin, William Wilson Jameson, to have a wee dabble, too.

Unfortunately, the distillery didn't have the best of reputations. The agent Neil Ryrie wrote to William Wilson and complained of the output having '*a singed taste*' with '*a flavour that was by no means good.*'

Then along came that old threat of a Stein bankruptcy. Rob recognised the signs and skilfully skedaddled.

On many a day, old JJ could be seen in his jaunting cart wobbling precariously as he and his pony negotiated the deep ruts of Lime Tree Walk. Without the aid of anti-inflammatory drugs, statins, and pacemakers, age was felt acutely. But at least JJ could keep his brain agile without the need for crosswords and puzzles. He remained the Bailie for the town of Alloa, cashier for the Harbour Trust, and Sheriff Clerk of Clackmannan. There were plenty of figures to tot up, reports to the Commissioners of supply, and sessions as Clerk of the Court. As an oldie, JJ was well set up to give his brain cells a run for their money.

For oldies, a version of the cruising industry was also coming into being. Paddle steamers were beginning to proliferate up and down the Forth. There was much to tempt as the steamboats threshed the water between Stirling, Alloa, and on to Newhaven for Edinburgh. Breakfast, luncheon, and tea were served with wines, porter, and ales of the best quality. The *Caledonian Mercury* advertised:

> *'Parties of pleasure must be highly gratified, in viewing the beautiful windings of the Forth, and the diversified scenery of the surrounding countryside.'*

Departures were subject to tides, but the regular three-hour journey from Alloa to Newhaven broke all records. *The Morning Star of Alloa* could comfortably land JJ at Newhaven Harbour by noon. A quick burst of Tourette's from the fishwives would be followed by a brisk trot up to town in a chaise.

For JJ, spacious accommodation was always available at James Haig's Lochrin House, and then a couple of days could be spent visiting old cronies.

One obligatory stop would be at York Place to call on John Francis at his terraced townhouse. The two old men would grunt and cackle away as the news was exchanged between Edinburgh and the wee county.

In 1816, talk would have been of the Grange distillery and the Steins, of whom John Francis was now not a huge fan.

'I have done them many a good turn, but money is the root of all evil,' he would comment primly.

JJ would chuckle at the paradox emanating from this earldom-seeking, overspending, land-owning, old toff.

And then talk would turn to JJ's pride and joy: his sons and his distilleries.

By 1816, JJ's youngest son, Andrew Jameson, was looking to branch out away from Dublin and into County Wexford.

Down by the River Urrin at Fairfield, near Enniscorthy, was a set of buildings called the Forge of Monart. The forge had originally been used to manufacture swords, and who knows, in later years, maybe to manufacture pikes for the nearby Battle of Vinegar Hill. The buildings had been converted into a distillery by a couple of Dublin rectifiers. Andrew saw his opportunity. With help from his dad chipping in, he bought up the rectifiers business. Leaving Marrowbone Lane behind, Andrew began distilling amongst the many shaded greens of County Wexford.

Soon after, James Jameson was to stretch his distilling wings, too, but he remained in Dublin. Jimmy went into partnership with James McCall and the famed George Roe. The partnership was based on George's distillery on Thomas Street. An eye-catching feature of the distillery was a massive windmill rising to over one hundred and fifty feet, known today as St Patrick's Tower. James negotiated a good deal for himself, as is recorded in Dublin's Registry of Deeds, with the premises, windmill, and business held in his name.

By 1819, James Jameson and Co. of Thomas Street, John Jameson of Bow Street, William Jameson of Marrowbone Lane, and Andrew Jameson of Fairfield were all firmly established Irish distillers.

Back in Alloa, a Regency romance was playing out. Captain Francis Stupart was a local lad and a hero of the Battle of Waterloo. As a lieutenant in the Scots Greys, he took part in their famed charge. Wounded, he recovered and returned home to Alloa, where he retired as a captain on half pay. Many a young Alloa lady sighed for the captain, but it was to the young Anne Jameson for whom this soldier came a-courtin'.

Calling at the House at the Shore, Stupart met his second Waterloo. The military did not impress the aged, growling JJ. But the soldier boy persisted, and Anne and Francis fell in love.

In 1821, the majority of Anne's close family was now living in Ireland. Whether that was the reason or there was an element of elopement, Dublin was the chosen venue for Anne's April wedding. In Prussia Street, JJ-2's house was filled to bursting with sister Janet, the four brothers, nephews, and nieces. The Reverend Dr James Horner officiated. A legendary Jameson revelry let rip.

A month later, the couple returned to Alloa, where the marriage was blest, and the rest of the families celebrated. JJ grunted his approval.

1821 was Coronation year, and the former Prince Regent and now newly crowned King George IV paid a state visit to Dublin. George was the first English monarch to come to Ireland without smashing the place up. The flags were out, triumphal arches were thrown across the streets, and Dublin cheered a welcome. The trip was a public relations coup. Even the Liberator Daniel O'Connell was a wee bit smitten and presented the King with a laurel crown.

On his arrival at Phoenix Park, George gave an impromptu speech to his fans gathered at the front door of Vice-Regal Lodge.

"*Go and do by me as I shall do by you!*" commanded the fat, boozy King. "*Drink my health in a bumper; I shall drink all yours in a bumper of good Irish Whiskey.*"

The Dublin distillers were understandably out in force to service the royal directive and wave the flag during the celebratory processions around the city. *The Freeman's Journal* of Dublin reported that '*Nothing looked so Majestically Grand as Messrs James Jameson of Thomas Street*'.

James had gone to town by fastening a flag to the dome of his one hundred and fifty-foot-high windmill: '*Fully equal to the height of Nelson's pillar.*'

Jimmy had also built a platform around the tower where the distillery's entire workforce was to dine as a demonstration of '*Real Irish Hospitality*'.

The newspaper added: '*On that occasion, when, no doubt, His Majesty's request will be complied with in drinking his health in flowing bumpers of the native*'.

The brothers had embraced the Irish way and learnt how to party and share their hospitality.

But the underbelly of poverty remained in the city. Within crumbling tenements, unscrupulous landlords crammed fifteen to twenty persons to a room. In rags, they slept on straw, alive with vermin. Disease spread, fevers abounded, and death was the great leveller.

On 5 December 1822, William Jameson died of typhoid at his house in Merrion Square. Irish farewells are legendary, and

Will's farewell spoke as to the man he was and, as reported in the *Saunders's News-Letter*:

> *'The funeral of the late William Jameson, Esq., of Merri-*
> *on-Square, took place yesterday; and although it was intended*
> *to be as private as possible, yet such was the esteem in which he*
> *was held during his lifetime, that his remains were followed to*
> *the place of internment at Donnybrook by a long train of private*
> *carriages, and, what no less marks the veneration in which he was*
> *held by all classes when living, a great number of poor men, whose*
> *countenance portrayed a keenness of sorrow for the deprivation*
> *of a kind and indulgent benefactor, also attended the funeral to*
> *the church-yard.'*

On Will's death, his estate and his Marrowbone Lane distillery were passed on to his younger brother, James Jameson. Leaving George Roe and his windmill in Thomas Street, James took over the ownership and running of Marrowbone Lane.

At Bow Street, John Jameson-2 continued to invest. Within the work's complex, Johnny had erected a new chimney from which a '*roaring*' was heard at all times of the day and night. Complaints came thick and fast. They included inmates at the local penitentiary, a night watchman who had his regular snooze on duty disturbed, and a Sandymount resident who thought an earthquake was approaching.

Apart from the bellows of laughter, these witnesses triggered at the resulting court case, the distillery's activities had all the hallmarks of the Steins and Haigs of thirty years ago. Both Bow Street and Marrowbone Lane had begun to fire up and speedily work off their stills by day and night to break even. The culprit was the licensing laws.

A licence fee was paid on every still according to its capacity. This fee was now paid monthly and was increasing. A still had to be worked at full tilt simply to pay its licence.

Back in 1788, Uncle Jim in Scotland had worked the system to his advantage. But for Uncle Jim, quality was not the issue, and fuel was cheap.

The Jameson brothers lobbied for change.

In 1823, the system of licence charges on stills was scrapped. Duty was to be paid instead on the spirit taken from the warehouse and sold. With the duty paid for at the end of the process, that process could be indulged. Distilling could now be slowed and repeated penalty-free. The pot still could come into its own to fully exploit the flavours. The spirit could then be racked in casks and stored till time percolated its mastery. 1823 was a new dawn for the Dublin distillers.

At his Wexford distillery, Andrew Jameson had an additional problem to that of the excise. His marriage to Catherine was falling apart.

When Andrew bought his works at Fairfield, he had decided, for some reason, not to move his family there. Maybe Wexford was too remote and far away from Dublin society. Perhaps Catherine was unsettled by Enniscorthy's rebellious nature and the distillery's nearness to the likes of Vinegar Hill. For whatever reason, Andrew and Catherine set up a home away from Fairfield. With their three children, they moved to Ruby Lodge in Booterstown, near the fashionable Dublin suburb of Blackrock.

Fairfield was a long commute of over seventy miles south of Booterstown. Every three weeks or so, Andrew travelled to the distillery and stayed away for up to a fortnight.

In Andrew's absence, a Mr Arthur Browne visited Catherine Jameson rather too frequently.

Nothing is very private in a house full of servants. At Ruby Lodge, the servants soon became aware of Mrs Jameson's rather furtive behaviour. There were the hushed voices at night, the mysterious turning of keys, and the sudden shifting of sleeping arrangements.

On certain nights, the youngest child, Miss Caroline, was parked in the governess's room instead of her mother's. On one such night, the butler was to observe Mr Arthur Browne entering Ruby Lodge via the greenhouse. Suspecting Mrs Jameson of infidelity, Mr Walsh, the butler, put the servants on high alert.

Two nights later, the butler and the coachman hid in a clump of trees outside the house. At eleven o'clock, they saw Arthur Browne arrive and slyly make his way through a wicket to the greenhouse. There he was met with a kiss from Mrs Jameson. She led Arthur into the house carrying her bedchamber candlestick.

The butler and the coachman tumbled out from their tree-clump hideaway and followed. Inside the house, they were met by Ann, the children's maid. Ann had witnessed Mrs Jameson and Mr Browne entering the upstairs bedroom.

The affronted servants swung into action. Bridget, another maid, was put on guard in the parlour beneath Mrs Jameson's bedroom. Then the butler and the coachman rushed up the stairs to the second landing and the boudoir. Outside the locked door, the butler and the coachman stopped for a moment, not quite knowing what to do next. Then the butler cleared his throat and, in a butler-styled delicate fashion, called out: "Robbers!"

Mrs Jameson unlocked and opened the bedroom door. Mr Walsh the butler announced to her that there were robbers in the house and proposed searching 'Madam's bedroom'. Madam refused. Instead, Catherine accused the butler and coachman of being drunk and threatened to send them to the police.

Downstairs, Bridget the maid, on hearing the upstairs commotion, dashed to the parlour window. From the window, Bridget caught sight of Arthur Browne sliding down a carpet from the room above. By the time the butler and coachman had run in and flung open the parlour window, Arthur had scarpered. All that was left was the incriminating evidence of Mrs Jameson's bedroom carpet lying on the lawn outside.

The Booterstown Casanova, Arthur Browne, had vanished, never to be heard of again.

It was only after Andrew's brother James Jameson had thoroughly interrogated all the servants that Andrew fully understood Catherine's naughtiness.

Thankfully, old man JJ would miss and never know of 'The Arthur Browne Affair'.

September 1823 at Alloa and the Ochil Hills had sucked in the last of the summer air; puffed out, they rolled away along the Forth in their autumnal tweedy browns.

The House at the Shore had the trappings of a life fading; the jaunting cart propped up, the pony stabled. Inside, a rat scurried, and a young terrier pounced. JJ chuckled and rasped up a cough. He sat like a toby jug with chunky legs glued to his chunky chair. Gently growling, JJ was breathing himself towards the last of his ancient breaths.

Alerted, JJ looked up. He had heard the clatter of hooves on the stone causey. A sporty two-horsed Phaeton drew up, and Robert Jameson leapt down. Hatted, booted, and quite the squire, he entered and clunked across the hall towards his papa.

JJ grunted as Rob handed him the minutes of the meeting of the Harbour Trust. JJ's watery eyes fused the words from the minutes into a continuous blur. Rob took them and read:

> 'Mr John Jameson who has long acted as cashier, is, from his great age, desirous of resigning that office. The meeting accepted his resignation.'

Over the past few months, the old man had been sifting and sorting out the details before his departure. His will was written, responsibilities and ownership of the distilleries were away with his sons in Ireland, and now all the town and county duties were passed onto his Prince Regent Robert. Only the title of 'Sheriff Clerk' would remain until he had gasped his last.

Helen joined her brother and father for the tittle-tattle of the day. Tea arrived on a tray and was poured fashionably. Rob chatted on without a pause.

"There is, in my opinion, a great worry for Mr Erskine of Mar's Grandson, a good man, inclined to religious melancholy, who is in Geneva, where my nephew—"

"Nephew?" interrupted JJ.

"Robert, your eldest grandson, Papa, who sends you both his love and who just happens to be busying himself in Geneva also, and where a physician was to inform him that Mr Erskine had been found in a perfect state of insanity, to which young Robert immediately paid a visit, to discover the man so delirious, raving, and incoherent that the doctor fears the distemper will either settle into confirmed insanity or terminate in death."

Rob paused to sip his tea.

"Geneva!" grunted JJ. "Geneva would inevitably incite insanity; it being placed too far from the oceans."

Helen laughed and squeezed her papa's hand.

The days shortened.

Autumn was swept clean by the first of the winter gales, and JJ retired to his bed. For convenience, the library downstairs had been adopted as his bedchamber. Oak shelves remained, climbing the walls and squashing books and parchments up to the ceiling. The scent of herbs, wood, wax, and coal fires filled the room. Like a billowing, draped sarcophagus, a posted and enclosed bed arose from the polished floor.

Whilst dreams wandered towards death, the House at the Shore was creaking back into life. Doors banged, bells clanged, trunks were dumped, and footsteps clipped from room to room. Voices were heard lowered; then, forgetful, raised with laughter.

By steamboat, horse, and carriage, the clan was gathering.

JJ slept within his room within a room, his head propped up against a cloud of pummelled pillows. His breathing was shallow and undecided. A lamp flickered, and he opened his eyes to see his four sons at the end of his bed. He chuckled a chainmail and gravel chuckle that rolled on into a choking cough. The brothers stood helpless as Helen, Anne, and Janet rushed in to prop and shake and revive the old man back to comfort.

"You have over excited Papa; I shall make him his toddy," said Helen, and she hurriedly left the room for the kitchen, followed by JJ-2.

Apart from the distillery's Martinmas payments, Johnny had brought for his father the best from Bow Street. A malt whiskey described in the *Saunders's News-Letter* as:

> *'This spirit so remarkably sweet, as to require but half the sugar generally used.'*

The pale gold was tipped, hot water was added, and sugar was stirred in sparingly.

Unflavoured and pure, the Irish offering was taken through to Papa.

Surrounded by his seven surviving children, JJ sipped his warm whiskey toddy and savoured the subtleties. He was enjoying the company; he was enjoying the attention; he was enjoying his whiskey. There was no need for words. But then JJ-2 could not resist.

"Papa, is the whiskey to your liking?" he asked.

"I think…" JJ wheezed as the three eminent distillers strained to hear counsel's opinion.

"I think, my judgement will be best given on reflection in the morning."

JJ almost chuckled but decided instead to take another sip of his toddy.

The morning came, and the day drifted away.

On Tuesday, 2 December 1823, in his eighty-fourth year, John Jameson slept through to the place of his beliefs.

The two distilleries of Bow Street and Marrowbone Lane
prospered and expanded. They were towns within the city.

Chapter 19

The Legacies

1823 – 2023

John Jameson takes up his residency at the Old Alloa Kirkyard; 1824–1909 – Andrew Jameson and the Marconi legacy; 1824– 1919 – The Haig legacy; 1824 – John Jameson-2 and James Jameson continue to distil; 1838 – Temperance; 1845 – The Famine; James Jameson and John Jameson-3 called on Downing Street; 1850 – Grandchildren and great-grandchildren take over the distilleries; Surfing on the waves of British colonialism; Home Rule; 1890 – James Sligo Jameson; 1899 – The Great Whiskey Case; 1916 – The Easter Rising; 1924 – John Jameson comes into his own; 1966 – Irish distillers; 1988 – Pernod Ricard; 1835 – An Alloa performance of Macbeth and the King of Irish Whiskey.

T HE BRAND-NEW CHURCH OF ST MUNGO now dominated the Alloa skyline, but within the town's pride of pinnacles, there were teething problems. Evidence came from the smell of dry rot and the absence of a bell. But the large crowds of mourners needed no summoning for the funeral of John Jameson, the county's departing Sheriff Clerk.

Daylight was almost gone; the platitudes of grief done; the towns-folk followed the cortège to the old kirkyard. The tower of the disman-tled St Mungo remained to toll. The surrounding railings were draped in black whilst behind them the frozen mist hung white amongst the shadows of the trees.

JJ lay light within his heavy coffin, lowered to rest beside the love of his life.

Soil drummed on wood; mortality's finger pointed; cold scraped; hearts chilled.

The mourners were fed, their penance was done, and they wandered away to lead what remained of their lives.

If John Francis Erskine had managed to attend, he would have hobbled home, waited for his earldom to arrive, and popped his clogs by the time the dry rot had been fixed.

With the business of death completed, the three brothers sailed back across the sea to Ireland. In the Land of Saints and Scholars, the brothers advanced what their father had bequeathed. Moving forward along the gifted socks of time, in their tens, in their hundreds, through temperance, famine, disputes, war, rebellion, civil war, prohibition, and more war, JJ's legacy survived.

In 1824, 'The Arthur Browne Affair' came to light shortly after the brothers returned to Ireland. A story then unfolded that led JJ not to a legacy but to a legendary connection.

Andrew and Catherine Jameson's marriage was over. They were separated, but closure was needed. There were no quickie divorces, and such was the sacredness of marriage to the state that the entire Feydeau farce of the 'Booterstown Casanova' had to be given a reading before the House of Lords. In 1827, to the relief of Andrew and Catherine and for the future benefit of science, the Lords granted the couple a Bill of Divorce.

Catherine went off to live in Edinburgh and sensibly went on to marry an accountant, Mr Donald Baine.

Andrew Jameson married Margaret Millar from Perth.

For the survival of his second marriage, Andrew decided to put his commuting days behind him. He and his new wife, Margaret Millar, rented an impressive home near his Fairfield distillery in Wexford. On the banks of the trout-filled River Urrin, Andrew Jameson's large house was set in twenty-three acres of parkland and known as Daphne or, on romantic days, as Daphne Castle. But Andrew's grand style of accommodation belied the fortunes of his distillery and the money he owed. His Wexford neighbours were also as volatile as ever.

In December 1828, the *Tipperary Free Press* reported that the distillery had been surrounded by '*the country people*' intent on destroying it. The locals suspected the precious potato was being used in the distilling process. Whatever Andrew was up to, distilling suddenly lost its appeal to him.

In 1831, strapped for cash, Andrew mortgaged the works at Fairfield to his brother John Jameson-2 for seven thousand pounds at an annual rent of one peppercorn. The distillery was then partly converted into a flour mill by installing two large steel water wheels. Success was patchy, and the works were frequently put up for sale.

In 1840, with distilling well into the past and heading into retirement, Andrew had a boost of youth. Margaret Millar gave birth to John Jameson's youngest granddaughter, Annie Jameson.

Annie's childhood was spent in Wexford, and when Daphne House was converted to a school, she spent much of her youth in Dublin, too. Growing up with elderly parents, Annie became strongly independent. Her ambition was to sing in opera as, like many of her cousins, she was gifted with an exceptional voice.

For a time, Annie followed her musical dreams and moved to Italy to study bel canto. It was in Italy near Bologna that Annie met and fell in love with an Italian landowner, Giuseppe Marconi.

Some years after her mother and father died, and to the family's raised eyebrows, Annie Jameson married her Italian, Mr Marconi.

In Bologna, Annie and Giuseppe had two sons. The eldest born was Alfonso, and the youngest was Guglielmo Marconi.

From a young age, Guglielmo Marconi had a passion for physical and electrical science. Championed by his mother, Annie Jameson, and through study, perseverance, and experimentation, Marconi invented wireless communication.

In 1909, Guglielmo Marconi won the Nobel Prize in physics. He and his company continued pioneering his work, and in 1912, Marconi's wireless telegraph transmitted the news and launched the rescue of the sinking RMS *Titanic*.

John Jameson's association with his great-grandson in the wireless scientific revolution was unexpected.

So, too, was Marconi's link to Arthur Browne, whose philandering precipitated one of the world's greatest inventions.

In 1824, a more predictable set of events was set into motion as a new chapter opened in the story of 'The House of Haig'.

The Haigs' Edinburgh distilleries were now at Lochrin, Sunbury, Bonnington, and Canonmills. Their success did not sustain; during the next thirty years, they gradually closed one by one. Across the Forth and over in Fife, a more lasting Haig legacy was beginning.

Peggie's youngest brother, William Haig, had taken over the Steins' Kincaple distillery beside St Andrews. Later, with financial help from John Jameson, William founded the larger Guardbridge distillery. But it was William Haig's son and Peggie's nephew John Haig who ensured the Haigs' long-term distilling success and a leg up to nobility.

In 1824, the young John Haig branched out on his own and built a distillery at Cameronbridge in Fife. The distillery was cutting edge, and by 1829 Haig had installed the continuous still. This ingenious invention, patented by John Haig's Kilbagie cousin Robert Stein, was an early version of a column still. Quantity and quality were assured, and the Cameronbridge distillery progressed and continued to innovate. It was here that Peggie's nephew established 'John Haig and Co', which has flourished to this day.

The continuous still may have also contributed to John Haig's reputation for becoming a little squiffy at times, but in 1839 he managed to focus on and marry Rachel Veitch. Rachel was the daughter of the Town Clerk of Leith and was reputed to have been one of the most beautiful women in Scotland.

Haig births followed.

John Haig's daughters, Mary and Harriet Haig, bolstered their distilling dynasty by marrying their first cousins, the Bow Street brothers John Jameson-4 and Willie Jameson.

John Haig's youngest son, Douglas Haig, preferred soldiering to distilling. As a field marshal, he played a leading if controversial role in 'Oh! What a Lovely War.' In 1919, Douglas Haig was elevated from trade to an earldom.

By 1824, JJ's legacy was well underway in Dublin. JJ-2 was at Bow Street, and James at Marrowbone Lane. Their whiskeys were sold under the names of John Jameson and James Jameson, in the tradition of using the distillery's proprietor's name. Occasionally, as published in the *Dublin Mercantile Advertiser* of May 1824, the brothers' whiskeys would be advertised as just Jameson's Whiskey. For your average punter to say 'Gimme a Jemmy!' it might mean a 'Ka-ching' for either brother, and neither would complain.

Through to the 1830s, and once Andrew Jameson had retreated into Wexford country life, there were just the two Jameson brothers to carry the legacy of distilling forward. Taking their papa's lead, JJ-2 and James diversified to prepare for any troughs that lay ahead, particularly from government. With banking at their base, the brothers expanded into the new industries of steamships and the developing railways.

In 1837, Victoria landed on the British throne. Agents and 'riders' from Bow Street and Marrowbone Lane distributed their gold throughout the land. The home market prospered, and JJ's legacy spilt abroad.

The families grew, too.

At Bow Street, JJ-2's son, JJ-3, joined up with his father, and from 1838 the Bow Street distillery was referred to as John Jameson and Son for the first time.

Within that year, a new challenge was arriving, not from the bogeyman revenue but from a priest in Cork. Father Theobald Mathew had begun a temperance movement that was to knock the industry sideways. By 1842, it was said that five million Irishmen had taken the pledge.

Temperance became all the rage amongst Catholics and Protestants alike. Even JJ-2's son, the Reverend William Jameson, and his wife, Elizabeth Guinness, the daughter of Arthur Guinness II, were converts. But temperance did not prevent Bill and Eliza from signing their marriage settlement for a very handsome alcohol-funded trust fund to secure their future.

The temperance movement was a sell-out, and whiskey sales plummeted.

Following close behind temperance came horror. From 1845 to 1850, the great Irish famine ravaged the land. The successive failures of the potato crop, the staple diet for millions, created a tragedy that is difficult to comprehend today.

At the time, far away in Westminster, they also found it difficult to comprehend. Many believed it was all false news and a conspiracy by Prime Minister Robert Peel to do away with the Corn Laws.

It was all too real among the population of Ireland, especially in the rural West. The famine's familiar overtures of terror and disease were there for all to see. Loose bones bagged beneath stretched skin. Fever, dysentery, cholera, and typhus festering. Ruined bodies ravaged by pain. The walking crawling dead, scavenging for food. Families slowly dying one by one, their grief killed. Corpses rotting by the roadside. Lives gone, forgotten, unaccounted for, alone in their homes to be eaten away.

Who was to blame? The blight, yes. But added was the rampant poverty in the land and the lines between subsistence, hunger, starvation, and death that were way too thin.

In September 1846, the Irish barrister James Burke called the government directly to account for the rising death toll. To an audience at the Conciliation Hall in Dublin, he described a man, a famine victim, who is returning home from a distant food depot. The man is taken into custody and delayed by the then-current curfew laws, only to discover that his entire family has been wiped out on his arrival home.

'*Murdered by the exquisite paradox of British legislation,*' accused James Burke.

Many of the politicians in Westminster, it appears, were wanton.

In June 1846, the Whigs came to power and undid much of the relief Peel had put in place. Their mantra was free trade. Their policy was non-intervention in Ireland. Their thinking was primitive and that of Sparta – 'The survival of the fittest'.

Over one million were to die from starvation in Ireland from 1845 to 1850.

'Close the distilleries!' came the calls, thick and fast. Opportunely, many of those calls came from the temperance movement, led at the time by the Rev. Dr Spratt. But the distilleries were practically Ireland's sole industry, a principal employer and exporter.

It was argued:

> '*To throw so many thousands out of work, would not be a prudent mode of relieving distress.*'

The distilleries remained open but reduced their consumption of corn. This they replaced with imported sugar. On the back of that came calls from the colonies to reduce the duty on their rum.

In January 1847, the colonial and free marketeer Chancellor Sir Charles Wood proposed slashing the duty on West India rum. The timing was not good for Irish distillers, and they predicted a '*ruinous*' outcome.

In February 1847, JJ's son James Jameson, with his nephew JJ-3, called at the Chancellor's residence at Downing Street in London. They were heading a deputation of distillers and Irish MPs, including Daniel O'Connell.

James was the principal spokesperson, saying that:

> *"We cheerfully accept any measure…that has the objective of alleviating distress, and for increasing food supplies for the people. But a sixpence differential of duty between colonial rum and home spirits, would result in transferring the manufacture of spirits from Ireland to the colonies."*

James and the rest continued their argument. Sir Charles listened with a few brief retorts. The toff was suffering from a nasty cold and a loss of voice. But he was also suffering from a loss of sympathy for anything Irish.

Of the famine, Sir Charles Wood had said:

> *"A want of food and employment is a calamity sent by Providence."*

Calamity, he believed, was there to buck your ideas up!

Eventually, the Chancellor shook his head and turned on his heels. The deputation returned to Ireland with little optimism.

However, James's arguments must have held some sway because the Chancellor backtracked a modicum a month later. He increased the proposed differential for duty on colonial rum from sixpence to ninepence.

The distilleries survived the famine, but James did not. That summer, James Jameson succumbed to a sudden and *dangerous* illness. Death announcements in the press followed close behind:

'Mr Jameson, the celebrated distiller and deputy governor of the Bank of Ireland, died on Tuesday night.' – the 24ᵗʰ of August, 1847.

Typhus was a disease of famine. Typhus had killed James's brother William, and it probably killed James. James's considerable wealth was no protection.

Age was creeping up on all the brothers, with Robert departing that same year in Alloa and JJ-2 taking his bow in 1851.

JJ's grandchildren and great-grandchildren were now running the distilleries. JJ-3 ran Bow Street, which retained the name of John Jameson and Son. Marrowbone Lane was now run by James's son William and Margaret's son John. For a short while, it was known as Jameson and Robertson and then established itself as William Jameson and Co.

The Victorian era was in full swing, with the British fast collecting territories, colonies, and dominions. Queen Victoria soon ruled over an empire on which the sun never set, so the sun was continuously over the yardarm to raise a glass of 'Irish'.

Following the famine, Ireland's people became a major export. They emigrated to England, Scotland, the colonies, and in the hundreds of thousands to America.

With the Irish went their longing for their homeland and a taste for their national drink of whiskey. For the distilleries, those emigrants, who had survived the coffin ships, became their leading ambassadors in America. Whiskey was shipped out in ever-increasing quantities.

As whiskey was exported to America, so the aphid *phylloxera* was imported back from America. This naughty little aphid had a par-ticularly ravenous appetite for the roots of the European vine, especially in the vineyards of Cognac and Charente. French brandy became almost unattainable, and the gentry of Europe was forced to sample the delights of whiskey.

The two distilleries of Bow Street and Marrowbone Lane prospered and expanded. They were towns within the city, with the kind of eye-watering statistics now applied to giant cruise liners or vast Hollywood studios. They had cooperage, coppersmiths, carpenters, painters, engineers, sawmills, smithy shops, and stables the size of cavalry barracks. Storage for over forty thousand casks and a combined output from the two distilleries of over two million gallons of spirit a year.

For John Jameson's clan, the wealth was immense. Grandchildren and great-grandchildren lived a charmed life and were now all aspiring toffs. Coats of arms were researched and registered; sons were sent off to Eton, followed by a spot of soldiering.

The distilleries only needed a certain number of distillers, so many of the offspring became professional gentlemen of leisure. They painted, fished, hunted, and sailed. Mansions and castles, together with their demesnes, were built or acquired. Yachts were bought, and shoulders were rubbed with kings and queens.

The Jamesons' collective and gilded dramas would make the *Downton Abbey* television series look like a trip up to the village post office. They journeyed through Europe with their expansive households. They staggered into the Uffizi Gallery with their paints, easels, and giant canvases to sit and copy the works of the Masters. Their daughters attended musical conservatoires and sang to dazzle after dinner. Come the dismal months of February and March, they would attend Grand Balls at Dublin Castle.

At one such, the Duke of Abercorn's Fancy Ball, my great-grandfather, who at the time was serving as a captain in the Kaiser's army, dressed as Mephistopheles in '*a magnificent dress of scarlet satin with deep crimson slashing, and handsomely trimmed in gold*'.

JJ's clan was surfing on the waves of British colonialism both at home and abroad. Some were labelled as 'Anglo-Irish' or, as Brendan Behan would put it, 'a Protestant with a horse'.

'You become what you are told,' said the poet Lawrence Hoo.

My great-grandaunt Ida knew she was Irish regardless of what she was told. Ida had two gold rings engraved with 'Eire'. One of them she gave to her close friend the suffragette and Irish Nationalist Maud Gonne. Together, they wore them for always. Ida Jameson and Maud shared their goal for Irish freedom and sang in concerts:

> *'Yes, old Ireland will be free, from the centre to the sea*
> *And hurrah! For liberty,' says the Shan Van Vocht.*

This new talk of Home Rule smacked the distilleries in the face. For the Raj to raise a glass of Irish as the sun came up over the yardarm now conjured trouble. Scotch began to become the preferred tiple abroad.

John Haig was now into his ascendancy. He and other Scottish distillers had been using an improved version of the continuous still, a column still patented by the Irishman Aeneous Coffey. Coupled with that, John Haig & Co, were bottling and blending their whiskies themselves.

Back in Dublin, the Jameson distilleries would have none of it. They proudly stuck to their superior pot stills and sold their whiskey sealed into sherry barrels and sold on for their agents to distribute. It was to their commercial disadvantage.

Jameson whiskey sales were not helped either by a scandal concerning JJ-2's grandson James Sligo Jameson.

In November 1890, a celebrated African expedition led by the explorer Henry Moreton Stanley began to receive bad press, notably in *The Times*.

Setting out as a mercy expedition for the relief of the Governor of Equatoria, Emin Pasha, it ventured deep into the Congo *'to save, relieve distress and to carry comfort'*. Contrary to these ideals, a brutal and murderous crusade for annexation was exposed, from which few had survived.

High on the list of acts against humanity was the case of a child slaughtered and cannibalised to satisfy the curiosity of the expedition's naturalist, James Sligo Jameson.

Sligo was unable to defend himself, dying shortly after, on the banks of the Congo, from haemorrhagic fever. However, his published diary was damning and startling in that it records his horror at the event but no grief or remorse.

It was shake-up time.

In 1889, the proprietors of William Jameson & Co. of Marrowbone Lane were James's sons, William and James. The two brothers were now getting on a bit and poor old James, Ida's dad, was away with the fairies or, as Maud Gonne reported:

'He had loved the golden fluid of his famous vats so well that, though he lived on, he had ceased to count amongst the living.'

Such was the health and safety hazards of inheriting a distillery.

For the benefit of the next generation, it was decided to sell William Jameson & Co. to the Dublin Distillers' Company for three hundred thousand pounds. The family retained a one-hundred-and-fifty-thousand-pound share in the company and remained at the helm.

Over on the other side of the Liffey, John Jameson & Son of Bow Street was owned by JJ's great-grandson, John Jameson-4, known as Jack. A couple of years later, Jack's business was reorganised, too, into a limited liability company.

The gap between the two distilleries and JJ's legacies was widening.

Until the mid-1880s, the two distilleries appeared to work in harmony as leading Dublin distillers. But in 1885, a rift appeared with William Jameson & Co. advertising that they were the senior distillery with the Jameson name. John Jameson & Son reposted by announcing for the first time that they were established in 1780. William Jameson

& Co. then rummaged deep into their leases and pushed back their birth date from 1779 to 1752.

The fuse had been lit. The competitive edge between the family businesses sharpened.

Over the next decade, the two distilleries separately developed their flagship brands of whiskey. John Jameson & Son's pride and joy was its quality 'Three Star' brand whiskey. William Jameson & Co. had a 'Harp' - branded whiskey of lesser quality that sold for half the price of the 'Three Star'.

An aggressive advertising campaign began for this cheaper 'Harp' by emphasising the Jameson and omitting the William. Large posters at railway stations declared:

Every Judge of whiskey drinks Jameson Harp Brand.

Three harps on the whiskey labels mimicked the three stars of John Jameson's 'Three Star'.

John Jameson & Son Ltd was none too pleased.

In 1899, 'The Great Whiskey Case' entered the Chancery Division of the Dublin high court. John Jameson & Son accused William Jameson & Co. of passing off the 'Harp' brand whiskey as their superior, more expensive 'Three Star' brand. They sought an injunction against Dublin Distillers to prevent William Jameson & Co. from selling their whiskey as Jameson Whiskey without the prefix 'William'.

Cousins were pitted against cousins. For the plaintiffs, there were JJ-2's grandsons, Managing Director John (Jack) Jameson-4, and his first cousin, Director Andrew Jameson. For the defendants, there were James's grandsons, Managing Director John Eustace Jameson and his first cousin William Bellingham Jameson. Nothing beats a family squabble.

Much of the argument wrangled over who was the more entitled to use the word 'Jameson' as a standalone. The debate rumbled back into antiquity as to which company was the founding Jameson company.

Many of the claims and counterclaims were as fictional as John Jameson fighting a giant octopus for a barrel of whiskey.

John Jameson & Son repeated the claim that the Bow Street distillery was founded in 1780. It was a dodgy claim to make under oath unless you allied someone making hooch in a tenement. They also grandly suggested that a Lord Mayor of London owned the Bow Street distillery at one time.

William Jameson & Co. doubled down on their claim that their distillery had existed since 1752. If so, it would have been no more than a pop-up dram shop with not a Jameson within range of a spittoon.

Why neither party challenged the other on their founding dates is a mystery, except that both knew each version was as fabricated as their rivals.

The family's dyscalculia was paraded.

William and JJ-2 were mentioned, but JJ, as father and enabler of both distilleries, was kept out of the dispute. This was an argument of division, and JJ's role in antiquity would have united the two.

During the hearing, the evidence of the posters at the railway stations seemed to distress the Vice-Chancellor the most. He was '*disgusted*' and considered it '*singularly bad taste*' to present a caricature of a judge with a tipple of whiskey.

Irrespective of the posters, the Vice-Chancellor came down in favour of John Jameson & Son and granted the injunction.

On the eve of the inevitable appeal, the families got together and settled their differences. It was agreed that William Jameson & Co. would always prefix Jameson with William. Each side was to bear its costs, and all charges of fraud were to be withdrawn.

Lord Justice Fitzgibbon was as pleased as Mr Punch at the settlement mutually arrived at, saying:

"No arrangement through the court could be as satisfactory, especially between families among whom there should be nothing

but good feeling respecting a business with which they have been connected for so many years."

Dublin Distillers' fortunes did not improve. Whilst John Jameson & Son Ltd held its own, in the turbulent years ahead, William Jameson & Co. began to sink out of existence.

As the Great War arrived, my great-grandfather, who at the sale of William Jameson to Dublin Distillers had been a part of the equivalent of a lottery rollover, was now anxiously totting up in his diaries every purchase, from herrings to margarine.

The Easter Rising of 1916 saw both Bow Street and Marrowbone Lane play their part. Due to wartime restrictions, they were not in production and were commandeered by volunteers. Their solid build provided excellent defences for rebellion.

My father, at the age of one, was also caught up in the excitement. Volunteers took over the top floor of No. 101 Seville Place. His mother and toddler brothers rapidly exited to the basement next door as the house was strafed with bullets. Independence was on its way.

The early Twenties saw Prohibition in America, followed by a trade war between the Irish Free State and Britain.

Despite a bumpy ride, JJ's legacy survived and lived on in John Jameson & Son.

In 1924, the distillery published *The History of a Great House*, illustrated by Harry Clarke. A truth floats through this eighteenth-century fairy tale. It places JJ as the first of the line and his desire to secure a future for his sons John and William.

Slowly, JJ took form from his origins in Alloa, his Sheriff Clerk role, and his unmistakable signature.

'Have you met John Jameson?' went the ads.

JJ's image began to appear, too.

Henry Raeburn, the prolific and cash-strapped Edinburgh portrait painter, had painted both JJ and Peggie back in the 1800s. Copies were dotted about the families.

The pair I met at my cousin's house had a narrow escape in the Twenties. During the Irish Civil War and following a dispute with the Farmers Union, armed raiders dumped the two outside and then burned Milestown House down to the ground.

The originals also survived and found themselves at the head office in Bow Street and later at the National Gallery of Ireland.

John Jameson was now an entity and given his place as the rightful founder.

Another World War, and by the 1960's Ireland's distilling industry was on its last legs. Prohibition, world wars, trade wars, government wrecking machines, and the continuing success of Scotch had almost wiped Ireland clean of distilling. Survival was at stake.

In the nick of time, to lead the way, along came JJ's three-times great-grandson and a chip off the old block, Aleck Crichton. After a century and a half, in 1963, John Jameson and Son finally began bottling their whiskey at Bow Street.

But Aleck didn't stop there. A collective strategy was called for. With his cousin Shane Jameson, he negotiated a merger with John Power & Son and the Cork Distillery Company to create 'Irish Distillers'. The merger led to a seismic change.

JJ had long needed to shake free from the confines of the city and the trappings of his old archaic distillery. From 1971, distilling ended at Bow Street, and production moved from Dublin to a brand-new distillery at Midleton in County Cork. Sacrilege, maybe, but JJ would have thoroughly approved this pragmatic decision by Irish Distillers and his three-times great-grandsons Aleck and Shane. It was all about survival and eventual success.

In 1988, that success was threatened by a hostile takeover. The French came to the rescue. Where they had failed for the United Irishmen at Bantry Bay, they now succeeded for Irish Distillers. My great-grandaunt Ida Jameson, who was swept off her feet by a Frenchman, would have rejoiced and sung her signature song:

'Oh, the French are in the Bay, they'll be here without delay.
And the Orange will decay,' says the Shan Van Vocht.

In the name of Pernod Ricard, the French stepped ashore peaceably and joined forces with Irish Distillers. Together, they conquered the world, with JJ leading as their standard bearer.

John Jameson's Whiskey has since made billions, and sales have increased yearly.

JJ would be chuffed, even though the billions would not be a figure he would have recognised from his Alloa bookkeeping course.

His whiskey of today, he would not recognise, either. It would interest him but might prove too smooth for his perfectly pitched but more rugged palate.

JJ's era is far away down the pegged lines of gifted socks to another world where a communal innocence once thrived.

In 1835, John Jameson had not been long gone, and Alloa remained a town he would have recognised well. In that year, a theatrical company from Edinburgh arrived to play a season at the Assembly Rooms. The details were recorded by actor and comedian Horatio Lloyd.

Robert Jameson had been in JJ's role as the Sheriff Clerk for twelve years. Rob welcomed the actors with open arms, and Alloa's hospitality kicked in. Members of the ensemble were invited to dine at various homes practically every day during their month's stay. It was all strangely Irish.

The final performance was to be *Macbeth*, with the actor-manager Montague Stanley playing the title role. A gifted artist, Montague had also painted the stage scenery onto sized brown paper. The comedian Horatio Lloyd was to play the First Witch, and he was to follow the tragedy with the comic song 'Humours of a Country Fair'.

The season's last night was a benefit performance for Montague Stanley, under the distinguished patronage of Philadelphia, the Countess of Mar.

Philly and Robert Jameson arrived together at the Assembly Rooms above the school. A large armchair had been placed in the front row as a private box for the Countess. Philly was not one for ceremony, and the armchair was removed whilst she and Rob sat down amongst the audience's warmth. The enticing theatrical smells of animal glue and stale socks prevailed.

'The Scottish Play' naturally drew a large crowd, and Montague Stanley was cramming them all in regardless, for this, his benefit night. The never-ending flow of townsfolk continued. Alarmed, Rob stood and called for the actor manager.

"*For God's sake, Mr Stanley,*" cried Robert, "*close the doors, or we shall all go through the floor into the school-room below.*"

The doors were closed, and the curtain rose.

All went swimmingly well until the climactic battle between Macbeth and Macduff.

A large bulldog belonging to the town constable found the performances far too convincing. Leaping over the shoulders of Rob and the Countess, he charged onto the stage and joined in the combat.

The audience erupted, hooting.

Barking savagely and baring his under-bite, the dog lunged from one player to the other. Macbeth and Macduff desperately tried to fend off this slobbering beast from hell.

Centre stage, the 'dug' stood his ground, his spindly tail twitching his fat bottom.

The crowd stamped and whooped and cheered on the doggy.

The Countess fell off her chair laughing.

With roars and whistles, the constable eventually managed to yank his dog away.

But it was a showstopper.

Neither Malcolm gaining the throne of Scotland nor Horatio Lloyd's 'Humours of a Country Fair' could have topped the bulldog's 'Method' performance.

This story of an impromptu turn by a bulldog who stole the show would have tickled old JJ hugely, as would another left-of-field tale. The man from Alloa who was told he was Scottish, who was neither distiller nor toff, but who was crowned the King of Irish Whiskey.

John Jameson didn't save the world, but from antiquity, he has bestowed us with a legendary good tipple.

As for me, I have long since ceased to be or do what I was told.

John Jameson & Son established 1780
(Tegestology /Alamy Stock Photo)

HAVE YOU MET

JOHN JAMESON?

THE PLEASURE IS ALL YOURS

MEETING John Jameson is very much like being introduced to a distinguished guest at your Club. For personality is just as marked in a whiskey as in an individual.

For 160 years John Jameson has been recognized as one of the finest of imported whiskies. Its flavor is mild and dry. Its high quality is assured by the fact that it is all whiskey—not a drop of which is less than 7 years old.

John Jameson is particularly pleasing as a highball . . . in a Manhattan . . . or Old Fashioned.

W. A. TAYLOR & CO.   New York City

SOLE AGENTS FOR U. S. A.   ●   ESTABLISHED 1888

WHAT IS JOHN JAMESON?

★ Pot still whiskey only
★ Made solely from barley, malt, wheat and oats
★ Matured at least 7 years in oak casks
★ Every drop distilled by John Jameson & Son, Ltd. at Bow Street Distillery, Dublin, Ireland

BLENDED IRISH WHISKEY
90 PROOF

1941 U.S. Magazine John Jameson Whiskey Advert
(John Frost Newspapers /Alamy Stock Photo)

Acknowledgements

Thanks:

To my cousin John Jameson, sailor extraordinaire, who has revitalised the family's passion for the sea and who first had the idea to write the story of his namesake and our ancestor.

To my cousin-in-law Michael Treays, who linked our relatives in a magnificent family tree and added many valuable stories and titbits in his wonderfully dry, witty, humorous way. To my son Joseph Jameson, who guided me with wisdom and expertise and issued the imperative always to go back to the written original; together, we proved his maxim at the Registry of Deeds in Dublin. To my son Jack Jameson, whose ambitions of founding his own Jameson micro-distillery was another catalyst in my quest to find out the facts. To my daughter Phoebe, whose calligraphy skills reflect those of her ancient ancestor and would win his admiration. To my sister Clodagh and my brother Tim, who read my drafts, smiled, corrected, and provided gems.

To John Finlay, Professor of Scots Law at Glasgow University, whose books and publications have been an invaluable source of information and who helped me eliminate some of my howlers. To the Rev. Bridget Spain from the Dublin Unitarian Church, who shed light on Jameson records of baptism and their connections to the United Irishmen. To Ian Friel, international maritime historian, who identified the type of ship on John Jameson's seal. To author David Haviland, in Brighton, who gave an invaluable editorial assessment. To Michael McConnell from St Louis, Missouri, USA, who copy-edited the manuscript with precision and generosity. To Sussex artist Helen Cann, who painstakingly drew the map of JJ's journey to Alloa. To Cambridgeshire heraldic artist Quentin Peacock, who brought John Jameson's two-hundred-year-old seal matrix to life. To proofreader Mark Swift from Blackpool Lancashire, who has performed the impossible feat of indexing despite multiple characters with the same name. To New York / Berwickshire graphic designer Latte Goldstein, who collaborated with Henry Raeburn to create the covers and cast his spell of invisible artistry throughout every page.

Notes & References

NRS - National Records of Scotland.

Chapter 1   **An Introduction Face to Face**

1. Pop: Martin Shaw MC (1891–1978). Maternal grandfather, army major, inventor. His brother Tommy was the last surviving Irish veteran of WWI.

2. JJ: John Jameson (1740–1823). The subject of this book and four-times great-grandfather.

3. Patsy Shaw (1919–2004). Patricia Margaret Alice Shaw, mother.

4. Our house: 15 New Street, Salisbury, now known as Maeve House.

5. School: Chafyn Grove School, Salisbury.

6. Richard Dawkins: *b.* 1941, author of *The Selfish Gene* and *The God Delusion*.

7. Lawrence Hoo: Poet and educator based in Bristol.

8. Father: Ian Eustace Jameson (1915–1991).

9. *'Paddy McGinty's Goat'*: A comic song written in 1917 by English songwriters Bert Lee and R. P. Weston.

10. Val Doonican (1927–2015). Twentieth-century Irish singer.

11. *Ulster Prince*: MV *Ulster Prince2*, Belfast Steam Ship Company. Originally named MV *Leinster* and built by Harland & Wolff Belfast in 1937 for B&I Line.

12. *Munster*: MV Munster, built by Harland & Wolff Belfast in 1947 for B&I Line.

13. Grandmother, paternal: Emma Elizabeth Galbraith (1877–1966).

14. Grandfather, paternal: James Frederick Jameson (1881–1960).

15. Uncle Charlie: Rev. Frederick Charles Jameson (1913–1980).

16. *'Slattery's Mounted Foot'*: A comic song by Percy French, written in 1889.

17. Milestown House: Castlebellingham, County Louth. Eighteenth-century house burnt down in 1923 and was rebuilt in 1925.

18. Peggie: Margaret Haig (1752–1815). Referred to as 'Peggie' in her marriage record. John Jameson also referred to Margaret Haig as 'Peggie'. Ref. NRS. CH12/24/22.

19. Portraits: John Jameson and Margaret Haig's portraits by Henry Raeburn are hung in the Grand Gallery of The National Gallery of Ireland, Merrion Square, Dublin.

20. Death of Milo: By Jean-Jacques Bachelier. Milo of Croton was a Greek wrestler who opened a split tree trunk, became trapped, and was devoured by wolves. Sir Arthur Guinness II presented the painting to the gallery.

21. *Truths About Whisky*: The book was published in London, which may have prejudiced the whisky spelling. Ref. Issued on behalf of Messrs John Jameson & Sons, William Jameson & Co., John Power and Son and George Roe Co. Printed by Sutton Sharpe and Co., London, 1878. Republished by Classic Expressions 2008.

22. Established: John Jameson Whiskey began to advertise that it was 'established in AD 1780' around 1885. Ref. *Sport (Dublin)*, 19 December 1885, page 3.

23. John Jameson's chosen motto: *Veritas Vincit* – Volume 1 of Admission Register of Notaries Public in Scotland, 1700–1799. Compiled by John Finlay, Publisher Scottish Record Society, 2012. Ref. page 311, 1645, John Jamieson 14 Jan 1763. *John Jameson's name is spelt with the addition of an 'i', a frequent misspelling in Scotland.

Chapter 2   Buried and Born in Alloa

1. German Ocean: The North Sea. Known as the German Ocean until hostilities with Germany in the early twentieth century.

2. Alloa: Derived from Ancient Gothic, aull waeg, way to the water or sea. Ref. The New Statistical Account, 1845, Vol. VIII – Parish of Alloa, page 1.

3. King James the First of Scotland (1394–1437). In 1406, James was captured by pirates or English sailors and taken as a prisoner to the royal court in London.

4. Dr John Jamieson (1759–1838). Scottish minister of religion and author of *An Etymological Dictionary of the Scottish Language*. Published 1808. The list of subscribers to the original edition included John Jameson Esq., Alloa.

5. Dr John Jamieson's meeting with John Jameson: Ref. *Tait's Edinburgh Magazine*, 1841, Volume 8, *Memoir of Dr Jamieson*, page 515.

6. John Jameson's original seal: Ref. Letter to the provost of Perth 1792, 'Perth and Kinross Council Archive'. NRS. B59/24/12/45.

7. The old kirkyard at Alloa: Surrounds the ruined west gable and tower of the fourteenth-century church of St Mungo, Kirkgate, Alloa. A mausoleum has been built over what was once the Mar aisle of the old kirk. Information – Clackmannanshire Council.

8. Alloa House and its tower: The fifteenth-century Alloa Tower was attached to an eighteenth-century mansion. The mansion

was burnt down in 1800, but the tower still stands today. Information from Canmore Historic Environment, Scotland, and the National Trust.

9. John Erskine, 6ᵗʰ Earl of Mar (1675–1732). John Erskine inherited the Earldom of Mar at the age of fourteen. He was responsible for Alloa's early industrial development. He led the Jacobite Rebellion in 1715 and died in exile. John Erskine, Earl of Mar, is often referred to in this tale by his nickname of 'Bobbing John'.

10. Gartmorn Dam: Originally constructed around 1700. As well as powering an assortment of mills, it served the Alloa Coal works by lifting water and coal to the surface. Ref. Statistical Accounts of Scotland, Number XL, 1793 Parish of Alloa. Drawn up from the communications of the Rev. James Frame and of John Francis Erskine, pages 602 & 614.

11. Bobbing John's nickname: Ref. *The Architectural, Landscape and Constitutional Plans of the Earl of Mar 1700-32* by Margaret Stewart, Four Courts Press, Dublin 2016. Preface, page xxi.

12. James Erskine, Lord Grange (1679–1754). Judge, politician, and younger brother to the 6th Earl of Mar. Grange was not directly involved in the rebellion of 1715. He claimed to be a strict Presbyterian but had a reputation as a libertine. Grange attempted to kidnap the wife of his brother. He also kidnapped his own wife and imprisoned her on the island of St Kilda. Some say this was to keep her quiet regarding his Jacobite activities. James Erskine, Lord Grange bought back the Alloa Estate with Lord Dun in 1724. References. *History of Parliament*, author Eveline Cruickshanks – 'National Galleries of Scotland' – *The Architectural, Landscape and Constitutional Plans of the Earl of Mar, 1700-32* by Margaret Stewart, Four Courts Press, Dublin 2016, page 95.

13. Lady Frances Erskine (1715–1776). Daughter of the 6th Earl of Mar – Married her first cousin James Erskine (1710–1785).

Her half-brother Thomas Erskine (1705–1766) died without issue. Her son John Francis Erskine claimed his right to the Alloa Estate and for regaining the Earldom of Mar through his mother's lineage.

14. William Jameson, (1718–1774). Father of John Jameson. He married Helen Horn from Kinross in 1737.

15. William Jameson feuar in Alloa: Ref. No. 1654 *Admission Register of Notaries Public in Scotland, 1700-1799* by John Finlay, Published by Scottish Record Society, Edinburgh 2012.

16. William Jameson's land: Ref. Sederunt books of the Mar Old Trust Ref. NRS. GD124/4/1 – Rent roll Crops 1757 & 1758. Also, land tax rolls for Clackmannanshire, Vol 04, 1802. Alloa Parish, page 6.

17. William Jameson occupation: Ref. Disposition & Assignation, William Jameson to John Jameson his son, 1772. Alloa Sheriff Court, Register of Deeds - Warrants - Bundle 1774. NRS. SC64/55/5.

18. John Jameson's baptism records: Ref. NRS. Old Parish Register of Births, Alloa, 1740.

19. The cottage at Woodgate: John Jameson's sister Margaret's baptism record states that William and Helen lived at Woodgate. This hints that they lived near to Alloa woods or certainly a wooded area in Alloa. Ref. NRS. Old Parish Register of Births, Alloa, 1739.

20. Diet: Ref. *The Social Life of Scotland in the Eighteenth Century* by Henry Grey Graham, Published by Adam and Charles Black, London 1899.

21. Stones connected to Kings and Wizards: Ref. Ordinance Survey Name Books of 1859–1862, – Scotland's Places.

22. Alloa Tower: Mary Queen of Scots and her son James VI both spent part of their childhoods at Alloa Tower under the guardianship of the Erskine family. Ref. National Trust of Scotland.

23. 'At Alloway a merchant may trade to all parts of the world': Ref. Letter XIII, *A tour thro' the whole island of Britain*, by Daniel Defoe, Volume 3. Published 1727.

Chapter 3   **The War**

1. War of the Austrian Succession (1740–1748). Ref. Encyclopaedia Britannica.

2. James Francis Stuart (1688–1766). Known as 'The Old Pretender'; son of James VII of Scotland, who was James II of England.

3. Prince Charles Edward Stuart (1720–1788). Son of James Francis Stuart. Known as 'The Young Pretender' and 'Bonnie Prince Charlie'.

4. Grange's letter: Ref. *History of Parliament*, Members Biographies, author Eveline Cruickshanks.

5. Naval engagement: Ref. *Dutillet's* Log, and *The Lyon in Mourning* from Conversations of the Rev. Robert Forbes with Duncan Cameron (Servant of Lochiel).

6. Eriskay: An island in the Outer Hebrides between Barra and South Uist. The SS *Politician* ran aground off Eriskay in 1941. Her cargo included twenty-two thousand cases of malt whisky, much of which was recovered by the islanders. The event inspired the book and film *Whisky Galore!* by Compton Mackenzie.

7. Loch Nan Uamh: A sea loch south of Borrodale House in the parish of Arisaig. Also referred to as Lochnanuagh.

8. 'Gang hame!': Whilst off Eriskay, Alexander MacDonald of Boisdale reportedly told Charles to return home, to which Charles replied, 'But I am come home.' Ref. *The Lyon in Mourn-*

ing Vol. 1, page 205, from Conversations of the Rev. Robert Forbes with Duncan Cameron (Servant of Lochiel).

9. Glenfinnan Railway Viaduct: Half a mile north of the head of Loch Shield. The viaduct was built in 1901 by 'Concrete Bob' McAlpine.

10. General Sir John Cope (1690–1760). An army officer and member of Parliament. Referred to by the Jacobites as Johnnie Cope. Ref. National Portrait Gallery, London.

11. The pay of two guineas and nine pence a day: Ref. *The Derby Mercury*, 6 September 1745, page 4, column 1, Letter from Edinburgh, September 3rd.

12. Military roads: Built in Scotland in the 1700s under the command of General Wade and later under Major Caufield. Ref. National Library of Scotland.

13. Corrieyairack Pass: A pass on General Wade's military road between Fort Augustus and Lagan. Ref. National Library of Scotland.

14. Lord George Murray (1694–1760). A Perthshire nobleman and soldier. Involved in the 1715 rebellion, he was later pardoned. He had sworn allegiance to George II and was Sheriff Depute to Sir John Cope until he joined up with Charles Stuart. After Culloden he went into exile in Europe. Ref. *Britannica*.

15. Duke of Perth: James Drummond, 3rd Duke of Perth (1713–1746). After Culloden he escaped on a French ship but died on the voyage. Info. National Galleries of Scotland.

16. General Cope's blunders: Reported by Henry Pelham. Ref. University of Nottingham – Ne C 1707.

17. Alan Ramsay (1713–1784). Scottish portrait painter. Ref. National Galleries of Scotland.

18. Farmers targeted: Ref. *Derby Mercury*, 3 November 1745, page 3, letter, column 2.

19. Admiral Byng (1704–1757). In 1745, as a rear admiral, Byng led a patrol along the east coast of Scotland against the threat of Jacobites. In 1757, Admiral Byng was shot dead by a firing squad after a court-martial found him guilty of cowardice and negligence for failing to engage with the enemy at the Battle of Minorca. Ref. Royal Naval Museum.

20. Newhaven blitz: Ref. *Caledonian Mercury*, 25 October 1745, page 2, column 2.

21. Newhaven Fishwives: Famous for their celebrated language and sharp tongue, which gave rise to the expression 'a tongue like a fishwife'. Ref. Newhaven Heritage Centre.

22. Three hundred wagons and livestock passing through Alloa: Ref. The *Caledonian Mercury*, 30 October 1745, page 1.

23. Captain Abercromby's attack: Ref. *Scots Magazine*, 'Domestic History', November 1745, page 537.

24. Archibald 1st Duke of Douglas (1694–1761). The Douglas family seat is Douglas Castle in South Lanarkshire. Ref. National Records of Scotland.

25. Humiliation of the Duke of Douglas: Ref. *Stamford Mercury*, 16 January 1746, page 4, columns 2 & 3.

26. Printing press carried from Glasgow: Ref. *Newcastle Courant*, 11 January 1746, page 2, column 3, under Edinburgh Jan 10.

27. Carpenters pressed: Ref. *Newcastle Courant*, 11 January 1746, page 2, column 3, under Edinburgh Jan 10.

28. Attack on the rebel brig at Alloa: Ref. Newcastle Courant, 18 January 1746, page 2.

29. Government attack on Airth: Ref. Newcastle Courant, 18 January 1746, page 3, column 1.

30. Prince William, the Duke of Cumberland (1721–1765) Cumberland was the third and youngest son of King George II. Ref. *Britannica*.

31. Charlie's aunt: A three-act comedy farce by Brandon Thomas, produced in 1892, that centres on the confusion created by impersonating an aunt.

Chapter 4   An Education

1. John Francis Erskine of Mar (1741–1825). John Francis's mother was Frances Erskine, the daughter of the 6th Earl of Mar; his father was James Erskine, son of the 6th Earl's brother, James Erskine, Lord Grange.

2. James Boswell (1762–1795). A Scottish diarist and lawyer born in Edinburgh. Friend and biographer of Samuel Johnson. Boswell was at Edinburgh University with John Francis Erskine in 1756 and friends of his parents, Frances and James Erskine. Ref. Boswell's diaries.

3. Navigation: The price of the navigation course was reported in the minutes of the Alloa Kirk Session Meetings, 1784–1805, 10 October 1786, page 80. Ref. NRS. CH2/942/2.

4. The Reverend William Jameson (1735–1792). John Jameson's first cousin. He married Mary Wilson, daughter of William Wilson, father of the Secession Church in Perth.

5. George Abercromby of Tullibody (1705–1800).

6. Ralph Abercromby of Tullibody (1734–1801). Son of George Abercromby. British soldier and politician.

7. Reverend James Syme (1723–1753). Ralph Abercromby's tutor.

8. Alloa Riot: Refs. *The Aberdeen Press and Journal*, 25 September 1750, page 3 & 16 October 1750, page 2. Also, *Caledonian Mercury*, 3 December 1750, page 2 & 14 January 1751, page 2.

9. Alexander Abercromby of Tullibody (1675–1753). Father of George Abercromby.

10. Mr James Moir's school: Ref. *Caledonian Mercury*, 26 May 1752, page 4, column 1.

11. Ralph Abercromby's education: Ref. *Lieutenant-General Sir Ralph Abercromby, K.B. 1793–1801. A Memoir by His Son, James Lord Dunfermline.* Published by Edmonston and Douglas, Edinburgh 1861, 'Family and Early Life', page 15.

12. Coach journey Edinburgh to London: Ref. *Caledonian Mercury,* 4 August 1752, page 4, column 1.

13. Robert Rollo (1691–1767). Clackmannanshire Sheriff Clerk from the age of twenty-one in 1712. Ref. Volume. 1 of *Admission Register of Notaries Public in Scotland,* 1700–1799, Compiled by John Finlay, Publisher Scottish Record Society, 2012. Entry 377.

Chapter 5   **Apprenticeship**

1. Robert Rollo's house: Ref. *Caledonian Mercury,* 3 February 1768, page 1, column 1, under 'House Sale'.

2. Robert Rollo's deteriorating eyesight: Ref. Letter from George Sandy, Underkeeper, and Clerk to His Majesty's Signet, to Sir Gilbert Elliot Minto, Keeper of his Majesty's Signet. NLS. Minto, MS 110033, Fos 110.

3. Katharine: Katharine Bruce of Clackmannan (1696–1791). Katharine's name is commonly misspelt as Catherine. Her last will and testament is signed as Katharine Bruce. Ref. Alloa Sheriff Court, Register of Deeds – Warrants, 1782. Bundle 1791. NRS. SC64/55/6.

4. Henry Bruce (?–1772). Husband to Katharine Bruce and the last of the Ancient House of Clackmannan.

5. 'Differences in politics and religious faith provoked no resentment': Ref. *Tait's Edinburgh Magazine* for 1841, Volume 8, *Memoir of Dr Jamieson,* page 515.

6. "What's wrang wi' mah mouth, man?": This quote from Katharine Bruce is also attributed to having been said to Robert

Burns. Ref. Collections by W Downing Bruce – Digitized by the Internet Archive in 2011 from National Library of Scotland, page 42, column 1.

7. Robert the Bruce artefacts: Ref. Details in the Last Will and Testament of Mrs Katharine Bruce, written and witnessed by John Jameson. Alloa Sheriff Court, Register of Deeds, Warrants, 1782–1797. Bundle 1791. NRS. SC64/55/6.

8. John Stein of Kennetpans (1697–1773). Farmer and distiller. Grandfather of Peggie Jameson (Margaret Haig).

9. James Stein (1740–1804). Son of John Stein of Kennetpans. James Stein is also referred to in this tale as 'Scallywag Jim' and 'Uncle Jim'.

10. James Stein, apprentice: Ref. James Stein and John Jameson both signed as witnesses and the servitors of Robert Rollo in a contract on 2 March 1757. Alloa Sheriff Court, Register of Deeds – Warrants, 1756–1768, NRS. SC64/55/4.

11. Lectures on the eye: Ref. *Caledonian Mercury*, 16 January 1759, page 3, column 1.

12. John Erskine of Carnock (1695–1768). Professor of Scots Law at the University of Edinburgh from 1738 to 1765.

13. Robert Dick: Professor of Civil Law at the University of Edinburgh from 1755 to 1792. He died in 1796.

14. Stage fright: Ref. Boswell's romp with a Covent Garden actress, Louisa, is recorded in Boswell's *London Journal*, 20 January 1763.

15. John Jameson, writer: Ref. Signatory 25 July 1759, at the Alloa Sheriff Court, Court Books, November 1748 to January 1760. NRS. SC64/1/8.

16. Robert Bruce of Kennet (1718–1785). Scottish advocate, legal scholar, and judge.

17. The Reverend James Frame (1706–1803). Minister in Alloa.

18. James Stein and the Alloa Kirk: Ref. Alloa Kirk Session minutes, 26 December 1760, & 2 January 1761, Alloa Kirk Session minutes, 1760–1770, Stirling Council Archives Services. NRS. CH2/942/1.

Chapter 6   **Good Prospects**

1. John Jameson N.P.: Ref. Admission Register of Notaries Public in Scotland, 1700–1799 by John Finlay (2012).

2. Lord Nisbet: The Hon. George Carre (1700–1766). Senator of the College of Justice and a Lord of Session.

3. Lord Coalston: George Broun of Coalston (d. 1766), a Lord of Session.

4. Putting affairs back in order: Ref. July 1800, House of Commons. *Return of the Sheriff Clerk of Clackmannan to the Questions of the Committee.* John Jameson reports that 'On 9 August 1764, when the keeping of these books having come under the charge of the reporter; he then began and has continued to enter the Minutes, Acts, and Interlocutors in the different processes in the said books'.

5. Appointment as Depute for Sheriff Clerk: Ref. Register of Deeds – Warrants, 1756–1768 – Bundle 1766. NRS. SC64/55/4.

6. Clerkship in his eye: Ref. Letters from George Sandy, Underkeeper and Clerk to His Majesty's Signet, to Sir Gilbert Elliot Minto, Keeper of his Majesty's Signet. NLS Minto – MS 11033. Fos 110r, 117r, 118v.

7. Honourable James Erskine of Alva Lord Barjarg (1723–1796). Scottish lawyer and senator of the College of Justice.

8. John Jameson appointment as Sheriff Clerk of Clackmannan: Ref. Alloa Sheriff Court Books, 16 Oct 1765 to 22 Jun 1768 – Entered 16 & 29 December 1766. NRS. SC64/1/10.

9. *Seven Chances*: Black and white silent film of 1925 directed by and featuring Buster Keaton as a bachelor desperate to marry on his twenty-seventh birthday so that he can inherit a fortune. In a climactic scene, Buster is pursued by an army of brides.

10. Penelope Prudence: Ref. *Caledonian Mercury* – 16 April 1760, page 1, columns 1 & 2 under the heading 'Modern Marriages'.

11. 'Look Aboot Ye': Ref. Attributed to Robert the Bruce but is also attributed to a local wit when Bruce was upset at losing his glove near Clackmannan Tower.

12. John Haig (1720–1773). Father of Peggie Haig. Referred to in documents of the time as a tobacconist. His grandson John Haig was the founder of John Haig and Co.

13. George Peirson (1716–1791). Married to John Haig's sister Janet Haig (1722–1804).

14. Brick and tile works: Ref. The ground for the brick and tile works was leased from the Erskine's by John Haig in 1762. The works were situated adjacent to the Glass House on the Shore of Alloa at Craig Ward.

15. Margaret Stein (1729–1794). Married John Haig in 1751. She was the eldest child and daughter of John Stein and Margaret Caldom. Mother of Margaret (Peggie) Haig.

16. Tron of Alloa: In Alloa, the Trongate led down to the Old Marketplace, parallel to the original High Street. John Haig's address at the Tron of Alloa was probably conveniently placed for trading by the market. Little of this historic area of Alloa now exists, with much now covered by car parks. John Haig lived at the 'Tron of Alloa' until he died. Ref. Window tax, 1748 - 1798 (Scotland's Places) & Church registers (Scotland's People).

17. Margaret Haig's nine children in 1767: The Haig's nine children (1752–1815). James Haig (1755–1833), Mary Haig (1756–1803), John Haig (1758–1819), George Haig (1760–1774

unvalidated), Ann Haig (1761–1802), Robert Haig (1764–1845), Janet Haig (1766–1828), and Caldom Haig (1767–?).

18. Dress Act: Part of the Act of Proscription (1746).

19. Peggie's Stein uncles: Uncle Robert, Robert Stein (1733–1816). Uncle Jim, James Stein (1740–1804). Uncle Andrew, Andrew Stein (1741–1828). Uncle John, John Stein (1745–1825).

Chapter 7   Distilling and Tantrums at Dawn

1. John Jameson's attendance at the Alloa Harbour Trust: Ref. Alloa Harbour Trust Sederunt Book dates 1754 -1788, page 135, 14 September 1768. NRS. BR/AHT/1/1.

2. Alloa Glass House Company: Ref. Tack between Erskine and Deas 1767, Register of Deeds, Warrants 1769–1781, Bundle 1777. NRS. SC64/55/5.

3. John Jameson's shares in Alloa Glass House Company: Ref. Agreement between John Jameson and James Miller 1767, Register of Deeds – Warrants 1756–1768 – Bundle 1767. NRS. SC64/55/4.

4. Dispute between John Haig and George Peirson: Ref. Petition for George Peirson and Spouse against John Haig Jnr 1760 – Register of Deeds – Warrants 1756–1768 – Bundle 1760. Ref. NRS. SC64/55/4.

5. Margaret Jameson (1769–1805). John Jameson's eldest child. Married William Robertson from Eyemouth in 1801 and had three children, Robert, John, and William.

6. Andrew Haig (1769–1824). Went into partnership with John Jameson-2 at the distillery at Tulliallan.

7. John Stein's wish for his distillery: Ref. 'A Disposition and Assignation – John Stein to John Stein his son, 1770.' Register of Deeds – Warrants 1782–1797, Bundle 1788. NRS. SC64/55/6.

8. Dear Kilbaigie: Ref. 'The Jolly Beggars,' a cantata by Robert Burns (1785). Kilbagie is referred to as Kilbaigie and also Kilbegie.

9. Robert Jameson (1771–1847). John Jameson's eldest son. Robert Jameson succeeded his father John Jameson as Sheriff Clerk and as the factor on the Alloa Estate.

10. William Haig (1771–1847). Youngest of the Haig brothers. Took over the Steins' Kincaple distillery and developed the Guardbridge distillery. William Haig's son John Haig founded the Cameronbridge distillery and the company of John Haig and Co.

11. The House of Haig: Ref. Published by John Haig & Co. Ltd Markinch, 1958.

12. John Jameson (1773–1851). John Jameson-2. John Jameson's third child. Writer in Edinburgh, a distiller in Tulliallan and a distiller at Bow Street. He was the second of John Jameson's sons to distil in Dublin.

13. Freemasons: Ref. A John Jameson joined the Convivial Lodge of the Dublin Freemasons on the 24th of June 1774. At the time, there were several others in Dublin named John Jameson.

14. 'To prevent tricks of the Sheriffs and Clerks': Ref. From a letter written by James Erskine, Lord Grange to Lord Marchmont in 1733. *History of Parliament* online; author Eveline Cruickshanks.

15. James Francis Erskine of Forest (1743–1806). The younger brother of John Francis Erskine.

16. Michaelmas Head Count 1773: Ref. Sheriff Court Book 1772–1777. NRS. SC64/1/12.

17. Sandy: Alexander Abercromby (1741–1804). Son of Alexander Abercromby who was a younger brother of George of Tullibody. Known as Sandy to his family, he became a Writer to the Signet in 1770.

18. James Abercromby, of Brucefield (1707–1775). MP for Clack-mannan from 1761 to 1768. The younger brother of George Abercromby of Tullibody. James Abercromby acquired a plantation in the colony of North Carolina.

19. The minutes of the election: Ref. Freeholders and Election Minute Book for the County of Clackmannan (1700–1869) NRS. SC64/62/1. Two pages of these minutes were torn from the Election Minute Book in 1796. The full minutes can be read from the original handed to John Jameson on the 9th of November, 1774. NRS. SC64/61/6.

20. The confirmation of Ralph Abercromby's election: Ref. Caledonian Mercury 12 April 1775, page 2, column 1, under the heading 'House of Commons'.

21. The duel between Abercromby and Erskine: Ref. *Caledonian Mercury* 26 April 1775, page 2, column 3, under the heading 'Edinburgh – Extract of a letter from London April 21'.

22. John Jameson becomes the factor: Ref. John Jameson cash account as factor for the trustees on the Estate of Mar. First entry: 4 December 1775. NRS. GD124/17/360/1, 2.

Chapter 8   **The House at the Shore**

1. Helen Jameson (1776-1847). John Jameson's fourth child. Evidence that Helen was at times called Ellen can be seen in a letter from her nephew Robert Robertson which refers to her as Aunt Ellen. NRS. GD124/15/1768.

2. The move to a new house: Ref. July 1800, House of Commons. Return of the Sheriff Clerk of Clackmannan to the Questions of the Committee. John Jameson reports that he has lived in his house for twenty-four years, i.e., in 1776 just after he became the factor.

3. The House at the Shore: Ref. The factors house in the Sederunt Books of the Old Mar Trust is referred to as The House at the Shore. Ref. NRS. GD124/4/1.

4. House at the Shore was later named Linden House: Ref. Ordnance Survey map of Alloa Town, Surveyed 1861–2.

5. In the earlier Plan of the Town of Alloa by John Wood published in 1825, the house is marked as belonging to Robert Jameson and being the Sheriff Clerk's office. John Jameson's will records the property as being purchased from the Erskines in 1802. NRS. SC64/42/1.

6. Causey: Ref. Sederunt Books of the Old Mar Trust – 1795, NRS. GD 124/4/1. Under Miscellaneous *'Pd Andrew Donaldson for causeying at the entry & before of the Offices of Factors House £1.6.'* Causeying was a traditional Scottish method of building a path and paved areas out of small stones, often used around cottages.

7. Purchasing lottery tickets for John Francis: Ref. NRS. GD124/16/129.

8. William Jameson (1777–1822). John Jameson's fifth child. The first Jameson to distil in Dublin.

9. William Pirrie, the manager of the tile works: Ref. *Caledonian Mercury*, 3 June 1775, page 3, column 3, under 'Sale of Tyles'.

10. Selling the half share of the snuff mill: Ref. 'Tack betwixt James Haig and George Peirson of the half of the Snuff mill at Jellyholm, 1776.' Register of Deeds – Warrants, 1769–1781 – Bundle 1777. NRS. SC64/55/5.

11. Gartlands: Also referred to as Gartland, Garland, or Garlet. Ref. The *Collections by William Downing Bruce* NLS, documents the ownership of the land and the 'Manor Place' by the Bruce Family. Five years after John Haig's death, the window tax record shows Mrs John Haig living at Gartland for about three

years. Ref. Scotland's Places – Window Tax Vol. 28, 1778-79, Clackmannan Town and Parish.

12. Lane from Gartlands to Kilbagie: Ref. Garlet – Rediscovery of a laird's house in Clackmannanshire, Paper by Dan Atkinson, Elizabeth Jones, Morag Cross, and Jacqueline Mulcair. Excavations with support from Historic Scotland were undertaken at Garlet House in February 2006, which revealed the path to Kilbagie.

13. Alexander Cumming (1739–1814). Scottish watchmaker and instrument inventor. Worked in London for much of his life and was a founding member of the Royal Society of Edinburgh.

14. Cumming and Garlet: Ref. Alexander Cummin(g), a London Merchant, acquired the land and property of Garland or Garlet in July 1763 and passed it on to Robert Bruce in 1766. Ref. *Collections by William Downing Bruce*, page 41, 6 August 1763. NLS. Also, Window Tax records show Alexander Cumming living at Garlet. Ref. Scotland's Places – Window Tax, Vol 28, 1767–68 Clackmannan Town.

15. School Inspection: Ref. *Caledonian Mercury*, 27 August 1783, page 1, column 1, Under 'Alloa 15th August 1783'. John Jameson's inspection of the Alloa school was reported in the *Caledonian Mercury* at the end of each school year.

16. Mary Jameson (1779–1781). John Jameson's sixth child. Another Jameson child was named Mary in 1794.

17. Life in the colliery: Ref. Statistical Account 1793 – Number XL, Parish of Alloa – Drawn up from Communications of the Rev. Mr James Frame and John Francis Erskine, page 614, under the heading 'Coal'.

18. Contract for the Alloa Coal Company: Ref. Sederunt Books of the Old Mar Trust, page 33, 3 September 1779, under 'Contract between the Trustees on the Estate of Alloa and John Fr

Erskine Esq, and James and John Stein and John Jameson' NRS. GD 124/4/1.

19. Alloa Coal trade: Ref. '*A General View of the Coal Trade of Scotland Chiefly that of the River Forth and Midlothian*' by Robert Bald 1808.

20. John Jameson, ship-owner: Ref. Stirling Council Archives, Customs and Excise Records, Register of Ships – 1786–1797. John Jameson also mentions one of his coaling ships in letters to the Provost of Perth. NRS. B59/24/12/45.

21. Debts of Haig and Deas: Ref. Letters from John Jameson to David Erskine, Clerk of the Signet, December 1779 – January 1780. NRS. GD124/17/565.

22. Cashier for the Harbour Trust: Ref. Harbour Trust Sederunt Book, 1754–1788. 10 November 1779, 'The meeting unanimously nominate John Jameson Writer in Alloa to be their cashier'. NRS. BR/AHT/1/1. John Jameson remained in his post as cashier of the Harbour Trust until the months before his death.

23. James Stein's spirits and poisoning: Ref. Edinburgh Advertiser 7 January 1780, page 14, column 3, under the heading – 'By James Stein Distiller at Kilbagie'.

24. American War of Independence: 1775–1783.

25. Ralph Abercromby Pro-American Independence views: Ref. *Lieutenant-General Sir Ralph Abercromby, K.B. 1793–1801, A Memoir by His Son, James Lord Dunfermline*', page 5. "He sympathised with Americans and their struggle for independence."

26. James Frame's views on Catholics: Ref. Alloa Kirk Session – Minutes 1766–1784. NRS: CH2/942/20.

27. No Popery Riots in London: Gordon Riots of June 1780.

28. James Jameson (1781–1847). John Jameson's seventh child. Distiller, director, and deputy governor of the Bank of Ireland. Married Elizabeth Woolsey in 1815. Three-times great-grandfather.

29. Jean Westland, b. April 1765. Ref. Scotland's Places, Clackmannan County Survey, Female Servant Tax 1785–1786.

30. John Francis Erskine's servants: Ref. Scotland's Places, Clackmannan County Survey, Female Servant Tax 1785–1786, Male Servant Tax 1789–1790.

31. Postilion: A person who rides the leading horse of a team or pair drawing a coach or carriage.

32. Maid slept under the kitchen dresser: The description of the maid sleeping under the dresser comes from a description of Robert Bruce of Kennet's house in Edinburgh – *Collections by W Downing Bruce*, page 43. NLS. The House by the Shore was also short on space at the time as complained of by John Jameson. Ref. 'Sederunt Book of the Old Mar Trust', 1777–1787, Edinburgh, 12 -13 August 1783, pages 220–221. NRS. GD124/4/4.

33. Mary's funeral on Friday, December 7, 1781: Ref. There are very few records of deaths registered in Alloa during this period. Mary's possible date of death comes from Kirk Accounts 1781. Morte Cloths and Bells December 7th, Mary Jameson. NRS. CH2/942/23.

34. 'It pleases a holy and wise God…': Ref. From the diary of George Turnbull, minister of Alloa and Tyninghame, 1657–1704.

Chapter 9   Volcano With Gin

1. Alexander Bald (1753–1823). Alexander was the Shore Master at Alloa and John Jameson's clerk and agent at the harbour. Alexander's brother Robert Bald was a distiller at Tulliallan.

2. Pow-Lords and Pow-Ladies: Ref. *An Etymological Dictionary of the Scottish Language* by John Jamieson (1759–1838) Volume 2 – 're. POW 4. The term seems hence transferred to the wharf or quay itself; as in the Pow of Alloa. Hence the males and females employed in driving coals to the quays are humorously called the Pow-Lords and Pow-Ladies.'

3. Distillery Act of 1779: Ref. *Caledonian Mercury*, 12 June 1779, page 1, column 1.

4. Edinburgh a booming city: In 1782, the Nor Loch had recently been drained, the North Bridge built, and Georgian Edinburgh was developing outside the city walls.

5. Long Haugh of Canonmills: Ref. Advertisement in the *Caledonian Mercury*, 27th of September, 1780, page 4. 'Piece of Ground above the Bridge of Canonmills, on the south side of the water, commonly called the Longhaugh, consisting of nine acres.' Also Ref. *'Plan of the Long Haugh of Canonmills'* by John Laurie 1784, Canmore image, Historic Environment Scotland.

6. Lochrin distillery: Ref. The origins of the Lochrin distillery are described in the *Journals of the House of Lords*, 18 April 1792 – Jameson, Maxwell, Haig v. Russel and Sawyer. 'Alexander Reid converted the place (Lochrin), which was formerly a brewery, into a distillery. In the year 1784, the ground and distillery were purchased by Mr Haig.'

7. Home Improvements: Ref. John Jameson's request for an enlargement to his house comes from the 'Sederunt Book of the Old Mar Trust', 1777–1787, Edinburgh, 12th & 13th August 1783, pages 220–221. NRS. GD124/4/4.

8. Andrew Jameson (1783–1857). John Jameson's eighth child. Distiller and grandfather to Guglielmo Marconi.

9. Charity Ball: Ref. Alloa Kirk, Poor Fund distribution, minutes and accounts, 4th May, 1784, '*Cash was received from Mr Jameson, produce of a Charity Ball £7,,0,,8.*' NRS. CH2/942/21 Alloa Tower as the venue for the ball is conjecture.

10. Lease of the Mills: Ref. Sederunt Book of the Old Mar Trust – 1777–1787 – Edinburgh 12th & 13th August 1783, page 221 – 'Mr. Erskine of Mar having represented that the Mills of Alloa with their house and kilns were in the greatest disrepair. And that Drysdale the present tenant having through cautionary engagements been unable to keep them, He had several communings with the Alloa Coal Company for a lease of them, and in consequence of instructions from some of the Trustees had procured estimates of the expenses of putting the mills houses & etc into a proper condition….' NRS. GD124/4/4.

11. Proclamation of Banns Matrimonial: Ref. NRS. Old Parish Register. Marriages, St Cuthbert's 1784.

12. The natural world as it once was: Ref. Statistical Account,1793. Number XL, Parish of Alloa. Drawn up from Communications of the Rev. Mr James Frame and John Francis Erskine, pages 596–597, 'Fishing, Islands, Waterfowls Etc.'

13. James Haig's house at Canonmills: Purchased by James Haig from the trustees of James McDowall, a surgeon. It was later to be bought by the brewer James Eyre along with the brewery. Canonmills House was demolished in 1879. The house was situated where the Eyre Medical Practice is in Eyre Place today. Ref. *Caledonian Mercury*, 27 September 1780, page 4. & *Caledonian Mercury*, 14 March 1789, page 4. Also, Sederunt Book for James Haig's creditors, page 136. NRS. CS96/2080.

14. Act of Proscription: Much of the Act of Proscription relating to the wear of Highland 'Garb' was repealed in July 1782.

15. Laki: Volcanic fissure and mountain in Southwest Iceland. An eruption began there on 8 June 1783 and lasted until February 1784. The eruption is considered to be the greatest lava eruption on Earth in historical times. Source: *Encyclopaedia Britannica*.

16. Canonmills Riots: Ref. *Caledonian Mercury*, 5th June 1784, page 3, columns 1 & 2, beginning, 'We are extremely sorry to mention...' & *Caledonian Mercury*, 9 June 1784, page 3, column 1, beginning, 'Monday night another mob'. Also, *The Scots Magazine*, June 1784, Historical Affairs, Affairs in Scotland, pages 331–333.

17. Grassmarket: An old marketplace below Edinburgh Castle. It was also the site for public executions.

18. Attack on James Haig's carriage: Ref. Old and New Edinburgh, Volume V, by James Grant. Originally printed as periodicals in the 1880s but now found online in Edinburgh Bookshelf, Chapter IX Canonmills and Inverleith, page 87.

19. The tiling of John Jameson's house: Ref. Sederunt Book of the Old Mar Trust, 1777–1787. Under Discharge,1785. NRS. GD124/4/4.

20. George Jameson (1784–1786). John Jameson's ninth child. George's birth was at a time of considerable family upheaval. There were extensive works on the House at the Shore, and it came not long after the riots at Canonmills, together with the general fallout from the Laki volcano. Peggie's sister-in-law Helen Haig had a son John who was born on the 24 April 1785, and he died very soon after. Helen had experienced the riots first-hand.

Chapter 10 **Let Battle Begin**

1. James Stein's four-wheeled carriage: Ref. Scotland's Places, Carriage Tax Rolls,1785–1798, Volume 9, page 33.

2. William Pitt the Younger (1759–1806). Prime Minister and Chancellor of the Exchequer (1783–1801), Prime Minister (1804–1806). It is recorded that William Pitt enjoyed drinking port by the bottle, especially before parliamentary debates.

3. James Stein's 'open and candid manner': Ref. *Memoirs of a Banking-House*, by Sir William Forbes of Pitsligo. Published by William and Robert Chambers, London, and Edinburgh, 1860.

4. Sir William Forbes of Pitsligo (1739–1806). A banker who took over the company of Messrs Coutts in Edinburgh, which eventually became Forbes Hunter and Co. A philanthropist, he was a founding member of the Royal Society of Edinburgh. Friend of Sir Walter Scott and Samuel Johnson. Ref. National Galleries Scotland.

5. Distiller Acts: Ref. Distiller Act of 1783-Published in the *Caledonian Mercury*, 24 September 1783, page 1. Distiller Act of 1784-Published in the *Caledonian Mercury*, 2 October 1784, page 1. Distiller Act of 1785-Published in the *Caledonian Mercury*, 6 June 1785, page 1.

6. John Bonar (1747–1807). Solicitor of Excise, eldest son of John Bonar the elder, minister of Cockpen. Ref. Dictionary of National Biography, 1885–1900, Vol. V.

7. Expectants and 'fore-hammer men': Ref. *Caledonian Mercury*, 14 December 1785, page 3, columns 2 & 3. Under the heading 'Distillery of Scotland'.

8. James Stein's prosecution of the Excise: Ref. *Newcastle Chronicle*, 10 August 1782, page 2.

9. Lord Advocate Against Mr Stein: Ref. *Saunders's News-Letter and Daily Advertiser*, 22 December 1786, page 1, columns 2 &

3, & page 2, columns 1 & 2, under the heading 'High Court of Judiciary in Scotland'.

10. Sir Ilay Campbell, Lord Succoth (1734–1823). Scottish judge and politician, in office as Lord Advocate from 1784 to 1790. Ref. *History of Parliament* & National Galleries of Scotland.

11. Henry Erskine (1746–1817). Lord Advocate 1783–84. The Dean of the Faculty of Advocates 1785–95. Legendary orator and adversarial lawyer. Ref. 'Electric Scotland' and National Galleries of Scotland.

12. Deacon William Brodie (1741–1788). Cabinet Maker and Edinburgh City Councillor who led a secret life as a House-breaker. Brodie was an inspiration for Robert Louis Stevenson's *Jekyll and Hyde* story.

13. Sir James Hunter Blair (1741–1787). Scottish politician, banker and Lord Provost of Edinburgh. He formed a banking partner-ship with Sir William Forbes.

14. Mr. James Craig: Baker, Deacon Convener of the trades of Edinburgh – Ref. Boswell's Edinburgh Journals – Wednesday, December 22, 1779.

15. Distillery of Scotland: Ref. *Caledonian Mercury*, 14 December 1785, page 3, columns 2 & 3.

16. Trip to London: Ref. John Jameson's trip to London is recorded in the Alloa Harbour Trust Sederunt Book, page 302 – Alloa 4th of February, 1786 – *'They authorise John Jameson, cashier, one of their number to go to London'*. NRS. BR/AHT/1/1.

17. Mary Haig (1756–1803). Peggie's sister. She married Andrew Mackenzie in 1783.

18. Andrew Mackenzie (b.1750). A Haig relative and a business partner to James Haig in London.

19. The Edinburgh and London Fly: Ref. *Caledonian Mercury*, 9 April 1785, page 1 – 'in four days only, the Edinburgh

and London Fly, by Kelso, Newcastle and York.' Also, James Boswell's diary, 27 January 1786.

20. *Gulliver's Travels*: A satirical work by Irish author Johnathan Swift and published in 1726.

21. Mr John Spottiswoode: A London solicitor who worked for John Francis Erskine and with James Boswell. Ref. *Boswell's Edinburgh Journals*. 1767–1786, the 20th & 23rd November 1784.

22. Alloa Harbour Bill: Ref. 'Journals of the House of Commons from January 4th, 1786, In the Twenty Sixth year in the reign of George the Third to December 14, 1786. In the Twenty Seventh year in the reign of George the Third. – Reprinted by order of the House of Commons 1803.' February 22nd, 1786, page 240. February 24th, 1786, page 254. March 1st, 1786, page 268, March 6th, 1786, page 293, March 29th, 1786, page 450.

23. Charles Wolfran Cornwall (1735–1789). Politician and Speaker of the House of Commons from 1780 to 1789.

24. Thomas Dundas (1741–1820). Member of Parliament 1763–1794. Became Lord Dundas on leaving Parliament. Dundas inherited his father's interest in the Forth and Clyde Canal and commissioned what was said to be the first practical steamboat, the *Charlotte Dundas*. Ref. *The History of Parliament*.

25. Andrew Mackenzie's address: Ref. *Stamford Mercury*, 18 April 1788, page 2, column 2.

26. Henry Beaufoy (1750–1795). Beaufoy was from a wealthy family of Quakers and vinegar brewers. He was MP for Great Yarmouth 1784–1795. He spoke in Parliament on behalf of the London Distillers. Ref. Pamphlet, 'In the House of Lords. Case of the Distillers of Corn Spirits in North Britain,' page 5.

27. Ultimatum: Ref. *Caledonian Mercury*, 13 February 1786, page 3, columns 2 & 3.

28. James Stein's bills and credit notes: Ref. page 72, *Memoirs of a Banking House* by Sir William Forbes of Pitsligo. Published by William and Robert Chambers, London, and Edinburgh, 1860.

29. London's Oxford Street in 1786: Ref. *Sophie in London* 1786: being the diary of Sophie V. La Roche; translated from the German. Johnathan Cape, 1933.

30. Gold pocket watch: John Jameson's possession of four gold watches exceeded those of everyone else in Clackmannanshire. Ref. Scotland's Places – The clock and watch tax listings for Clackmannanshire in 1797–98, Volume 1.

31. Paid Mr Spottiswoode: Ref. John Spottiswoode's and John Jameson's payments for the trip to London are recorded in the Alloa Harbour Trust Sederunt Book – Minutes and Reports from the 10th of July 1786. NRS. BR/AHT/1/2.

32. Anne Jameson (1786–1861). John Jameson's tenth child. Anne was born on the 20th of March and was baptised three weeks later on the 11th of April, which suggests that the late baptism was to accommodate John Jameson's return to Alloa. Ref. Old Parish Register Births Alloa. Anne married Francis Stupart.

Chapter 11   Reckless

1. Distiller Act of 1786: Ref. *Caledonian Mercury*, 24 July 1786, page 1, column 3.

2. Stephen Maxwell (1740–1794). Known as Stephen Maxwell of Morriston. Maxwell was a coppersmith who also worked in tin, brass, and pewter. Some of his work is still collected today. Maxwell gave his name to Maxwell Street in Glasgow, where he built a tenement to house the Merchant's Hall Bank in which he was a partner. Stephen Maxwell's works and foundry were also situated on Maxwell Street. When Maxwell died at the age of fifty-four, he was bankrupt.

3. The increase of the export of Scottish spirit to England: Alderman Watson's opening statement to Parliament on the debate *'Petition of the Corn Distillers of England'* on the 7th of February, 1788: 'The Quarter before the Licence, they (the Scotch) imported into the English Market 245,700 Gallons; the next Quarter, the Number of Gallons imported amounted to 900,000; the first quarter of 1787, the importation was 752,000, since which time they had the whole Consumption of Scotland free of Duty, and a surplus for the English Market.' Ref *Caledonian Mercury*, 9 February 1788, page 3, column 1.

4. Kilbagie distillery output: Ref. Statistical Account of Clackmannan 1796, by Rev. Mr Robert Moodie, page 625.

5. Blootert: Scots word for drunk.

6. Nook: Scots word for hole.

7. Christian Jameson (1766–1841). The daughter of John Jameson, a merchant in Leith.

8. Wedding: The Jameson-Haig wedding took place at the parish church in South Leith at St Mary's. There are no records of where the reception took place. The old Leith Assembly Hall was at the Boar's Head Tavern, and a brand-new Assembly Hall was at the end of Constitution Street.

9. Bab at the Bowster: Also known as Babbity Bowster. Bab is Scots for 'bob', and Bowster is Scots for 'bolster' or 'cushion'.

10. John Stein (1769–1854?). Son of James Stein of Kilbagie. John Stein took over the Canonmills distillery after the bankruptcy. He was involved in various banking enterprises with his brothers Robert and James, but these eventually failed, as did his distilling at Canonmills. He became an MP for Bletchingley as a paying guest (1796–1802). It was said of John Stein, 'A man entirely devoted to the service of his country wherever it did not interfere with his own interests.'

11. Don Corleone: A fictional mafia character from Mario Puzo's novel *The Godfather*, 1969.

12. Strathspey: A slow, graceful Scottish country dance.

13. Bank reduces the extent of engagement: William Forbes wrote, 'I was resolved to endeavour gradually to reduce the extent of our engagement within more moderate bounds, and we began to take measures to bring this about.' Ref Page 72, *Memoirs of a Banking House* by Sir William Forbes of Pitsligo. Published by William and Robert Chambers, London and Edinburgh, 1860.

14. James Stein's fishing trip: Ref. Sederunt book for James Haig's creditors, pages 8 to 9. NRS. CS96/2080.

15. Janet Jameson (1787–1861). John Jameson's eleventh child. Janet was sometimes referred to as Jennet. She married John Woolsey, a brewer in Castlebellingham, Co. Louth, Ireland.

16. The Parliamentary debate on the Petition of the Corn Distillers of England: Ref. *Northampton Mercury*, 9 February 1788, & *The Scots Magazine*, Parliamentary reports for February 1788, pages 72 & 73.

17. Sir James Johnstone (1726–1794). MP for Dumfries 1784–1790. 'He was remarkable for his laconic style of speaking, being seldom more than a minute and a half on his legs'. Ref. Member Biographies, *History of Parliament* 1754-1790, author R. G. Thorne.

18. Sir William Cunynghame (1747–1828). MP for Linlithgow-shire West Lothian, 1774–1790. Championed Scottish Inter-ests, including Scots distilling. He opposed William Pitt on many issues. Ref. Member Biographies, *History of Parliament* 1754-1790.

19. Ceres: Sloop, launched on the 20th of April, 1787. Owned by John Stein. She had one deck, and two masts, and weighed 143 tons. Thomas Jameson, the ship's captain, was not a close relative

to John Jameson. Ref. Stirling Council Archives, Customs and Excise Records, Register of Ships, 1786–1797.

20. David Sandieman and Andrew Graham: The Steins' agents at John Street, American-Square, London.

21. Bills of Lading: A legal document issued to a carrier that details the goods and their destination. The carrier, i.e., the ship's captain, was instructed to deliver and hand over the goods to a named consignee, i.e., David Sandieman; the consignee needed a corresponding bill that an assignee had endorsed. In the case of the *Ceres*, it was likely that the assignee was the bank of Sir William Forbes.

22. Kennetpans and Kilbagie excise duty: Ref. Statistical Account 1796. Parish of Clackmannan, by Rev. Robert Moody, page 626.

Chapter 12   **Picking up the Pieces**

1. The Royal Exchange: Designed by John Adam and opened in 1760. Situated on the High Street, it contained two coffee houses and a piazza where merchants could meet and 'exchange'. Today, the building houses the City Chambers.

2. The Luckenbooths: A row of seven tenements built in the fifteenth century along the High Street, parallel to St Giles Cathedral. It was an early shopping centre containing permanent shops and accommodating various artisans, including publishers and printers. The Luckenbooths were demolished in 1817.

3. The Old Tollbooth: Attached to the western end of the Luckenbooths. As well as the Council chambers, it housed the borough prison. Built onto the side of the building was a two-storey extension with a gallows on the roof where from 1785, public executions took place. The building was demolished along with the Luckenbooths in 1817.

4. Walker's Tavern: A well-known meeting place in Writers' Court at the Royal Exchange. It is mentioned in Robert Fergusson's poem 'The Election' and Walter Scott's *Scottish History*, chapter 18. It is recorded as the location for the interim creditors meeting on the 3rd of March, 1788. Ref. Sederunt book for James Haig's creditors, page 6. NRS. CS96/2080.

5. 'A man of whom too much good cannot be said': Ref. *The Journal of a Tour to The Hebrides with Samuel Johnson* By James Boswell. – Sunday, 12th August.

6. David Steuart (1747–1824). Edinburgh Provost, property developer, antiquarian book collector, banker, and corn merchant.

7. Glasshouse sale: Ref. Register of Deeds and Warrants, 1782–1797, 'Articles of Roup of the Alloa Glassworks and Minutes Thereon, 1788'. NRS. SC64/55/6.

8. Alloa Coal Company dissolved: Ref. Sederunt book for James Haig's creditors, page 24. NRS. CS96/2080.

9. Wood and iron company wound up: Ref. Sederunt Book for James Haig's Creditors, page 26. NRS. CS96/2080.

10. James Stein lobbies for his son to take over Canonmills: Ref. Sederunt Book for James Haig's Creditors, page 31. Ref. NRS. CS96/2080.

11. Margaret Haig and brick and tile works: Ref. Sederunt Book for James Haig's Creditors – page 66. NRS. CS96/2080.

12. Stephen Maxwell's purchase of the Lochrin metal: Ref. John Haig's creditors Sederunt Book, page 92. NRS. CS96/2081.

13. Purchase of Lochrin: Ref. John Haig's creditors Sederunt Book, pages 63–68. NRS. CS96/2081.

14. The Krames: Booths used as shops and built against and along the wall of St Giles. They ran parallel to the Luckenbooths. Many of these booths sold toys, and they brightened up the Gothic walls of St Giles, with hobby horses and toys from Holland.

15. John White of Penicuik (1753–1820). Married to Ann Haig, Peggie's sister. John White owned the two cotton mills of Eskmills, Penicuik. By 1804, they had been sequestered.

16. Peter Williamson (1730–1799). Known as Indian Peter. Williamson's kidnap from Aberdeen into slavery eventually resulted in him exposing the scandal of children being sold into slavery and suing officials in Aberdeen.

17. Francis Erskine Jameson (1789–1790). John Jameson's twelfth child. Born on the 24th of May, baptised on the 17th of June 1789. Source: Old Parish Registers Birth Alloa.

18. David Steuart's letter to his nephew Charles: Ref. *David Steuart: An Edinburgh Collector* by Brian Hillyard, page 17 – Published by Edinburgh Bibliographical Society, 1993.

19. Purchase of Kennetpans: Ref. Letter from John Francis Erskine to Thomas Dundas on the 24th of March 1791. NRS. GD124/15/1681.

20. Sale of Canonmills: Ref. Sederunt Book for James Haig's Creditors, page 136. NRS. CS96/2080.

21. Lochrin appeal in the House of Lords: Ref. 'Journal of the House of Lords,' 23 April 1792, John Jamieson, Sheriff Clerk of Alloa, Steven Maxwell Merchant in Glasgow, and John Haig, Distiller in Lochrin V. John Russel, and John Sawyers of Bell's Mills, Water of Leith.

22. Canonmills distillery resumes work in 1792: John Stein entered a contract on 20 April 1792 to supply spirits from Canonmills to two Leith merchants. Ref. 'Cases decided in the house of Lords, upon appeal from the courts of Scotland' John Stein Distiller at Canonmills V. Thomas Stewart and James Sommervail & Co., 1796.

23. James Stein in Russia: Ref. 'The case of Lady Haddington V Stein'. Reported in the *Sun* (London) 12 February 1811, page 3,

columns 2 & 3. Under the heading – Edinburgh, Feb 1. Court of Session (1st division).

Chapter 13 **To Ireland**

1. Elizabeth Jameson (1791–1791). John Jameson's thirteenth child. Born on the 21st of June & baptised on the 3rd of July 1791. Ref. Old Parish Registers Birth Alloa.

2. Henry Jameson (1792–1801). John Jameson's fourteenth child. Born on the 4th of September & baptised on the 20th of September 1792. Ref. Old Parish Registers Birth Alloa.

3. Mary Jameson (1794–1800). John Jameson's fifteenth child. Born on the 26th of January & baptised on the 15th of February 1794. Ref. Old Parish Registers Birth Alloa. Giving your child's name from a previously departed child was quite common, but for JJ and Peggie, this only applied to Mary.

4. Alison Jameson (1797 – 1802). John Jameson's sixteenth child. Born on the 16th of August & baptised on the 1st of September 1797. Ref. Old Parish Registers Birth Alloa.

5. The wagonway, the most complete railway in Britain: Ref. Statistical Account 1793 – Number XL, Parish of Alloa – Drawn up from Communications of The Rev. Mr James Frame and John Francis Erskine, from page 614, under the heading 'Coal'.

6. Robert Jameson admitted Procurator: Ref. Sheriff Court Book 1791–97, page 26. NRS. SC64/1/15.

7. John Jameson-2. Writer: In the Register of Game Certificates 1793, three Jameson game certificates are entered together on the 10th of August: 'Mr John Jameson Sheriff Clerk of Clackmannan, Mr Robert Jameson Alloa, Mr John Jameson Junr Writer in Edinburgh.' Ref. NRS. SC64/1/15.

8. Robert Bald (1776–1861). Celebrated mining engineer. Son of Alexander Bald, the Shore Master, and John Jameson's clerk and agent at the harbour.

9. William Jameson and Robert Bald, clerks to John Jameson: Ref. William and Robert are named as John Jameson's clerks when witnesses to the transfer of ownership of the Vessel Mary of Alloa on the 5th of April 1792. Stirling Council Archives, Customs and Excise Records, Register of Ships, 1786–1797.

10. William Jameson, writer: By 1794, William Jameson, (aged sixteen) is referred to in the Court Books as a 'Writer' - Sheriff Court Book 1791 to 1797, 16 October 1794. Ref. NRS. SC64/1/15.

11. Robert Bald, reformer: Ref. *A General View of the Coal Trade of Scotland Chiefly that of the River Forth and Midlothian* by Robert Bald, 1808.

12. Rights of Man: Rights of Man, Being an Answer to Mr Burkes attack on the French Revolution, by Thomas Paine, 1791.

13. The Society of the Friends of the People: Founded in 1792, it advocated parliamentary reform by encouraging a broader variety of men to take part in government.

14. General Abercromby's views on republicanism: Ref. *Lieutenant-General Sir Ralph Abercromby, K.B. 1793–1801. A Memoir by His Son, James Lord Dunfermline,* Published in Edinburgh by Edmonston and Douglas, 1861. 'Family and Early Life' – page 37.

15. A series of commercials for Jameson Whiskey: 'Tall Tales' was a TV advertising campaign for Jameson Whiskey that started airing in 2009.

16. Gift of coal: Ref. The letters recording John Jameson's gifting of coal to the poor of Perth are kept in the Perth and Kinross Council Archive. NRS. B59/24/12/45 and B59/24/12/47.

17. John Buchan (1875–1940). Perth-born author of *The Thirty-Nine Steps* – awarded Freedom of Perth in 1933.

18. Winston Churchill (1874–1965). Statesman. Awarded Freedom of Perth in 1948.

19. John Jameson's note to James Watson, surveyor of taxes: The note is dated 'Alloa 15ᵗʰ October 1794' and contained within the survey of the Inhabited House Duty in the County of Clackmannan from the 5ᵗʰ of April 1794 to the 5ᵗʰ of April 1795. Ref. Scotland's Places, Inhabited house tax, Vol 10, County of Clackmannanshire 1778–1798.

20. 'Desiring to secure the future of his sons, he visited Ireland...': Ref. '*The History of a Great House*', illustrated by Harry Clarke. John Jameson and Son Ltd. Dublin, 1924.

21. Wolfe Tone (1763–1798). Founding member of the Society of United Irishmen in 1791.

22. Catholics' right to vote: Catholic Relief Act of 1793.

23. Boke: Scottish slang for to retch or vomit.

24. The Court's move from Clackmannan to Alloa: Ref. Sheriff Court Book 1791–1797, the 17ᵗʰ of October, 1791 – 'That the Sheriff Court in Future be held in the house of James Younger Founder in Alloa.' NRS. SC64/1/15.

25. James Waddell: Appointed Sheriff Substitute of Clackmannanshire in 1790.

26. Sheriff William Tait (1755–1800). A Writer to the Signet, he became an Advocate in 1780. Sheriff from 1790 to 1797. Became the MP for Stirling in 1797. Supporter of William Pitt and an ally of Henry Dundas.

27. Riding the clerk: Ref. *Community of the College of Justice* by John Finlay – page 233 – Under the heading – Judges Clerks.

28. James Waddell and the Alloa Kirk: Ref. Alloa Kirk Session Minutes, March 2nd & 13th, 1792. NRS. CH2/942/2.

29. John Jameson and James Waddell's disagreement in court: Ref. Alloa Sheriff Court Book 1791–1797, the 12th of November 1793. NRS. SC64/1/15.

30. Robert Haig's lease of land near Dublin: Ref. Registry of Deeds Dublin, Book 502, page 461, Memorial No. 326035.

31. James Allan's bankruptcy: Ref. Sederunt Books of the Mar Old Trust, 1796–1800. Minutes of the Trustees, the 24th of December 1795. NRS. GD124/4/7.

32. Robert Jameson factor for the creditors: Ref. Sederunt Book for the creditors of James Allan, pages 7 & 8. NRS. CS96/730.

33. Sale of Alloa Dry Dock: Ref. Articles & Conditions of Roup and Sale of the Dry Dock and other heritable subjects which belonged to James Allan. 1795 – Register of Deeds – Warrants 1782–1797. Bundle 1795. NRS. SC64/55/6.

34. Route to Glasgow: Ref. *A Guide from Glasgow to some of the most remarkable scenes in the highlands* by James McNayr' – 1797 – page 9, 'From Glasgow to Stirling, by Cumbernauld.'

35. St Ninians church tower: The church of St Ninians, near Stirling, had been used to store gunpowder that exploded during the Jacobite retreat in 1746. The remains of the church tower still stand today.

36. Battle of Bannockburn: Fought from the 23rd to the 24th of June 1314. It resulted in the victory of the Scottish King Robert the Bruce over the English King Edward II.

37. Saracen's Head Inn: Famed Glasgow inn (1755–1905). Frequented by James Boswell and Dr Samuel Johnstone, Robert Burns, John Wesley, William Wordsworth, and his sister Janet.

38. Glasgow to Donaghadee: Details of John Jameson's journey to Dublin are taken from various letters and journals of the time. Ref. Letter to John Francis Erskine from John Erskine, his uncle, concerning his forthcoming journey from Ireland to Alloa, 3rd

of April,1792. NRS. GD124/15/1683. & 'Sketch of a Short Excursion Lately taken in the West of Scotland.' *Belfast Monthly Magazine*, Volume 2, 1809, page 341. Also, *Caledonian Mercury*, August 1st, 1791, page 4. Under the heading 'Cheap and Expeditious Travelling from Glasgow to Ayr, Portpatrick, Dublin.'

39. Portpatrick: A village in the county of Wigtownshire in Southern Scotland, on the west coast of the Rhins of Galloway. It is only twenty nautical miles from Portpatrick to Donaghadee in Ireland.

40. Donaghadee: A small market town in County Down in the north of Ireland on the Ards Peninsula. It was a popular gateway from Scotland to Ireland in the eighteenth and early nineteenth centuries.

Chapter 14   **Dublin**

1. The Ale of Muirthemne: 'To Findia is served up sumptuously, The Ale of Muirthemne' is a quote from the *Poem of Cano* in praise of the various celebrated ales of Ireland translated and transcribed by Eugene O'Curry (1794–1862) from an ancient Irish manuscript. Professor O'Curry singled out Castlebellingham beer in the early nineteenth century as still maintaining the reputation of the Ales of Muirthemne. Ref. *On the manners and customs of the Ancient Irish, a series of lectures delivered by the late Eugene O'Curry, M.R.I.A. Volume 1, Introduction*, pages 374–375. Published by Williams and Norgate, London & Edinburgh, 1873.

2. O'Brien Bellingham (1742–1798). Third son of Alan Bellingham (1709–1796). Alan Bellingham gave over the lease of a malt house and land to O'Brien Bellingham, on which he built the Castlebellingham brewery in 1781–82. Ref. Registry of Deeds, Dublin, Book 661, page 442, Memorial No. 544681.

3. William Bellingham (1753–1826). The fourth son of Alan Bellingham. He was the MP for Reigate and was a private secretary to William Pitt. He was appointed the Commissioner for the victualling of the Royal Navy in 1789. Bellingham Bay and the City of Bellingham, Washington State, were named after him, and he was made a baronet in 1796.

4. The Battle of the Boyne: Fought on the 11th of July 1690. It resulted in the victory of the Protestant William of Orange over his Catholic father-in-law, James II. The Boyne battlefield is within a loop of the River Boyne, upstream from Drogheda.

5. Lying in hospital: The Rotunda Hospital was founded by Bartholomew Mosse. Mosse was appalled at the suffering from the 1742 potato famine. He was motivated to create a lying-in training hospital to provide food, shelter, and medical care for destitute mothers. Much of the building of 1752 continues to be used to this day as a maternity hospital.

6. Carlisle Bridge: Built in 1794. Rebuilt and renamed in 1880 as O'Connell Bridge.

7. Custom House: Built in 1791 and remains a landmark today.

8. Trinity College Dublin: Established in 1592. Well-endowed by the nearby Protestant Parliament of the time. Much of the eighteenth-century buildings and squares had taken shape by 1795.

9. 'Dear Dublin': Ref. Letters from John Francis Erskine to his Grandson – Bundle 3 of 5, No. 43. NRS. GD124/15/1735.

10. A tax upon coffins: Ref. *The Stranger in Ireland* by John Carr, 1805, page 290.

11. Roe, Power, and Teeling: Ref. *Wilson's Dublin Directory* 1795 – Nicolas Roe Distiller at 33 Pimlico, John Teeling, Distiller at 11 Marrowbone Lane, James Power, 109 Thomas Street.

12. The Pidgeon House: Named after John Pidgeon, the caretaker of a storehouse during the building of the South Wall

that stretches out into Dublin Bay (1765–95). Pidgeon began serving refreshments to travellers on the packet-boats. Later, he built a small hotel to accommodate them. By 1793, a more prominent hotel had been built that still stands today.

13. Ringsend: Ref. *The Stranger in Ireland* by John Carr, 1805, page 30. Described as 'One of the most horrible sinks of filth I have ever beheld.'

14. Viscount Fitzwilliam (1745–1816). 7th Viscount of Merrion. He was responsible for much of the urban development in Dublin at the time, i.e., Merion Square. The Fitzwilliams were originally an Irish Catholic Family, but that faith was relinquished by the 5th Viscount so that he could enter politics.

15. Arthur Guinness I (1725–1803). Founder of the Guinness porter brewery at St James's Gate Dublin in 1759.

16. Underground cistern: Ref. *Saunders's News-Letter*, 3 July 1804, page 3, column 2. Sale of a distillery at No. 16 Bow Street. 'It is well worthy the attention of the public, as having an uncommon supply of water, with the most extensive and secure storage.'

17. John Swan and William Dodd: Ref. Wilson's Dublin Directory 1794 – 'John Swan Distiller 52 Smithfield.' *Wilson's Dublin Directory 1795* – 'John Swan Table beer & Brewer 52 Smithfield.' *Wilson's Dublin Directory 1796* – 'William Dodd distiller 1 Bow Street.'

18. Land for sale, Bow Street: Ref. *Dublin Evening Post*, 3 May 1794, page 4, column 2, under the heading 'Sale of Lands and Tenements' – No. 6.

19. John Stein and Roscrea: Advertisements appeared in the press in 1797 and 1798 - 'To be Sold by Private Contract, by order the assignees of John Stein, a bankrupt, all the said Stein's right title and interest in the large new distillery, Malt House, Still, Worm, and all necessary utensils, in the Town of Roscrea.' Ref.

Dublin Evening Post, 28 October 1797, page 4, column 3, second from top.

20. Dublin to Roscrea: By 1795, the route from Dublin to Roscrea by canal and then road was well established. Ref. *Saunders's News-Letter*, 23 May 1795, page 2, column 1.

21. Monasterevin: County Kildare, where the Grand Canal crosses the river Barrow. Monasterevin has been referred to as the Venice of Ireland.

22. Canal travel: Ref. *The Stranger in Ireland* by John Carr, 1805, page 255.

23. Timetable: Ref. *Dublin Evening Post*, 17 February 1787, page 4, column 4, under the heading 'Grand Canal Passage Boats.'

24. Book of Dimma: An eighth-century Irish Gospel Book from the Abbey at Roscrea, now held at Trinity College in Dublin.

25. Bog of Corbally: Ordnance Survey maps of 1838 show a canal from the Birchgrove distillery to the nearby bog at Corbally. Whether John Stein cut this is uncertain, but it is a Stein hallmark repeated at other Stein distilleries in Ireland.

Chapter 15   Nastiness Then Opportunity

1. Meeting of Commissioners on the 16th of May: Ref. NRS. CS96/3968.

2. The Battle of the Diamond: A confrontation at a village called the Diamond near Loughgall, County Armagh on the 21st of September 1795. Its aftermath was viewed by many, including Ralph Abercromby, as the catalyst for the rebellions that followed. Ref. *Lieutenant-General Sir Ralph Abercromby, K.B. 1793–1801, A Memoir by His Son, James Lord Dunfermline*, Published in Edinburgh by Edmonston and Douglas 1861, 'Command in Ireland', page 62.

3. Election advice from Lord Dundass: Ref. *'The History of Parliament'*, Clackmannanshire, 1788 to 1811. Article by R. G. Thorne.

4. Fighting the French in the West Indies: West Indies Campaign, 1796.

5. Election 1796: Ref. Freeholders' and Electors' Minute Book, 1700–1869. NRS. SC64/62/1.

6. John Jameson resignation, Alloa Coal Company: Ref. Sederunt Books of the Mar Old Trust 1788–1797. Minutes of the meeting of the 24th of November 1796. NRS. GD124/4/1.

7. Pernod Ricard: A French company formed in 1975 from the merger of two anise-based spirits companies. In 1988, it acquired Irish Distillers, which included Jameson Irish Whiskey as its foremost brand.

8. Ralph Abercromby in Ireland: Ref. *Lieutenant-General Sir Ralph Abercromby, K.B. 1793–1801, A Memoir by His Son, James Lord Dunfermline*, Published in Edinburgh by Edmonston and Douglas 1861, Command in Ireland.

9. Sale of Roscrea distillery: Ref. *Dublin Evening Post*, 13 December 1798, page 3, column 1.

10. Unpaid duty: In 1797, the Steins owed £31,225 in licence duty in Scotland. Ref. *History of Parliament*, Biography of John Stein 1769-1854.

11. John Stein (1775–1854). The Eldest son of John Stein of Kennetpans. A distiller and farmer. He was in partnerships at Marrowbone Lane and Bow Street, Dublin; Thomond Gate, Limerick; and Marlfield near Clonmel. He married Eliza Bellingham in 1817 and had a daughter, Monique, born in 1819. He moved to Dorset in the late 1820s with residences at High Cliff, Lyme Regis and Chalmington in Cattistock. He was High Sheriff of Dorset in 1836. He died *'suddenly whilst sitting in his chair at the Birlington Hotel London at an advanced age.'*

12. Marrowbone Lane Lease 1798: Ref. Registry of Deeds, Dublin, Book 523, page 308, Memorial No. 345530.

13. John Jameson ends his role as factor and the credit he is owed: Ref. 'Memorial for John Jameson concerning his position as creditor of the Mar estate in respect of Alloa mills and his accounts as factor'. NRS. GD124/17/382. Also, John Jameson cash accounts – NRS. GD124/17/360/1, 2.

14. Death by cabbage stalks: Ref. *Dublin Courier*, 24 June 1763, Page 1, 3rd column.

15. John Teeling's premises for sale: Ref. *Saunders's News-Letter*, 28 August 1799, page 4, 2nd column under 'Distillery and Utensils by Auction'.

16. Atkinson Brewery: Ref. Registry of Deeds, Dublin, Book 531, page 262, Memorial No. 349599.

17. Marrowbone Lane Lease, Jameson and Stein: Ref. Registry of Deeds, Dublin, Book 530, page 457, Memorial No. 348935. A later deed confirms that this deed was signed by John Stein Junior and not John Stein Senior. Ref. Registry of Deeds, Dublin, Book 661, page 365, Memorial No. 455196.

Chapter 16   **Bow Street**

1. Grange brothers: Edmond Grange, b. 1766, John Grange, b. 1768, Richard George Grange, b. 1771. The Grange brothers were sons of the Reverend Richard Capel Grange and Mary Rochfort.

2. Buying up land in Bow Street from 1796: Ref. Registry of Deeds Dublin, Book 578, page156, Memorial No. 386955.

3. Grange's large-scale ambitions: Ref. Account book of Edmund and Richard Grange and Co. of Dublin, brewers and distillers. Essex Records Office – D/DGd B3. & Balance sheets and

statements of accounts of Edmund and Richard Grange and Co. of Dublin, brewers and distillers. Essex Records Office – D/DGd B4.

4. Mary Rochfort (1744–1803). Mary Rochfort was the daughter of the Honourable William Rochfort of Clontarf (1719–1772). William Rochfort's brother was Robert Rochfort, 1st Earl of Belvidere, who famously and cruelly imprisoned his second wife.

5. Sisters: Mary Rochfort's sisters were Harriet Sperling (1758–1854), married to John Sperling; Lady Diana Hadley D'Oyly (1747–1803), married to Sir John Hadley D'Oyly.

6. Bow Street earmarked as a brewery: Ref. Copy of Memorial of Deed 1798 between Grange brothers and Sperling. Essex Records Office – D/DGd B4.

7. John Sperling (1763–1851). The son of Henry Sperling of Dynes Hall in Essex. John Sperling features in a series of watercolours by his daughter Diana Sperling collected in the book *Mrs Hurst Dancing & Other Scenes from Regency Life 1812–1823*. Publisher Victor Gollancz, 1981.

8. Sir John Hadley D'Oyly (1854–1818). Worked for the East India Company in India, where he married Diana Rochfort. He returned to England because of Diana's ill health. He was MP for Ipswich from 1790 to 1796.

9. Sperling and Hadley D'Oyly's investment: Ref. Essex Records Office – D/DGd B4.

10. Plans for Bow Street distillery 1799: Ref. Document – '*Resolutions made and agreed by Sir John Hadley D'Oyly Bart, John Sperling, Edmond Grange and John Grange Esquires the acting and anonymous partners in a Brewery Malt House Mill and Distillery in the city of Dublin and its environs the 10th of April 1799.*' Essex Records Office – D/DGd B4.

11. Gustavus Rochfort (1750–1824). Son of George Rochfort and Alice Hume, and a cousin to the Rochfort sisters. He continued

a family tradition and sat as MP for Westmeath. He was also Sheriff of County Westmeath from 1796 to 1797 and commanded the Moyarshell and Magheraderen mounted yeomanry as captain.

12. Rochfort borrowed money at a high interest: Ref. High Court of Chancery, Judgement Date 19 August 1836. From the Court of Chancery in Ireland, Sir Gerard Noel V Gustavus Rochfort and others.

13. William Robert Robertson of Eyemouth (1761–1833). Robertson was from a well-established county family, the Robertsons of Prenderguest, Berwickshire.

14. Eyemouth: As well as exporting corn, it was a notorious area for smuggling. John Nisbet was a smuggler who built Gunsgreen House, which today commands the view of Eyemouth. William Robertson's father and brother Alexander bankrupted Nisbet and took over Gunsgreen House.

15. Margaret Jameson's dowry: John Jameson's settlement on his daughter Margaret Jameson can be found in his will. Ref. NRS. SC64/42/1 – Alloa Sheriff Court, page 39.

16. Tulliallen distillery: Previously owned by John Bald, brother of Alexander Bald, the shore master. In 1799, John Bald built a larger distillery for himself at Carsebridge. Ref. Sederunt Books of the Old Mar Trust, Minutes of Trustees 24 November 1796. NRS. GD124/4/1.

17. John Jameson-2 and distilling: In 1799, John Jameson-2 was recorded in the Games Certificates register as a 'Writer in Edinburgh'. In 1800, John Jameson-2 was first recorded as a distiller in Tulliallan from a report of those present at a Lowland Distillers meeting. Ref. *Caledonian Mercury* 26th of June, 1800, page 1. In 1803, John Jameson-2 was referred to as 'John Jameson Distiller in Tulliallen' in the will of his aunt Janet Haig. Ref.

Register of Deeds and Warrants, 1798–1818 – In bundle for 1804. NRS. SC64/55/7.

18. Alloa House Fire: August 28th, 1800. There was no organised local fire brigade, and much was lost in the fire, including an original painting of Mary Queen of Scots.

19. Curse of Alloa Tower: A curse supposedly placed on John Erskine, 17th Earl of Mar, by the Abbot of Cambuskenneth in the sixteenth century. Any misfortune that befell the family over the centuries was attributed to this curse, including the fire of 1800. This story was exaggerated at times to include the death of John Francis's wife in the fire, but she had died two years earlier.

20. Isabella Stein (1784–1861). 6th daughter of John Stein of Kennetpans (1745-1725). Married her 2nd cousin John Jameson-2 in 1802. She is buried in John Jameson's tomb in Alloa.

21. Rags of every colour: The use of cast-offs by the Irish was observed by Sir Walter Scott when he visited Ireland in 1825. 'Sir Walter rather irritated a military passenger (a stout highlander) by asking whether it had ever occurred to him that the beautiful checkery of the clan tartans might have originated in a pious wish, in the part of the Scottish Gael, to imitate the tatters of the parent race.' Ref. *Sir Walter Scott's Tour in Ireland in 1825* by D.J. O'Donoghue, first published in 1905.

22. Begging in Dublin: 'I wish God had made your heart as tender as your toes.' Ref. *The Stranger in Ireland* by John Carr, published 1806, page 36.

23. The death of Abercromby pantomime: Ref. *Saunders's News-Letter*, 8 January 1802, page 2, column 2, under the heading 'Amphitheatre Royal'.

24. Battle of Alexandria: A battle in Egypt fought on the 21st of March, 1801, between Napoleon's French Republic and a British expeditionary force under General Abercromby. It was a British victory, but Abercromby entering the fray of battle at

the age of sixty-six, was wounded by a spent ball. Although at first it was thought he would recover, he died from the wound a few days later. The heroics of the general dying victorious and selflessly caught the nation's imagination, as did Nelson's death at Trafalgar four years later.

25. The death of Abercromby pantomime review: Ref. *Saunders's News-Letter*, 4 January 1802, page 2, bottom of column 1.

26. Proclamation from Dublin Castle: Ref. *Caledonian Mercury*, 20 October 1801, page 3, column 3, under the heading 'Distilling of Whisky.'

27. Renewal of Bow Street lease 1801: Ref. Registry of Deeds Dublin, Book 578, page156, Memorial No. 386955.

28. John Stein Senior at No. 1 Bow Street: Ref. Registry of Deeds Dublin, Book 562, page 349, Memorial No. 374400.

29. Andrew Haig and the Kirk: The Tulliallan Kirk session minutes recorded that 'In the course of an inquiry by sessions at Tulliallan and Kincardine, Andrew Haig (Distiller), after being accused of the sin of fornication, admitted by letter to being the Father of the child of Janet Sheddan.' Ref. Tulliallen Kirk Session – Minutes, 1745–1820, May 18th, May 29th, July 19th, 1803. NRS. CH2/710/4.

30. Robert Robertson (1802–1865). The eldest child of Margaret Jameson. Advocate and Sheriff Substitute of Stirling. Died at Airfield House Donnybrook, Dublin, Ireland.

31. The Charlotte Dundas: Designed by William Symington, commissioned by Thomas Dundas and named after his daughter. The vessel was said to be the first practical steam-powered boat. On March 28th, 1803, and after various experiments and rebuilds, the Charlotte Dundas successfully towed two sloops along the canal from Wynford to Port Dundas in Glasgow.

32. Robert Jameson's trip to London: Ref. Alloa Harbour Trust Sederunt Book, 12th of July, 1803, NRS. BR/AHT/1/2.

33. William Jameson and the Emmet uprising: When Alfred Barnard visited Marrowbone Lane distillery in 1785-6, he wrote – 'Marrowbone Lane is not far from the scene of the rising under T. A. Emmet in 1803, and an ancestor of the present proprietor was dining in his house – now used as the offices of the Distillery – when it commenced, and heard the first shots, and cries of the wounded,' Ref. *The Whisky Distilleries of the United Kingdom* by Alfred Barnard, first published by the proprietors of *Harpers Weekly Gazette*, 39 Crutched Friars, London 1887. Republished by Birlinn Ltd. Edinburgh, 2008, page 369.

34. Robert Emmet (1778–1803). Brother of Thomas Addis Emmet, a friend of Wolfe Tone. As a supporter of the United Irishmen, Emmet was expelled from Trinity College Dublin in 1798. After the defeat and suppression of the United Irishmen, he sought to re-establish the cause. He led the rising on July 23, 1803, which ended in confusion and Emmet's eventual arrest for treason.

35. John Stein's partnership with John Kennedy dissolved: Ref. Registry of Deeds Dublin, Book 562, page 349, Memorial No. 374400.

36. The bankers and Bow Street: Ref. The bank's connection to the distillery's insolvency is given in a letter from Mr Bailie acting for Rochfort and Sperling, the 21st of November, 1804, 'Said co-partnership became so far insolvent as not to be able to pay a very considerable debt claimed by a banking house in London'. Essex Records Office –D/DGd B4

37. Bow Street distillery for sale: Ref. *Dublin Evening Post*, 2 February 1804, page 1, 3rd column, under 'MESSRS. E. And R. Grange and Co' – 'MESSRS. E. And R. Grange and Co intending to confine themselves entirely to the Porter Brewing business, will dispose of their interest in the following concerns – The distillery Malt-House and Stores, situate in Smithfield

and Bow Street, newly erected and on extensive scale now in complete order and ready for immediate work.'

38. Baby JJ-3: John Jameson-3 (1804–1881). Born in Scotland. Ref. Trinity College Dublin Alumni P435. He was the grandson of John Jameson, and he was the original son of 'John Jameson & Son.' He was active in running the Bow Street distillery with his father and later with his son. He married his second cousin, Ann Haig, daughter of William Haig. Ann Haig's nieces, in turn, married her sons Jack and Willie Jameson.

39. Sackville Street: When signing the Bow Street contract, John Jameson-2's address is given as Sackville Street. Ref. Registry of Deeds, Dublin, Book 578, page 156, Memorial No. 386955.

40. The Bow Street purchase price: Ref. Balance sheets and statements of accounts of Edmund and Richard Grange and Co. of Dublin, brewers and distillers from the 2nd of October 1804 to the 2nd of April 1805. Essex Records Office – D/DGd B4.

41. Bow Street contract: Ref. Registry of Deeds, Dublin, Book 578, page156, Memorial No. 386955.

42. Sale of John Stein's possessions: Ref. *Freemans Journal*, 9 June 1806, page 1. 'To be Sold by Auction, On Thursday 12th June 1806'; By order of the assignees of John Stein, a bankrupt, At his house, No. 1, Bow-Street.'

Chapter 17   **A Whiskey in Its Youth**

1. John Jameson Robertson (1804–1882). 2nd son of Margaret Jameson. He partnered in running the Marrowbone Lane distillery in Ireland for a short time.

2. William Robertson (1805–1882). 3rd son of Margaret Jameson. Minister of Greyfriars Church in Edinburgh.

3. The poor quality of malt on the market: Ref. *Saunders's News-Letter*, 31 January 1793, column 2, under the heading 'At a meeting of the Distillers of Dublin'.

4. Made solely from malt: Ref. *Saunders's News-Letter*, 9 July 1819, page 1, 2nd column, under the heading 'Certificate'.

5. Duty-free warehousing: Ref. *Morning Post*, 26 July 1804, page 2, under 'Imperial Parliament'. Also Ref. 'Irish Whiskey' by E.B. McGuire, published 1973. Gill and Macmillan Ltd. Dublin, page 196.

6. Prussia Street: The large eighteenth-century house in Prussia Street was acquired around 1804 by John Jameson. The numberings for this house have changed through the years as listings in the various Dublin almanacks show, from 38 to 33 to 38 to 42 and eventually 55.

7. James Jameson's house: 19 Harcourt Street was built on the site of the south wing of Clonmell House.

8. Eustace Street Congregation and Unitarianism: Many of John and James Jameson's children were christened at Eustace Street. The last christening was James Jameson's daughter Mary Anne in 1824, but she was christened again elsewhere two years later. By 1828, most of the congregation of Eustace Street had become Unitarians, i.e., Nontrinitarian. All the brothers eventually went on to join their local Church of Ireland congregations. However, John Jameson's one-time Alloa apprentice and cousin, William Wilson Jameson, went on to support the Unitarians at the High Court of Chancery in January 1842.

9. James Whitelaw (1749–1813). He took over the Protestant Parish of St Catherine's, encompassing the Marrowbone Lane distillery and the Guinness brewery like its Catholic counterpart. In 1805, Whitelaw published 'Essay on the Population of Dublin in 1778'. It was a census gathered during the rebellion of 1798 with the object of improving social conditions amongst the

poor of Dublin. James Whitelaw died after contracting typhus at the Cork Street Fever Hospital, which he had founded.

10. Daniel O'Connell (1775–1847). Lawyer and Irish Nationalist politician and leader. Known as the Liberator, he petitioned for Catholic emancipation and founded The Catholic Association in 1823. In 1826, JJ's grandson, John Jameson-3, joined the association.

11. Catherine Jameson (1792–1846). Daughter of Dr Macmillan Jameson, Surgeon General of Artillery. After Catherine divorced Andrew Jameson, she married Donald Baine, an accountant in Edinburgh. She died of erysipelas.

12. John Stein's debts: Ref. *Saunders's News-Letter*, 13 December 1811, page 4, second column: 'John Stein, a bankrupt … debt due by James Ward Bow Street.'

13. Marlfield distillery: Ref. Registry of Deeds Dublin, Book 646, page 38, Memorial No. 441518 – In the 1850s, the distillery was taken over fully by Jameson and run by JJ's grandson Henry Jameson.

14. John Woolsey (1778–1853). Son of the Reverend William Woolsey of Priorland and Mary Ann Bellingham. Woolsey married Janet Jameson, the daughter of John Jameson, in 1812.

15. Reverend William Woolsey of Priorland (1746–1832). Rector of Kilsaran Parish, Castlebellingham.

16. Rev. William Woolsey's support for Catholics: Ref. Lothian MSS 73 1905, pages 327–378, James Fortescue to Earl of Buckingham, 1st of April, 1778.

17. William Cairnes (1787–1863). Cairnes married John Woolsey's sister, Mary Anne Woolsey.

18. Woolsey Cairnes & Co.: Ref. Registry of Deeds Dublin, Book 661, page 442, Memorial No. 455681. Book 660, page

365, Memorial No. 458250. Book 660, page 382, Memorial No. 458273.

19. Janet Jameson's marriage settlement: Ref. Registry of Deeds, Dublin, Book 656, page 519, Memorial No. 452783.

20. Priorland: Lands from the ancient Monastery of St Leonards in Dundalk, a priory of an order of Augustinian Hospitallers.

21. Haggardstown: Townland on the shores of Dundalk Bay.

22. Elizabeth Sophia Woolsey (1795–1873). Eighth child of Rev. William Woolsey and Margaret Bellingham of Priorland.

23. The Jameson and Woolsey partnership: The partnership was dissolved after William's death in 1822, but the link continued. Ref. *The Drogheda Journal*, 11 January 1823, page 1, column 2.

24. Sheriff Clerk deputation: Ref. Register of Deeds – Warrants 1798 – 1818, Bundle 1813. NRS. SC64/55/7.

25. John Jameson's illness and Peggie's death: Ref. Dewar Stein and Company, distillers, Grange of Alloa. Letter book, 1808–1816, letters from Neil Ryrie on the 17th & 19th of January,1815. NRS. CS96/1856.

26. Election 1815: Ref. Freeholders and Electors Minute Book 1700–1869. NRS. SC64/62/1.

27. Arthur Guinness II (1768–1855). Second son of Arthur Guinness I. He took over the brewery on his father's death in 1803.

28. Palmer family: George Palmer was an early director of the Bank of Ireland and governor from 1803 to 1805.

Chapter 18   The Gloaming

1. Legal action by John Francis against Andrew Haig: Ref. NRS. GD124/6/31.

2. St Mungo: The church was declared ruinous and unsafe in 1815. In 1817, the new St Mungo's foundation stone was laid. The new

parish church was completed in 1819. With a seating capacity of 1561, it was then one of the largest churches in Scotland.

3. William Wilson Jameson (1775–1855). The son of John Jameson's first cousin and secession preacher, the Reverend William Jameson. William Wilson was an apprentice clerk to John Jameson and later a merchant in Alloa and a member of the Harbour Trust. After the collapse of the Grange distillery, he moved to Ireland and was in partnership with William Jameson and John Woolsey in Drogheda. He moved to Dublin, living at 11 Smithfield. In 1842, he was a defendant in the High Court of Chancery for the Unitarian Protestant Dissenters.

4. Neil Ryrie (c.1770–1830). A brewer by trade who acted as an agent or 'rider' for the Grange distillery. He lived at the Grassmarket and later Royal Terrace in Edinburgh. As he travelled the central belt between Edinburgh and Glasgow, he enjoyed a life of drinking and going to the races. He was a model eighteenth-century gentleman.

5. Grange distillery complaints of *'a singed taste'*: Ref. Letter Book, the 24th of March 1811, NRS. CS96/1856.

6. Stirling to Edinburgh steamboats: Ref. *Caledonian Mercury*, 1 April 1815, page 1. column 1, 'The Stirling Steamboat'. & *Caledonian Mercury*, 21 August 1815, page 3. column 5, 'The Lady of the Lake'. Also, *Caledonian Mercury*, 11 April 1816, page 1. column 1 – 'Morning Star of Alloa.'

7. Lochrin House: The house was surrounded by extensive, landscaped gardens south of the distillery. Today, it would have been opposite the King's Theatre on Leven Street. Ref. Edinburgh map by Robert Kirkwood in 1817.

8. York Place: John Francis Erskine was living at 24 York Place in 1817, but by 1821, he had moved to Shandwick Place. Ref. Scottish Post Office Directories.

9. John Francis's opinion on the Stein family: Ref. Letter from John Francis to his grandson, John F. M. Erskine, Letter 83 of Bundle 5, NRS. GD124/15/1735.

10. Origins of Fairfield distillery: Ref. Registry of Deeds Dublin, Book 873, page 446, Memorial No. 580446.

11. Financial assistance from John Jameson to Andrew Jameson: At John Jameson's death in 1823, Andrew owed his father £500. Ref. John Jameson's Will, NRS. SC64/42/1 Alloa Sheriff Court.

12. James Jameson's co-partnership with George Roe: Ref. Registry of Deeds, Dublin, Book 731, page 247, Memorial No. 498782.

13. Captain Francis Stupart (1781–1860). Son of John Stupart of Clackmannan.

14. Dr James Horner (1750–1843). A leading light in the Irish Presbyterian movement. He was ordained at Mary's Abbey in 1791, where he remained with that congregation until he died in 1843.

15. The blessing of Anne Jameson's marriage in Alloa: Ref. NRS. Old Parish Registers Marriages 465/70295 Alloa – page 295.

16. King George IV (1762–1830). George became Prince Regent in 1811 because of his father, George III's illness. He succeeded to the throne on the 29th of January,1820. He was crowned on the 19th of July,1821. The coronation was followed by a state visit to Ireland the next month, arriving on Sunday, the 12th of August.

17. 'Drink my health in a bumper.': King George's advice to Dublin. Ref. *Cassell's Illustrated History of England*, Vol 7, Chapter VI, published in 1873.

18. James Jameson's windmill: 'Nothing looked so Majestically Grand'. Ref. *Freeman's Journal*, 16 August 1821, page 3, 3rd column.

19. Poverty in Dublin: Ref. An Essay on the population of Dublin being the result of an actual survey taken in 1798, to which is

added the General Return of the District Committee in 1804. By the Rev. James Whitelaw, M.R.I.A. vicar of St Catharine's. Dublin 1805.

20. William Jameson's funeral: Ref. *Saunders's News-Letter*, 9 December 1822, page 2, 3rd column, 'The funeral of the Late William Jameson Esq of Merrion Square'.

21. William Jameson left his distillery to his brother James: Ref. Registry of Deeds, Dublin, Book 855, page 287, Memorial No. 571287.

22. Bow Street distillery complaints: Ref. *Saunders's News-Letter*, 23 January 1823, page 2, column 2, under the heading 'The Infernal Machine.'

23. The Excise Act 1823: Ref. *Saunders's News-Letter*, 27 August 1823, page 4, 2nd column, 'Excise Office, Dublin.

24. Andrew and Catherine Jameson's marriage problems: Ref. 'Journals of the House of Lords,' Vol. L1X page 58, the 12th of February, 1827.

25. John Jameson's resignation as cashier: Ref. Alloa Harbour Trust, the 16th of September, 1823. NRS. BR/AHT/1/2.

26. John Francis Erskine's grandson: John Francis Miller Erskine (1795–1866). 9th Earl of Mar.

27. Letter from Geneva: Letter from Robert Robertson to his uncle Robert Jameson concerning the mental health of John Francis Erskine's grandson. Ref. NRS. GD124/15/1768.

28. Martinmas payments to John Jameson from Bow Street: Ref. NRS. Reference SC64/42/1 Alloa Sheriff Court – the Bow Street distillery's Martinmas payments are recorded in John Jameson's will.

29. John Jameson whiskey description: 'This spirit so remarkably sweet.' Ref. *Saunders's News-Letter*, 14 June 1820, page 2, column 1, under the heading 'Pure Malt Spirit'.

Chapter 19   The Legacies

1. Dry rot: Discovered at St Mungo two years after its opening in 1819. In 1824, pavement was laid to prevent the dry rot. The St Mungo bell was added in 1825.

2. Earldom: In June 1824, an act was passed to restore to John Francis Erskine 'the honours, dignities and titles of the Earl of Mar'. Due to his 'bodily age and infirmity', the act excused him for the necessity of a trip down to London to take the oaths of allegiance. He died in August 1825.

3. Andrew Jameson's divorce bill: Ref. Globe, 3 April 1827, page 3, column 1, 'Private business of the House of Commons'. Read for the third time and passed in the House of Commons on April 2nd, 1827.

4. Catherine's marriage to Donald Bain: Ref. NRS. Old Parish Registers Marriages 685/2 420206 St Cuthbert's, page 206. Dated 25 April 1831.

5. Andrew's marriage to Margaret Millar: Ref. NRS. Old Parish Registers Marriages 465/70334 Alloa, page 334. Dated 19 June 1827.

6. Daphne (Castle). Andrew Jameson took up residence at Daphne in about 1827. Ref. *Dublin Evening Mail*, 30 June 1826, page 1, column 2, *'County Wexford to be let'*. By 1844, four years after Annie Jameson was born, Daphne House was converted into a school by Mr Ormsby. Ref. *The Wexford Conservative*, 3 July 1844, page 3, column 5, under the heading 'Fashions for July'. By 1846, Daphne House is referred to as 'Daphne Castle' Ref. *The Evening Packet*, 1 August 1846, page 1, column 3, under the heading 'Daphne Castle Collegiate School'.

7. Fairfield distillery surrounded: Ref. *Tipperary Free Press*, 13 December 1828, page 3, column 3, under the heading 'Attempt on a distillery'.

8. Fairfield distillery mortgaged: Ref. Registry of Deeds, Dublin, Book 873, page 446, Memorial No. 580446.

9. Fairfield flour mill: Ref. *Dublin Evening Post*, 4 October 1834, page 1, column 4, under the heading 'Distillery and flour mill'.

10. Annie Fenwick Jameson (1840–1920). Granddaughter of John Jameson and mother of Guglielmo Marconi.

11. Annie's childhood: Annie Jameson lived between Wexford and Dublin. When Annie was twelve years old in 1852, Andrew Jameson lived at Kiltrea, about four Kilometres from Fairfield. Annie was sixteen years old in 1856 when her mother, Margaret Jameson, died at Clifton Ville, Monkstown, Dublin. In 1857, when Annie was seventeen, her father, Andrew Jameson, died at Carysfort Avenue, Blackrock, Dublin.

12. Giuseppe Marconi (1823–1904). Married Annie Jameson in 1864, seven years after Andrew Jameson's death.

13. Guglielmo Marconi (1874–1937). Second son of Annie Jameson and Giuseppe Marconi. He was an Italian physicist and inventor of the successful wireless telegraph.

14. Haig's Edinburgh Distillery Closures: Distillery closed at Lochrin by 1851. Ref. Midlothian OS Name Books, 1852–1853 / Midlothian Volume 110. OS1/11/110/13. Distillery closed at Sunbury by 1856. Ref. Midlothian OS Name Books, 1852–1853 / Midlothian Volume 90. OS1/11/90/23. Distillery closed at Bonnington by 1853. Ref. *The Book of the old Edinburgh Club* Vol 19, page 175. Distillery closed at Canonmills by 1840. Ref. Midlothian OS Name Books, 1852–1853 / Midlothian Volume 94. OS1/11/94/36.

15. Financial help from John Jameson: John Jameson's financial assistance to William Haig is recorded in his will, which notes

an 'Arrears of interest on debt over the lands of Seggie belonging to Mr William Haig – £270 9s 6d.' Ref. NRS. SC64/42/1 Alloa Sheriff Court – John Jameson's will – page 35, Item 10.

16. John Haig (1802–1878). Founder of John Haig and Co. Born at Kincaple near St Andrews in Fife. John Haig married Rachel Mackerras Veitch of Stewartfield, Bonnington, daughter of Hugh Veitch, Town Clerk of Leith. John Haig raised his family in Edinburgh and at Cameron Bridge House, Markinch.

17. Mary Elizabeth Haig (1843–1918). Eldest daughter of John Haig. Married John Jameson-4, her first cousin.

18. John Jameson-4 (1839–1920). Eldest son of John Jameson-3. Known in the family as Jack. Together with his younger brother Willie, he built and raced several famous racing cutters, including Queta, Enriqueta, Samoena, Irex and Iverna. He had no children.

19. Henrietta Frances Haig (1851–1924). Youngest daughter of John Haig. Married William George Jameson, her first cousin. Henrietta dabbled in the supernatural and forewarned King Edward VII, a friend of her husband, of his imminent death.

20. William George Jameson (1851–1939). Youngest son of John Jameson-3, known in the family as Willie. He was a gentleman sportsman and very successful at it both on the turf and being a world-class helmsman and shipmaster. He struck up a friendship with the Prince of Wales (Edward VII) and was entrusted with the building of the royal racing cutter *Britannia*. He had no children.

21. Field Marshall Sir Douglas 1st Earl Haig (1861–1928). Youngest son of John Haig.

22. *Oh! What a Lovely War*. A musical satire on World War I and war in general. It was developed by Joan Littlewood and her ensemble company at the Theatre Royal Stratford East in 1963. It was later adapted into a film by Richard Attenborough.

23. Jameson's whiskey is advertised with the Jameson name alone in 1824: Ref. *Dublin Mercantile Advertiser and Weekly Price Current*, 24 May 1824, page 1, column 1, under the heading 'Old Whiskey'.

24. Queen Victoria (1819–1901). Succeeded to the throne of Britain in 1837. Over Victoria's sixty-three-year reign, the British Empire became a global industrial power. The wealth of the new industrialists and entrepreneurs grew immeasurably.

25. Bow Street distillery first referred to as John Jameson and Son: Ref. *Freeman's Journal*, 23 March 1838, page 1, under the heading 'Choice Old Whiskey'. Jameson John and Son, Licenced distillers Bow Street, appeared in the *Dublin Almanac* of 1840.

26. Theobald Mathew (1790–1856). Priest and President of the Cork Total Abstinence Society.

27. The Reverend William Jameson (1811–1886). Third son of John Jameson-2. He married Elizabeth Guinness, the daughter of Arthur Guinness II, on the 12 April 1844.

28. Jameson Guinness marriage settlement: £6000 from John Jameson-2 and £10,000 from Arthur Guinness II were put into a trust fund for William and Elizabeth Jameson, administered by John Jameson-3 and Benjamin Guinness. Ref. Registry of Deeds Dublin, Year of registry 1844, Volume 6, Memorial No. 209.

29. 'Murdered by the exquisite paradox of British legislation': Ref. *The Freeman's Journal*, 29 September 1846, pages 3 & 4.

30. Call to close the distilleries: Ref. *Essex Standard*, 29 January 1847, page 3, column 4, under the heading 'Famine in Ireland'.

31. Sir Charles Wood (1800–1885). Whig politician and Member of Parliament. Chancellor of the Exchequer from 1846 to 1852. He later became 1st Viscount Halifax.

32. Meeting at Downing Street: Ref. *The Freeman's Journal*, 8 February 1847, pages 2 and 3.

33. Death of James Jameson: Ref. *London Evening Standard*, 28 August 1847, page 1, column 3, under the heading 'Death of Mr Jameson'.

34. Distillery statistics: Ref. '*The Whisky Distilleries of the United Kingdom*' by Alfred Barnard, first published by the proprietors of *Harpers Weekly Gazette*, 39 Crutched Friars, London 1887. Republished by Birlinn Ltd. Edinburgh, 2008.

35. Mansions and castles: Many Jameson houses survive through to today. James Jameson's Donnybrook house 'Montrose' is now the grounds and crèche for the Irish broadcaster RTE. John Jameson-3 built a house at Portmarnock that is now a hotel.

36. Great-grandfather: James Robert Jameson (1849–1924). Born Airfield House Donnybrook. Eldest son of James Jameson (1821–1829), the co-owner of the Marrowbone Lane distillery.

37. Duke of Abercorn's Fancy Ball: Ref. the *Cork Constitution*, 15 March 1876, page 4, column 5, beside the title 'Captain JR Jameson Airfield'.

38. Brendan Behan (1923–1964). Irish Republican, poet, novelist, and playwright.

39. 'A Protestant with a horse': Quote from Brendan Behan's play in 1958, *The Hostage*, Act 1.

40. Great-grandaunt Ida: Ida Isabel Jameson (1870–1945). A very individual and colourful character. Maude Gonne described Ida as 'a strange girl with curious psychic faculties'. Ida married French diplomat Robert Boeufe and lived in New Zealand for a time. During WWI, Ida journeyed from New Zealand to France and to the trenches to seek out her son Alic. Alic married a French girl, Marguerite. Ida persuaded Marguerite to pose for a photo dressed in her son's lieutenant's uniform. At that time, the photo was considered very risqué and probably would be today.

41. Maud Gonne MacBride (1866–1953). Irish patriot, actress, feminist, and a founder of Sinn Féin. In her book *A Servant of the Queen*, she references her friendship with Ida Jameson.

42. *The Shan Van Vocht*: A political ballad sung in Ireland throughout the nineteenth century. It dates from the United Irishmen Rebellion of 1798, with a particular reference to the French attempt to land at Bantry Bay.

43. Aeneous Coffey (1780–1839). A customs and excise officer who went on to work for the distilling industry. He patented an improved version of the continuous column still in 1831. Coffey worked at Robert Haig's distillery at Dodderbank for a time.

44. James Sligo Jameson (1856–1888). The grandson of John Jameson-2. He was born in Alloa, where his father, Andrew Jameson (1812-1872), was the third and last Jameson to hold the office of Sheriff Clerk of Clackmannanshire.

45. Henry Morton Stanley (1841–1904). Welsh-American explorer of Central Africa. On an expedition to find the Scottish missionary and explorer Dr Livingstone, he is famous for his quote, 'Dr Livingstone, I presume?'

46. The Times, November 1890: The Times, report centred on an affidavit written by Assad Farran, an interpreter on the Stanley expedition.

47. Emin Pasha (1840–1892). Naturalist, physician, and explorer. He was appointed Governor of the Egyptian province of Equatoria on the Upper Nile by General Gordon. There he succeeded in abolishing slavery in the region. During the Mahdist uprising, he became isolated, prompting Stanley's expedition.

48. James Sligo Jameson's diary: Ref. *Story of the Rear Column of the Emin Pasha Relief Expedition* by the Late James S Jameson, Naturalist to the Expedition, edited by Mrs J. S. Jameson.

49. William Jameson (1818–1896). Grandson of John Jameson and son of James Jameson (1781-1847). Inherited the Marrowbone

Lane distillery with his younger brother James. Lived at Montrose House Donnybrook.

50. James Jameson (1821–1829). Grandson of John Jameson and son of James Jameson (1781-1847). Inherited the Marrowbone Lane distillery with his elder brother William. He lived at Airfield House, over the road from his brother at Montrose House Donnybrook. Two-times great-grandfather.

51. James Jameson 'Had ceased to count amongst the living': Ref. page 87 – *A Servant of the Queen* by Maud Gonne MacBride. First published in 1938, re-edited edition published by Colin Smythe Ltd., Gerrards Cross1994.

52. The Sale of William Jameson & Co.: Ref. Registry of Deeds, Dublin, Year of registry 1889, Volume 44, Memorial No. 53.

53. The competitive edge between the family businesses: In 1885, an advertisement appeared, 'William Jameson, Marrowbone-Lane Distillery, The Original Dublin Distillery of the Name, working 130 Years'. Below this advertisement, 'John Jameson & Son, Bow Street, Please Observe the above firm is not connected with any other distillery.' Ref. *Sport*, 14 November 1885, page 2.

54. Established first appearances: In December 1885, John Jameson & Son added 'Established 1780'. Ref. *Sport*, 19 December 1885, page 3. In February 1886, William Jameson & Co. added 'Established 1752'. Ref. *Sport*, 13 February 1886, page 2.

55. Andrew Jameson (1855–1941). Irish politician and chairman of John Jameson and Son Ltd. Born in Alloa, he was the brother of James Sligo Jameson.

56. John (Jack) Eustace Jameson (1852–1919). Irish politician, soldier, and cavalier businessman. He was involved for a short time with his cousin Guglielmo Marconi. Born Airfield House Donnybrook, Dublin. The younger brother of great-grandfather.

57. William Bellingham Jameson (1859–1940). Born Montrose House, Donnybrook, Dublin. Grandson of James Jameson

(1781-1847) and second son of William Jameson, co-owner of Marrowbone Lane distillery.

58. Vice-Chancellor: Hedges Eyre Chatterton (1819–1910). Vice-Chancellor of Ireland from 1867 to 1904.

59. Lord Justice Fitzgibbon: Gerald Fitzgibbon (1837–1909).

60. 'Have you met John Jameson?': A series of advertisements for U.S. magazines in 1941.

61. Henry Raeburn (1756–1823). Edinburgh portrait painter. He became bankrupt in 1807 and was left to pay off his creditors for the rest of his life.

62. JJ and Peggie rescued: Milestown House was burnt down on the 13th of January, 1923. As with most tales, there are different versions of events. My father, who moved to Milestown soon after the fire. He spoke, of how the young IRA men helped the family remove some of the furniture before they set the house alight.

63. Aleck Crichton - Alexander Cochrane Crichton (1918-2017). Grandson of Andrew Jameson, the politician and former chairman of John Jameson and Son. As chairman and managing director of John Jameson and Son, Aleck initiated the merger in 1968 and guided the company to success. He was described in an obituary as dutiful, painstaking, and cautious. These attributes could have also been applied to his three-times great-grandfather, John Jameson.

64. Shane Jameson - William Shane Musgrave Jameson (1924-1994). He was the last named non-executive director of John Jameson & Son, from 1963-1988. Three-times great-grandson of John Jameson.

65. 'Irish Distillers': Formed in 1966 with a merger of John Jameson, John Power, and Cork Distilleries Company.

66. The visit by a theatrical company to Alloa in 1835: Retold from an extract from '*Life of an Actor an Autobiography by H.F. Lloyd, seri-*

alised in the Evening Times, Glasgow from 19 May 1886. The original can also be found on the website – www.arthurlloyd.co.uk.

67. Montague Stanley (1809–1844). Actor, landscape painter, and evangelist.

68. Horatio Lloyd (1807–1889). Actor and comedian. Horatio was the father of Arthur Lloyd (1839–1904), singer, songwriter, comedian, and impresario.

69. Philadelphia the Countess of Mar (1794–1853). Married to John Francis Miller Erskine, 9th Earl of Mar.

Bibliography

Abercromby, James. *Lieutenant-General Sir Ralph Abercromby, K.B. 1793-1801, A Memoir by his son, James Lord Dunfermline* Published by Edmonston and Douglas, Edinburgh, 1861. Republished by Forgotten Books, London 2018.

Aitchison, Peter & Cassell, Andrew. *The Lowland Clearances, Scotland's Silent Revolution 1760-1830.* Published by Tuckwell Press, East Linton, Scotland, 2003.

Bald, Robert. A *General view of the Coal Trade of Scotland, Chiefly that of the River Forth and Midlothian. To which is added, an Inquiry into the condition of the Women who carry coals underground in Scotland, known by the name of Bearers.* Published by Oliphant, Waugh, and Innes, Edinburgh 1812.

Barnard, Alfred. *The Whisky Distilleries of the United Kingdom.* First published by the proprietors of *Harpers Weekly Gazette*, 39 Crutched Friars, London 1887. Republished by Birlinn Ltd. Edinburgh 2008.

Boswell, James. *Boswell's Edinburgh Journals 1767-1786.* Edited by Hugh M. Milne Published by Birlinn Ltd. Edinburgh 2001.

Boswell, James. *Boswell's London Journal 1762-1763.* Edited by Gordon Turnbull, Published by Penguin Classics, 2010.

Campbell-Smith, Duncan. *Masters of the Post, Authorized History of the Royal Mail.* Published by Allan Lane, London 2011.

Carr, John. *The Stranger in Ireland or A Tour in the Southern and Western part of that Country in the year 1805.* First published by Lincoln and Gleason, 1806. Republished by Franklin Classics 2018.

Casey, Christine. *Dublin (The city within the Grand and Royal Canals and the Circular Road within Phoenix Park.) 'The Buildings of Ireland'* Published by Yale University Press, Newhaven and London 2005

Clarke, Harry. *The History of a Great House, Origin of John Jameson Whiskey. Containing some interesting observations thereon, together with The Causes of its Present Scarcity*. Published by John Jameson and Son Ltd. Dublin 1924.

Finlay, John. *Community of the College of Justice, Edinburgh and the Court of Session, 1687-1808*. Published by Edinburgh University Press, Edinburgh 2012.

Finlay, John. *Admission Register of Notaries Public in Scotland, 1700-1799*. Published by Scottish Record Society, Edinburgh 2012.

Fleet, Christopher & MacCannell, Daniel. *Edinburgh: Mapping the City*. Published by Birlinn Ltd. Edinburgh 2014.

Forbes, William. *Memoirs of a Banking House*. Published by William and Robert Chambers, London and Edinburgh 1860.

Foyster, Elizabeth & Whatley, Christopher A. *A History of Everyday Life in Scotland, 1600 to 1800*. Published by Edinburgh University Press Ltd, Edinburgh 2010.

Hall, Donal & Maguire, Martin. *County. Louth and the Irish Revolution 1912-1923*. Published by Irish Academic Press, Newbridge 2017.

Hillyard, Brian. *David Steuart Esquire: An Edinburgh Collector*. Published by Edinburgh Bibliographical Society, Edinburgh 1993.

Jameson, James, S. *The Story of the Rear Column of the Emin Pasha Relief Expedition*. Published by John W. Lovell Company, New York 1890.

Jameson, John & Son, Jameson William & Co., Power John & Son, Roe, George & Co. – *Truths About Whisky*. Printed by Sutton Sharpe and Co., London. 1878. Republished by Classic Expressions, 2008.

Jameson, John & Son Limited. '*Soverign Liquor*', *A brief investigation into the making and maturing of good Irish Whiskey*. Published by Jameson, John & Son Limited. Bow Street, Dublin 1950.

Laver, James. *The House of Haig*. Published by John Haig and Co. Ltd., Markinch 1958.

MacBride, Gonne, Maud. *A Servant of the Queen*. First published 1938, Re-edited edition – Colin Smythe Ltd. Gerrards Cross, 1994.

McGuire, E. B. *Irish Whiskey - A History of Distilling, the Spirit Trade and Excise Controls in Ireland*. Published by Gill and Macmillan Ltd. Dublin, 1973.

Oakley, C. A. *The Second City*. Published by Blackie & Son Ltd. Glasgow and London, 1946.

Riding, Jacqueline. *Jacobites: A New History of the '45 Rebellion*. Published by Bloomsbury Publishing, London 2016.

Russell, John. *The Book of the Old Edinburgh Club, Nineteenth Volume*. Printed by T. and A. Constable Ltd for the members of the club. 1933.

Sperling, Diana & Mingay, Gordon. *Mrs Hurst Dancing and other scenes from Regency Life 1812-1823.* Published by Victor Gollancz Ltd. London 1981.

Stewart, Margaret. *The Architectural, Landscape and Constitutional Plans of the Earl of Mar, 1700-32.* Published by Four Courts Press. Dublin 2016.

Turnbull, Rev. George. *Diary of the Rev. George Turnbull Minister of Alloa and Tyninghame, 1657-1704,* Edited from the original manuscript by Robert Paul. Scottish History Society. Edinburgh, 1893.

Whatley, Christopher, A. *Scottish Society 1707-1830.* Published by Manchester University Press. Manchester 2000.

Young, Arthur. *A Tour in Ireland, 1776-1779.* Edited by Henry Morley. Published by Dodo Press. Moscow 2008.

Archives Consulted

Chelmsford:
Essex Records Office

Dublin:
Dublin City Library and Archive
National Archives of Ireland
National Library of Ireland
Registry of Deeds

Edinburgh:
National Records of Scotland (NRS)
National Library of Scotland (NLS)

Perth:
Perth and Kinross Council Archive

Stirling:
Stirling Council Archives

Online Archives Consulted

Ancestry.

Edinburgh Bookshelf.

EDINA, University of Edinburgh.

Irish Newspaper Archives.

Irish Times Archives.

JSTOR.

National Library of Scotland – Maps.

Scotland's People.

Scotland's Places.

The Book of the Old Edinburgh Club.

The British Newspaper Archive.

Index

Figures in **bold** refer to illustrations.

About the Author

Brian Jameson is an Early Boomer of Irish parentage who grew up in Salisbury, England.

After training at RADA, he worked as an actor for twenty years. He was a Play School presenter for a time, which led him to write, direct, and produce for children's TV. He won a BAFTA for his creation of the children's soap *Balamory*. His BBC series *Woolly and Tig* has spawned books and billions of views worldwide. He now lives in Edinburgh with his wife Donna Krachan. *JJ* is a new departure.

Printed in Great Britain
by Amazon

40961747R00185